THE LIFE

OF

ISRAEL PUTNAM

Israel Putnam

THE
LIFE
of
GEN. PUTNAM.

BY WILLIAM CUTTER.

THE LIFE

OF

ISRAEL PUTNAM,

MAJOR-GENERAL IN THE ARMY

OF THE

AMERICAN REVOLUTION.

COMPILED FROM

THE BEST AUTHORITIES.

BY WILLIAM CUTTER.

FOURTH EDITION.

KENNIKAT PRESS
Port Washington, N. Y./London

KENNIKAT AMERICAN BICENTENNIAL SERIES

Under the General Editorial Supervision of
Dr. Ralph Adams Brown
Professor of History, State University of New York

THE LIFE OF ISRAEL PUTNAM

First published in 1850
Reissued in 1970 by Kennikat Press
Library of Congress Catalog Card No: 78-120874
ISBN 0-8046-1267-6

Manufactured by Taylor Publishing Company   Dallas, Texas

KENNIKAT AMERICAN BICENTENNIAL SERIES

PREFACE.

THERE are three sources to which the writer of biography may repair, for materials to accomplish his work. The first is an intimate personal acquaintance with his subject, derived from long intercourse, and a daily participation in the scenes which it is his purpose to describe. The next is, a detailed narrative of incidents and events, taken down from the lips of his subject, giving to his delineations the spirit and authenticity of an autobiography. The third is found in the testimony of neighbors and acquaintances, corroborated by contemporaneous history, correspondence, &c. When the veracity and honesty of the party are unimpeachable, there is no source so reliable as that which is here placed second in the list. No person can possibly be so well acquainted with the acts of another as himself. And when, to the proper appreciation of these acts, it is necessary to know something of the motives and purposes from which they sprung, and the feelings with which they were accompanied, this is the only source to which we can look. And when to this is added an intimate personal acquaintance of a compiler of approved integrity and faithfulness, it affords the highest species of evidence in favor of his narrative, which can possibly be desired.

Of this nature is the evidence in favor of the prin-

cipal incidents in the life of General Putnam. His
original biographer, Colonel David Humphreys, was
intimately associated with him, having served as *Aide-
de-camp* in his staff, during a portion of the Revolutionary War. He had many parts of the narrative
direct from the lips of the General. That he was
competent to discharge well the duties of a biographer
—that he was entitled to the confidence of his readers
—will not be questioned by any who have honestly
consulted the history of the times, and weighed the
opinions of those who knew him best.

When General Putnam's health failed, in 1779, and
he was compelled to retire from the service, Colonel
Humphreys served, for a short time, as Aid to General
Greene; after which he became a member of General
Washington's family, and served him as *Aide-de-camp*,
during the remainder of his military career. That he
occupied a very high place in the esteem of " the
Father of his country," and of others eminent in the
councils of the nation, is abundantly manifest in the
correspondence of Washington.

Among a multitude of letters which might be referred to, an extract from one only will be given. It
was addressed to Colonel Humphreys in Europe, under date of the 25th of July, 1785. General Washington, apparently in reply to a suggestion from Humphreys, that he (Washington) should apply himself
to preparing commentaries upon the Revolutionary
War, says : " In a former letter, I informed you, my
dear Humphreys, that if I had talents for it, I had no
leisure to turn my thoughts to commentaries. * * *
I should be pleased indeed to see you undertake this

business. *Your abilities as a writer, your discernment respecting the principles which led to the decision by arms, your personal knowledge of many facts as they occurred in the progress of the war, your disposition to justice, candor, and impartiality, and your diligence in investigating truth, all combining, fit you, when joined with the vigor of life, for this task.* I should, with great pleasure, not only give you the perusal of all my papers, but any oral information of circum·stances, which cannot be obtained from these, that my memory will furnish; and I can with great truth add, that my house would not only be at your service, during the period of your preparing this work, but (I say it without an unmeaning compliment) I should be exceedingly happy if you would make it your home. You might have an apartment to yourself, in which you could command your own time. You would be considered and treated as one of the family, and meet with that cordial reception and entertainment, which are characteristic of the sincerest friendship."

Colonel Humphreys returned home in May, 1786; after which he was often at Mount Vernon, a member of Washington's family. *It was there that he wrote the Life of General Putnam,* in 1788, under the eye of Washington, and with the best possible means of knowing that great man's opinion of the subject of his work. The work was written for the Society of Cincinnati, of Connecticut, and by them, and under their sanction, presented to the world. This Society was composed of surviving officers of the Revolution, the compeers of Putnam, and the sharers and eye-witnesses of his heroic and daring achievements.

1*

In addition to the testimony of Colonel Humphreys, we have that of a large number of the cotemporaries of General Putnam. Numerous letters, written at the time when, and on the spot where, the several prominent events occurred, as well as the verbal testimony of the few aged witnesses who yet remain among us, confirm, and more than confirm, the narrative of his original biographer. It would appear that Putnam had not been disposed to estimate his own services very highly, or to present in any very strong colors his own acts of heroism; since Colonel Humphreys, who gathered much of his material from personal conversations with his subject, is far more modest and unpretending, in many of his statements, than authentic documents, furnished both by friends and by foes of that period, would warrant.

In bestowing the above high commendation on Colonel Humphreys, it is not intended to hold him up as infallible; but only to say, that, with respect to the general truthfulness and fidelity of his sketches, and the degree of reliance to be placed upon his narrative, though there may be some slight errors and misconceptions, the testimony is unquestionable, and the character of the witness above suspicion.

The present compilation is, of course, indebted to the original memoir, for its main outline, and principal incidents. It will be seen, however, to have deviated from it, in some points, upon a careful comparison of authorities; while large additions have been made from other authentic sources.

Brooklyn, L. I., Oct., 1846.

In the preparation of this work, the following authorities have been consulted. There are some discrepancies among them, in relation to several points of considerable importance. Without attempting to account for these discrepancies, I have endeavored as far as possible to reconcile them, by a rigid and laborious comparison of each with all the rest, and by an impartial consideration of the amount of responsibility attached to each. How far I have succeeded in doing justice to all, and to my subject, it must be for others to decide.

The Life of General Putnam. By Colonel David Humphreys. With Notes and Additions. Boston. 1818.

The Life of Israel Putnam. By Oliver W. B. Peabody. Sparks' American Biography, Vol. vii.

Memoirs of the American Revolution, &c. By William Moultrie. New York. 1802.

History of the American Revolution. By Bernard Hubley. Northumberland, Penn. 1805.

History of the Origin, Progress and Termination of the American War. By C. Stedman. London. 1799.

Annals of the American Revolution, &c. By Jedediah Morse, D.D. Hartford. 1824.

History of the American Revolution. By Paul Allen.

Botta's American Independence.

History of the Rise, Progress and Establishment of the Independence of the U. S. A. By William Gordon, D. D. New York. 1789.

Pemberton's Historical Journal of the American War.

Thatcher's   do.

Holmes' Annals of America. Second edition. Cambridge. 1829.

Sandford's United States and Aborigines. Phil. 1819.

Anecdotes of the Revolutionary War in America. By Alexander Gordon. First and Second Series. 1822 and 1828.

Marshall's Life of Washington. Second Edition. 2 vols. Phil. 1832.

Ramsay's Life of Washington.

Sparks'   do.   do.   Boston. 1839.

Writings of Washington. 12 vols. Edited by Dr. Sparks. 1829.

Rogers' Biographical Dictionary. Phil. 1829.

Gorton's   do.   do.   London.

Library of American Biography. By J. Sparks.

American Portrait Gallery.

History of Massachusetts. Ay Alden Bradford. Boston. 1829.

History of Connecticut. By J. Trumbull.

History of the Battle of Bunker Hill. With a plan. By S. Swett. Third Edition. With Notes.

Life of Aaron Burr. By Matthew L. Davis.

American Archives—consisting of a collection of authentic records, state papers, debates, letters, and other notices of public affairs; &c., &c. Prepared and published under the authority of an Act of Congress. Fourth Series, in six quarto vols.

Almon's Impartial Remembrancer. London. 1775, et seq.

Mante's History of the French War. London. 1772.

Historical Journal of the Campaigns in North America, for 1757, 1758, 1759 and 1760. By John Knox. London. 1769.

Journals of Major Robert Rogers, &c. London. 1765.

Also numerous pamphlets, MS. Orderly Book, &c.

TABLE OF CONTENTS.

CHAPTER IV.

THE CAMPAIGN OF 1756.   PUTNAM'S SERVICES AS A RANGER

CHAPTER V.

THE CAMPAIGN OF 1757.

CHAPTER VI.

CAMPAIGN OF 1758. ABERCROMBIE'S ASSAULT UPON TICON-
DEROGA.

CHAPTER VII.

CAMPAIGN OF 1758 CONTINUED. MAJOR PUTNAM A PRISONER.

CHAPTER VIII.

THE CAMPAIGN OF 1759 AND 1760. EXPEDITION AGAINST THE WEST INDIA ISLANDS.

CHAPTER IX.

THE PONTIAC WAR.

CHAPTER X.

CAUSES OF THE REVOLUTION.

CHAPTER XI.

AGITATIONS PRECEDING THE WAR OF INDEPENDENCE.

CHAPTER XII.

FIRST ACT IN THE DRAMA OF THE REVOLUTION.

2

CHAPTER XIII.

THE BATTLE OF BUNKER HILL.

CHAPTER XIV.

ARRIVAL OF WASHINGTON AT CAMBRIDGE. ORGANIZATION OF THE ARMY. FORTIFICATIONS.

CHAPTER XV.

BOSTON EVACUATED BY THE BRITISH.

CHAPTER XVI.

PUTNAM IN COMMAND AT NEW YORK.

CHAPTER XVII.

THE BRITISH FLEET AND ARMY AT STATEN ISLAND.   PUTNAM'S CONTRIVANCES TO ANNOY THEM.

Comparative force of the English and Americans—Two fri-

CHAPTER XVIII.

THE BATTLE OF BROOKLYN, AND RETREAT FROM LONG ISLAND.

CHAPTER XIX.

RETREAT OF THE CONTINENTAL ARMY FROM NEW YORK.

CHAPTER XX.

LOSS OF FORT WASHINGTON, AND RETREAT THROUGH NEW JERSEY.

CHAPTER XXI.

PUTNAM'S COMMAND AT PHILADELPHIA AND PRINCETON

2*

CHAPTER XXII.

PUTNAM'S COMMAND IN THE HIGHLANDS.

CHAPTER XXIII.

COMMAND IN THE HIGHLANDS CONTINUED. LOSS OF FORTS
MONTGOMERY AND CLINTON.

CHAPTER XIV.

DISSATISFACTION WITH PUTNAM'S COMMAND IN NEW YORK.

CHAPTER XXV.

NEW FORTIFICATIONS IN THE HIGHLANDS. PUTNAM DISPLACED FROM THE COMMAND.

CHAPTER XXVI.

RETIREMENT AND LAST DAYS OF THE HERO.

APPENDIX.

THE LIFE

OF

GENERAL PUTNAM.

CHAPTER I.

EARLY LIFE AND YOUTHFUL ADVENTURES OF PUTNAM.

His ancestry—His birth—The old homestead—His early life—
Deficiency of the means of education—Early development of character—The bird's nest—Hazardous exploit—Coolness and intrepidity in danger—Singular escape—Perseverance in pursuit of
an object—The prize secured—His activity, industry, and wit—
His first visit to Boston—Insulted in the street—His able defence
—Slavery—Anecdote of Cudge—The sequel.

AMONG the earliest settlers in Salem, in the Province of
Massachusetts, was JOHN PUTNAM ; who, for the free
enjoyment of the rights of conscience, and the liberty of
worshipping God in the manner which his own judgment,
enlightened by a careful study of the Scriptures, approved
and required, left the home of his youth, and the sepul-
chres of his fathers, and cast in his lot with the heroic,
self-denying Pilgrims, under the banner of the venerable
Endicot. He was a man of eminent piety, and acknowledged moral worth ; having blended in his character those
elements of Christian heroism which distinguished our
Pilgrim Fathers above every other body of men, that
ever effected a great revolution in the world, and eminently fitted them, not only to endure the hardships of a
pioneer life in a savage wilderness, but to give substance

and permanency to the new institutions, which it was their destiny to found in that wilderness.

The original name of the family was Puttenham. They resided in Buckinghamshire, one of the southern counties of England, and but a short distance from the metropolis. The emigrant brought with him three sons, Thomas, Nathaniel, and John, and two brothers, younger than himself. They pitched their tents, in 1634, in that remote part of Salem which, for a century past, has been included within the limits of Danvers, where they soon established themselves as successful, independent farmers ; and where many of their posterity still reside, in circumstances of respectability and affluence.

ISRAEL PUTNAM was the son of Captain Joseph Putnam, grandson of Thomas, and great grandson of the worthy John, who planted the family tree in this country. He was born on the seventh day of January, 1718, and was the eleventh of a family of twelve children. His mother's maiden name was Elizabeth Porter. The house in which he first saw the light is still standing, in good order and well-conditioned; having, like the hardy old settlers who founded it, been built of the best materials which the times afforded. It is an old-fashioned, gambrel-roofed house, two stories in height, with dormer windows in the attic, and painted yellow. It is at present occupied by Mr. Daniel Putnam, grand nephew of the General. It stands on the main road from " The Plains," in Danvers, to Middletown, being the last house on the right before the intersection of that road with the Newburyport turnpike. By the turnpike, it is exactly half way between Newburyport and Boston.

A little above this house, near the angle of a small hill, on the right side of the road, stands a locust tree, in a gentle hollow. On that spot formerly stood a small, one story house, which the General once occupied, and where he kept a sort of bachelor's hall, previous to his marriage. When the house was taken down, some fifty years ago, the locust tree was planted there by one of the family, to designate the spot where it had stood.

Of the early life of the General, however it might have been marked by incidents illustrating or foreshadowing those eminent traits of character which were developed by the stirring scenes of his after years, we have no authentic records, and but few reliable traditions. To use the words of a kind correspondent, and a talented antiquarian of Salem,*—to whom application was made for materials for this part of the memoir—" Putnam migrated from Massachusetts more than a century ago, while he was young and undistinguished. His neighbors and relatives were employed in rural pursuits, and while he dwelt with them they did not regard him as a future great man— they noticed not ' the lambent flame on the crest of Tullius.' "

The few incidents, relating to this period that have been preserved, are in perfect keeping with the character which he exhibited in after years. The same fearless daring, the same insensibility to danger, the same generous, manly disposition, and the same ready good humor, which made him through life the boon companion and the idol of his friends, as well as the foremost leader in all kinds of adventure. Unfortunately, we have nothing of his school-boy days. Schools, especially in the scattered settlements of the country, were more rare at that period than now, and the advantages of education difficult to be obtained by those whose circumstances and mode of life, like those of our hero, demanded the unceasing application of their energies in cultivating the soil. The want of those advan-

* Benjamin Merrill, Esq.

tages, and of the benefits which he might have derived
from them, was sensibly felt in all his subsequent career.
And it is probable, had he been permitted, at the close of
his life, to address the youth of the country, or to leave a
legacy of caution and instruction to coming generations,
he would have dwelt much and strongly upon the duty
and privilege of a thorough early education. He would
have urged the young to neglect no opportunity for acquiring knowledge, and preparing themselves, not only to win
an honorable eminence in society, and adorn it when won,
but to enjoy it with that conscious ease and self-reliance
which, to an ingenuous mind, constitutes its principal
attraction.

There are few who have the native strength of character
to rise above the inauspicious circumstances of early life,
and carve out their own fortunes, by the mere dint of their
own irrepressible genius. Putnam was one of the few.
The times in which he lived demanded marked and striking peculiarities in the class of men, whose duty it was to
go forward and " guide the current of events." And it is
one of the most interesting and instructive cases of the
history of that exciting period, to notice how wonderfully
its leading characters were fitted for the crisis, and how
wisely and kindly the various " gifts " required for the
service were distributed among them.

That the heroic character of Putnam was inborn, a part
of his very nature, and not the result of temporary excitement, or a transient exhiliration of spirits, will appear from
the following anecdote, which is related of his boyish
days. It exhibits a cool serenity and self-possession in
times of great peril, which are of inestimable value to the
leader of an enterprise, placing him, in a manner, above the
vicissitudes of fortune, and making him the master, rather
than the slave, of circumstance. The charge of cruelty,

which attaches to it, must be set down to the score of the heedlessness of youth ; for his whole subsequent life shows that he had a kind, generous, noble heart, keenly alive to the sufferings of others, and ready, almost to a fault, even to aid his enemies. Friends and foes alike accord him this praise.

In common with most boys in the same situation in life, Putnam found great amusement in " bird's-nesting." Like many other boys, too, whose experience has not been written, he found it a very hazardous sport, having nearly lost his life in one of his hair-brained attempts to perpetrate this species of heartless piracy. It was customary, on these occasions, for several boys to go out in company ; but Putnam was always the leader of the band. In the case referred to, they had discovered a fine nest, lodged on a frail branch, near the top of a very high tree. The tree stood apart from others, and was difficult to climb. The nest was so far out of the way that it could not be reached by a pole, or any other contrivance, which they could command. The only possible way, therefore, to secure the prize, was for some one to venture upon one of those frail branches, neither of which, in the opinion of all the party, was sufficient to sustain the weight of any one of their number.

Putnam regarded the nest and the limb in silence for some minutes. At length he said :

" That bird has some of the qualities of a good soldier ; she has selected her post with excellent judgment, and fortified it with great skill. I'll wager there is not a boy within ten miles that can reach that nest."

No one was disposed to accept the implied challenge. They were about quitting the spot in quest of some more practicable sport, when Putnam, deliberately taking off his jacket, and rolling up his pantaloons to his knees, said,

3

" There's nothing like trying," and proceeded to climb the tree.

His companions used their utmost eloquence to dissuade him from the mad attempt; but all to no purpose. He never flinched from any undertaking when he had once made up his mind to it. The tree was ascended, and the limb gained, nearest to that which held the nest. It seemed stouter than the others. The daring boy placed his foot on it by way of trial. It creaked ominously ; while the mother-bird, with a shrill cry, abandoned her nest, hovering anxiously around, and uttering many a touching complaint.

Stepping boldly out upon the limb, it bent under him. The boys below warned him of his danger, and entreated him not to venture any further. Getting down upon one knee, he reached toward the nest, but before he could grasp it the limb cracked. His comrades shouted to him to come down, but still he persevered. His fingers touched the wished-for prize. In his eagerness he cried, " I've got it—it is mine." At that instant the limb broke quite off, and Putnam fell; but not to the ground. His fall was arrested by one of the lower branches of the tree, which caught in his pantaloons, and held him suspended in mid air with his head downward.

" Put, are you hurt ?" inquired one of the boys.

" Not hurt," answered the undaunted heart, " but sorely puzzled how to get down."

" We cannot cut away the limb for you because we have no knife."

" You must contrive some other way to relieve me then, for I cannot stay here till you get one."

" We will strike a light, and burn the tree down."

" Ay ; and smother me in the smoke. That will not do."

G.F.PEASE.Sc.   MATTESON.Del.

Birds-Nesting.—Putnam suspended in the Tree. PAGE 36

There was a boy named Randall in the group, who was noted for being a crack marksman, and who afterwards fought bravely at Putnam's side. Fortunately, he seldom went out without his rifle, and had it with him on this occasion.

"Jim Randall," said he, "there's a ball in your rifle."

"Yes."

"Do you see that small limb that holds me here?"

"I do."

"Fire at it."

"What! to cut you down?"

"Of course; for what else could I ask it."

"But I might hit your head, perhaps."

"*Shoot; better blow out my brains at once*, than see me die here by hanging, which I shall certainly do in fifteen minutes. *Shoot.*"

"But you will fall."

"Jim Randall, will you fire?"

Randall brought his rifle to his shoulder. Its sharp crack rang through the forest—the splinters flew—and Putnam fell to the ground. He was severely bruised by the fall. He laughed it off, however, and nothing more was thought of it.

Not many days after, Putnam, who could never endure the thought of being defeated in an enterprise, returned alone to that tree, and succeeded, though with the greatest difficulty, in securing the nest, which he bore away in triumph to his companions.

Though we cannot apologize for the cruel act of robbing a harmless bird of her home and her young, nor do otherwise than censure the fool-hardiness of the boy, who could twice put his life at hazard for such a prize, we cannot but see in this incident the germ of that indomitable spirit, which was so often displayed amid the more fearful perils of his subsequent career. His conduct, while suspended in the tree, displays the same coolness and self-possession, and the same promptness of action, which characterized his daring leap at Horseneck, and his perilous trip down the rapids of the Hudson.

As would naturally be expected from those traits of character which have already been exhibited, Putnam was eager to excel in all the manly athletic exercises, which constitute so large a part of the sports of a country village. In running, leaping, wrestling, pitching the bar, and in feats of horsemanship, he displayed great agility and physical power, and was scarcely ever second among his competitors. Even in the labors of the field and the wood, it was his early ambition to do the part of a man, and not to be outdone, even by his elders, in anything, which patient, persevering toil could achieve.

But with all his restless activity, and his fondness for athletic amusements, he never loved a quarrel. He was not easily provoked. His disposition was frank, generous and confiding, and his uniform good humor often preserved the peace among his more inflammable companions, when, as is too often the case, the heat and excitement of their game began to wear a threatening aspect, and parties at play to assume the tone and bearing of combatants. His wit and humor gave him great influence on such occasions, and he always employed it in allaying excitement, and harmonizing and adjusting difficulties. It seems to have been his principle, that a man should never fight except with his enemy, and with him only when he could not manage him in any other way.

On his first visit to Boston he was rudely assailed in the street by one of the young aristocrats of the town, who was considerably his superior both in age and size. The coarse homespun dress and awkward air of the country boy, as he sauntered along, gazing into the shop-windows, and wondering at the number, size and magnificence of the buildings, excited the mirth of the well-dressed and self-important city boy, whose superior education did not restrain him from showing his contempt in the most rude and ungentlemanly manner. His insults were borne in silence for a considerable time. At length, disgusted and exasperated by this unprovoked and continued abuse, and finding that it was attracting the attention of the people who were passing in the streets, he turned fiercely upon his assailant, and gave him so complete and satisfactory a drubbing, that he was glad to haul down his colors, and beat a retreat, much to the amusement of a large number of spectators, who made a ring to watch the issue of the contest.

At that period there were slaves in all the colonies. It is true, they were not very numerous in New England. Still, slavery existed, and African bond-men, and bond-women, and bond-children, were found—tell it not in Gath!—in all the towns, and scattered over the farming districts of Massachusetts. It fell to the lot of one of Putnam's neighbors to have one of these slaves in his family, who was noted and feared for his fierce, ungovernable temper, and a disposition that would have served a savage or a fiend. There seemed to be no way to subdue him but with the lash; and that, though often repeated, was far from being as effectual as could have been wished.

On one occasion, when Cudge had been particularly unruly, so that his master could do nothing with him, he called upon Putnam to assist him in administering the proper chastisement.

"Well, neighbor, what do you propose to do?" he inquired.

"I intend to tie him up in the barn, and give him such a flogging as he will be likely to remember."

3*

"Very well," replied Putnam, "you catch him, and I will tie him up. You can then do what you please with him."

Accordingly, the exasperated master went out into the field, seized Cudge, and brought him into the barn. Putnam, in the mean time, had fastened his rope to a beam, and prepared a noose. Cudge resisted, and his master was obliged to exert all his strength to hold him. In this position, Putnam threw the noose over them both, so as completely to secure their arms, and render it impossible for them to help themselves, or each other, drew them up together, and left them to their reflections.

Going coolly into the house, he lighted his pipe, sat down and smoked it out. Then, calling to the mistress of the house, he proposed to her to go out with him and see how the Captain and Cudge were getting along.

Arrived at the barn, the good woman was almost thrown into hysterics, on seeing her husband bound up in this manner with that terrible negro, whom she feared scarcely less than she did a certain other character in black, whose name it would not be polite to mention, and of whom she regarded Cudge as the living representative, or counterpart. After a little persuasion, and some words of stronger import, Putnam unbound his prisoners, endeavoring to pacify the now doubly enraged master by assuring him, that, however disagreeable to himself, the effect upon Cudge would be better than a dozen floggings.

The event justified the assertion. Cudge was so delighted with the joke, that he did not get out of humor for a long time after. At the same time, with that kind of instinctive regard which the slave naturally feels for his master, he could not help being hurt on his account. His heart was softened. He was more respectful and more obedient than he had ever been before.

The sequel of Cudge's history is too good a story to be lost ; and, though it has no relation to the subject of this memoir, we take leave to preserve it here, for the special benefit of those peculiar friends of Africa, who claim for New England an entire freedom from the plague-spot of slavery, and from any participation in " the price of blood."

By some means, his mistress had grievously offended the negro. He became so enraged, that he swore he would take her life ; and neither soothing words, nor threats, had any `effect to pacify him. The family was thrown into the greatest alarm, knowing that his temper was of that ungovernably savage character that nothing would restrain him from indulging it. In this state of things, his master devised a plan for the permanent relief of his family. Having made his arrangements, he went out into the field with his hoe in his hand, and said—

" Cudge, you have had rather hot work getting in the potatoes."

" Yes, massa, hot enough."

" Well, I am going to give you a play-day. I have sold fifty bushels, to be delivered on board a vessel at the wharf in Salem, and if you would like it, you may go in with the load."

" Oh ! yes, massa ; like it very well."

" You may have the whole day, Cudge. You can take your fiddle with you, and play a jig for the sailors, and so get a few coppers for yourself."

Cudge was highly pleased with the proposal, and started off in great glee.

Having unloaded his potatoes, the sailors, who had been let into the secret and received their instructions beforehand, called upon Cudge to bring out his fiddle and play them a jig, that they might have one merry dance before going to sea.

The negro showed his teeth, and his fiddle too ; and presently the deck of the brig was as merry as a country ball-room at Thanksgiving. Meanwhile, the dancers were not niggardly in " paying the piper." The coppers fell on this side and that, and Cudge was somewhat disconcerted in his measure, by the necessity of breaking off and running after them, to prevent them from going out at the scuppers. Presently, one of the sailors said—

" Cudge, your fiddle is getting dry ; you must go below and *rosin your bow.*" This was another phrase for " wetting his whistle," or taking a dram.

Cudge took the hint with alacrity, and adjourned with two or three of the party to the forecastle. Here, with drinking, fiddling, singing and dancing, two or three hours passed away, and Cudge had almost filled his pockets with coppers. At length, starting up, as from a dream, he exclaimed :

" Yah ! I must go up, and see how the cattle stand."

He went up; but, to his utter amazement, there was neither cattle nor cart to be seen ; no, nor houses, nor wharf. The brig was many miles out at sea, and Cudge was bound to a southern clime, where slaves could be more easily managed than on the hardy soil of New England. He went to the same market with his potatoes, and was sold for the same account.

CHAPTER II.

In 1739, at the age of twenty-one years, Mr. Putnam was
married to Miss Hannah Pope, daughter of Mr. John Pope,
of Salem, by whom he had ten children, four sons and six
daughters. The following year he removed from his native place, and settled upon a tract of land which he had
purchased in Pomfret, in Connecticut. This is an inland
town in Windham County, thirty-six miles east of Hartford, and situated on the Quinnebaug, or Mohegan river,
one of the tributaries of the Thames. It is blessed with a
good soil, and all the ordinary requisites for a thrifty and
successful husbandry.

In those days of comparative simplicity, the expenses
of living, particularly in the farming districts, were very
moderate, and easily acquired. Few of the costly luxuries of the present day were known. The hard and burdensome yoke of European fashion, which grinds so many
of us into the dust, was not then laid upon the colonies.

It is a singular anomaly in the history of Independent America, that she wears, without complaint, the fetters of a voluntary slavery, ten times more expensive and burdensome than that which roused the dependent colonies to resistance, and severed for ever the bonds which had so long united them to the mother-country. Our good old fathers and mothers, particularly those who maintained the independent life of cultivators of the soil, would have scorned the servile imitation of the multitude in our day. They would have deemed it the extreme of folly to sacrifice one real comfort to the mere outside show of equality to the rich and the great.

With these simple, unaffected tastes, and no merely artificial wants to drain off all the fruits of their toil, the industrious and skilful were almost sure of success. This was the issue of Mr. Putnam's labors upon his new farm. A very few years found him in the enjoyment of a comfortable and substantial home ; his clearings well fenced and cultivated ; his pastures handsomely stocked ; and his entire establishment, with one exception, in the full tide of prosperous increase. This exception, as it serves to illustrate the heroic and independent character of our subject, and furnishes the explanation of one of the peculiar sobriquets, by which he was often distinguished among his military comrades in after life, deserves particular notice.

Mr. Putnam's pastures were well adapted to the cultivation of sheep. With his usual promptness he availed himself of this facility to carry on quite an extensive business in wool. His flocks were numerous and thrifty, and he prided himself not a little in having as extensive folds, and as good fleeces, as any in New England. He was, therefore, particularly nettled when this part of his extensive establishment was selected as the object of nightly ravages, by some of the farmers' enemies, that were prowling about in that region. His fields had suffered occasionally from drought in summer, and mildew in harvest. The severity of the winter had carried off some of his cattle. But these inroads upon his folds had come to be exacted as an annual tribute, and were quite too severe to be tolerated. His losses were very great, so much se as to threaten the entire destruction of that department of his business. All this havoc appeared to have been com mitted by one she-wolf, and her annual whelps ; though it is not improbable they were sometimes accompanied by a stronger force. The young were usually destroyed in the course of the season by the vigilance of the hunters and their dogs ; but the old one was too sagacious to allow herself to be caught, or even to be seen. ˅She had once unwarily set her foot in a trap that was laid for her, but had escaped by leaving her toes behind. When too closely pursued to carry on her depredations any longer with safety, she would abandon the vicinity altogether for the season. But she invariably returned the ensuing winter, with another family of hungry whelps to feed.

Mr. Putnam was not the only sufferer by these annual visits of the wolf. His neighbors, all around, shared in his losses, though none of them were quite as heavily taxed as he. At length, finding the nuisance intolerable, he entered into a combination with five of his neighbors to watch and hunt alternately, and never abandon the pursuit till she was destroyed. Two of them, by turns, were to keep on her track until she was overtaken, or driven home to her den. Commencing the pursuit immediately after a light fall of snow, in the opening of winter, they were soon on a trail that could not be mistaken. The accident of the steel trap had made one foot much shorter than its mate, so that the fugitive robber made her mark as she went.   In this manner she was pursued over hill and valley, through forest, and brake, and swamp, to the bank of the Connecticut river.   Arrested in her flight here, she turned back in a direct course for Pomfret, with the hunters in close and vigilant chase.   Early in the morning, the day after their return, they had driven her into a den, about three miles from the house of Mr. Putnam.   Here she was carefully guarded, till a large company of men and boys had assembled, with dogs, guns, straw and sulphur, prepared to finish the work which had been so well begun, by inflicting summary vengeance upon the common enemy.

, It was a scene of general interest and excitement.   Rare sport was expected by some of the younger and less experienced.   It was, soon found, however, that the enemy had chosen her retreat with good judgment ; and was prepared, not only to stand an obstinate siege, but to defend herself with a fierceness and bravery that were quite appalling.   Some of the hounds, who had become heated in the chase, ventured into her fastness, but soon retreated, yelping bitterly and covered with wounds.   And no urgency could induce them to return to the charge.

It was now attempted to smoke her out.   The mouth of the cave was filled with straw.   The torch was applied. The smoke rolled up in heavy volumes, and filled every crevice of the cave ; but the wolf came not forth.   She seemed resolved to die where she was, rather than suffer herself to be taken, or face the weapons of such a company of exasperated foes.   The fumes of sulphur produced no better effect.   It is probable, indeed, that the imprisoned animal was not so much annoyed by them as her tormentors supposed.   There may have been some fissure by which they escaped, without finding their way into the inner recess of the cavern where the wolf was.

In these fruitless efforts to dislodge her, the time had flown by, till it now wanted only two hours of midnight. It was clear that something more effectual must be done, or all their labor would be lost. Another effort was made to induce the dogs to go in, but without success. They had had enough of that sport already, and would not budge an inch. Mr. Putnam then proposed to his servant to take a torch and a gun, and descend into the cavern and shoot the wolf. As his master doubtless expected, he declined the honor of so hazardous an enterprise. Finding no one in the company who was willing to attempt the perilous descent, and declaring he was ashamed to have a coward in his family, he resolved at once to go in himself, and put a certain end to the ravager of his flocks, lest she should escape by some unknown passage, and become once more the scourge of the country.

His neighbors remonstrated against so mad an exposure of his life, but in vain. He was bent on accomplishing, that very night, the death of his victim. He knew that all wild animals have instinctive dread of fire. He, accordingly, provided himself with a quantity of birch-bark, which he tore into strips convenient for use—these being the only torches which he could then command. Thus provided, he stripped off his coat and waistcoat, lighted one of his torches, and crawling on his hands and knees, without any weapon in his hand, commenced the bold descent.

" The aperture of the den, on the east side of a very high ledge of rocks, is about two feet square ; from thence it descends obliquely fifteen feet ; then, running horizontally about ten feet more, it ascends gradually sixteen feet towards its termination. The sides of this subterranean cavity are composed of smooth and solid rocks, which seem to have been divided from each other by some for-
4

mer earthquake. The top and bottom are also of stone,
and the entrance, in winter being covered with ice, is exceedingly slippery. It is in no place high enough for a
man to raise himself upright, nor in any place more than
three feet in width.

" Having groped his passage to the horizontal part of
the den, the most terrifying darkness appeared in front of
the dim circle of light afforded by his torch. It was silent
as the house of death. None but monsters of the desert
had ever before explored this solitary mansion of horror."
It required no slight care and presence of mind, to keep
alive the flame by which his course was guided. Though
creeping on all fours, he was obliged several times to pause
and renew his torch, at the imminent hazard, each time, of
being left in utter darkness in the depths of the cave.
" Cautiously proceeding onward, he came to the ascent,
which he slowly mounted on his hands and knees, until he
discovered the glaring eye-balls of the wolf, who was sit-
ting at the extremity of the cavern. Startled at the sight
of fire, she gnashed her teeth, and gave a sullen growl."
Having fully reconnoitered the position of the enemy, and
formed his plan of attack, the bold scout gave a hearty
kick upon the rope, which, by way of precaution, had been
secured around one of his legs. His friends, who were
waiting in breathless suspense and anxiety at the mouth of
the den, hearing the fierce growl of the wolf, which showed
that she was yet unhurt, and supposing that Mr. Putnam
must be in imminent danger, responded vigorously to the
concerted signal, dragging him forth with such violence,
" that his shirt was stripped over his head, and his skin
severely lacerated."

Having adjusted his clothes, and loaded his gun, he took
another handful of torches, and descended a second time
into the narrow cave. Encumbered with his musket, this

Putnam and the Wolf drawn out from the Cave.   PAGE 39.

descent was much more difficult than the first, though, armed as he was, and somewhat familiar with the bearings and distances of his journey, and the position of his foe, it was certainly much more safe and agreeable. As he approached the object of his pursuit somewhat nearer than before, she manifested the most decided symptoms of uneasiness at his presence. Her appearance was exceedingly fierce and terrible ; " howling, rolling her eyes, snapping her teeth, and dropping her head between her legs, she was evidently in the attitude, and on the point, of springing at her assailant. At that critical moment he levelled his piece, aiming directly at her head, and fired. Stunned with the shock, and suffocated with the smoke of the powder, he immediately found himself drawn out of the cave," though somewhat more gently than on the former occasion.

Having refreshed himself a few moments in the open air, and given time for the smoke to clear away from the long passages of the cavern, he went down the third time to secure and bring away his prize. His shot had taken good effect. The animal lay stretched on the floor of her inner chamber, weltering in her blood. Applying his torch to her nose, and finding her perfectly insensible, he seized her by the ears ; and, giving the usual signal to his friends without, by kicking the rope, was drawn heavily, but exultingly out, dragging his victim after him.

On emerging into the air, and bringing out, amid the fitful glare of a score or two of torches, that fearful creature, that had so long been the terror and scourge of their fields, he was received with such a shout as made the old woods of Pomfret ring again. Its echoes reverberated along the valley, and reached the wakeful ears of the anxious wives and mothers, whose fears, increasing as the midnight hour approached, had led many of them more than once to exclaim, "I wish they would leave the old wolf alone. I would rather lose every sheep in the fold, than have my husband or child brought home dead or wounded."

The nature of that shout could not be mistaken, even by a woman. It hushed all their fears in a moment; and when, some half an hour after, the party was seen winding down the valley, with flaming torches, escorting the victor in triumph to his home, with the trophy of his daring valor borne on a sort of litter on the shoulder of the larger boys, who claimed the honor as their perquisite for keeping awake so long—the tables were all laid, and a generous hot supper provided for all the volunteers in that cold midnight campaign.

Mr. Putnam's frank, open, agreeable manners, his generous spirit and uniform good humor, had already secured him the good will of all his neighbors; while his activity, enterprise, good sense and sterling integrity of character had won for him their entire esteem and regard. He now became, as will naturally be supposed, the hero of the village and the surrounding country. The story of his daring exploit with the wolf travelled far and wide, and received many poetical embellishments, in the course of its travels. In some cases the dimensions of the cave, and the difficulty of access to it, formidable as it really was, were greatly exaggerated. In some, the den was full of wolves, as that of Daniel was of lions; while one version represented the hero, like Samson or David, as entering her hold unarmed, seizing the wolf, and strangling her in his arms. Another substituted a bear and two cubs for the wolf, and represented the bear as going off with Putnam's sow in her mouth, while he pursued her with a club, descending into the den, and destroying the whole family without the assistance of any other person. The story, with all its exaggerations, found its way into the papers

and journals of England and France, so that Putnam came
to be familiarly known abroad as "the old wolf." This
was a common designation among his fellow-officers during
"the seven years' war."

The description of the cave, given above, is in every
particular accurate and exact, and was no doubt the result
of actual measurement on the part of Colonel Humphreys

Mr. Putnam was a man of great personal strength, as
well as courage. His frame was large and athletic. His
motions were rapid, nervous and impulsive. And though
he seldom undertook what he did not successfully accomplish, it often seemed as if he rushed to an act without
thought, and achieved it without a purpose. The truth
was, that the movements of his mind were as nervous and
impulsive as those of his body. His perceptions were
quick and accurate, and he jumped to conclusions at which
other men would arrive by slow and careful inquiry. This
was the true secret of his successful daring. It was not
thoughtlessness, but an instantaneous perception of all the
bearings of his position, and a consequent calmness and
self-possession which made him master of circumstances,
over which other and less active minds would have had
no control.

An incident is related of him at this period, which,
though it may seem too trifling of itself to be preserved,
will illustrate this peculiar impulsiveness, at the same
time that it affords a striking proof of his uncommon
strength. He had among his cattle a very fine bull, whom
he valued highly for his noble proportions and great
strength, but whose fierce, unruly temper made him the
terror of the whole neighborhood. Coming up to him in
the pasture one day, when he had been peculiarly savage
and ugly, he suddenly seized him by the tail, and twisting
it round a small tree, held him fast, while he administered

4*

a severe and effectual chastisement with an ox goad. The furious animal bellowed and tore the ground in his rage, but it was of no avail. The rod was laid on with such determined energy and good will, that every stroke had its desired effect, while the strong arm that held him gave him no chance of escape. From that time he was master of the bull, and had only to show the rod in his hand, to make him comparatively quiet and submissive.

The untiring industry and prudent husbandry of Mr. Putnam, during the ten or twelve years that intervened before the breaking out of the French War, placed his affairs on a very sound basis, and secured for him a comfortable independence for life. And when he was afterwards called to engage in the active service of his country, in the camp and the field, and to undergo the hardships and privations of war, he had the satisfaction of leaving his family well provided for, and having a quiet retreat to fall back upon, whenever the fortunes of war should either compel or permit him to retire. In this respect, he was more favorably situated than many of his compeers, who, in hazarding their lives for a cause which was too poor to reward them for their services, sacrificed their all, and returned, when their liberties were achieved, to wear away the evening of their days amid the cares and privations of poverty, as broken in fortune as in physical constitution.

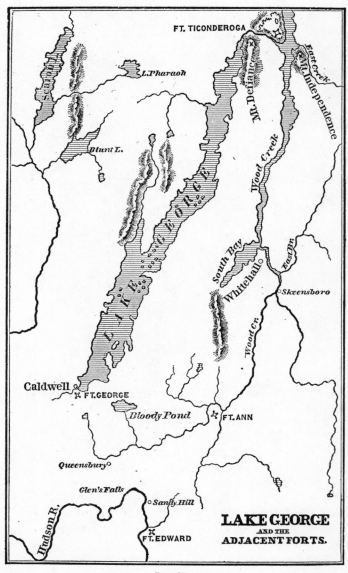

FT. TICONDEROGA

L. Pharaoh

East Creek

Mt. Defiance

Mt. Independence

Wood Creek

Blunt L.

LAKE GEORGE

South Bay

East Bn

Whitehall

Skeensboro

Wood Cr.

Caldwell

FT. GEORGE

Bloody Pond

FT. ANN

Queensbury

Glen's Falls

Sandy Hill

Hudson R.

FT. EDWARD

LAKE GEORGE
AND THE
ADJACENT FORTS.

CHAPTER III.

THE fearless courage, the generous and ready benevolence,
and the open, frank, confiding manner of Mr. Putnam, won
the admiration and regard of all who knew him. His
early popularity was remarkable ; and so enduring was it,
that the few individuals who have assumed the ungracious
office of detracting from his well-earned fame, have been
compelled to admit the fact, while they deny him every
pretension to that distinguished merit on which it should
have been founded.

So great was his reputation, however accounted for,
that, without any previous military experience, he was
appointed to a captaincy, in the regiment of Connecticut

provincials, on the breaking out of the French War. He found no difficulty in beating up recruits. His personal friends and admirers flocked to his standard, and his company was soon complete.—A company, not of vagabonds and bar-room adventurers, who follow the beat of a drum for the rations .which it promises without the drudgery of daily toil—but of hardy, industrious, respectable young men, the very flower of the yeomanry of Connecticut. None of them had been educated in the use of arms, or the evolutions of the camp and the battle-field. They had bold hearts and strong arms, and a confidence in their leader that made the service light.

The regiment, of which this company composed a part, was commanded by General Lyman. Putnam's command, however, was so often detached on special and peculiar service, that it held, during all the war, rather the position of an independent corps, than that of a limb of the army. Though not specifically drafted as Rangers, nor organized under that distinctive name, the duty assigned to it, and performed by it, was of that hardy, bold, adventurous character, which is usually rendered by that portion of a well appointed army. It was a service to which the genius of Putnam was peculiarly adapted. He delighted in scenes of daring excitement. He revelled in adventure. The ordinary monotony of camp duty would have been insupportably irksome. In the active and perilous duty of reconnoitering the enemy's posts, surprising their pickets, cutting off or capturing detached parties, waylaying convoys of provisions, destroying barracks and batteaux, and making prisoners, he found ample employment for his spirit of restless enterprise, as well as ample scope for that fruitfulness of invention and stratagem for which he was distinguished.

Never, perhaps, was there a war between two civilized

nations in which this peculiar kind of service was so indispensable, or where it was attended with so great and fearful hazards, as this, in which the English and French contended for the mastery in the Western Continent. The Indian tribes were nearly all enlisted on the side of the French. The mountains, the forests, the river banks, the shores and inlets of the lakes, were infested with straggling parties of these ruthless marauders, whose stealthy movements and peculiar mode of attack, rendered them far more formidable and annoying than many times their number of ordinary soldiers. Skulking in every thicket, and prowling in the outskirts of every wood, they were ever ready to spring upon the foe; who oftener fell by an unseen hand, than by an open enemy, against whom they might defend themselves, either by skilful manœuvre or the prowess of their arms. To contend with the difficulties of such a service, and render effective aid in its prosecution, the utmost coolness, prudence, sagacity and watchfulness, as well as fertility and readiness of resource, and promptness of action, were demanded. Bold, resolute, unflinching hearts, and hands that could almost anticipate the promptings of the will, were requisite to any degree of success.

The war commenced in earnest in 1755, with the unfortunate expedition of General Braddock against Fort Duquesne; the fruitless one of General Shirley against Fort Niagara; and the brilliant victory of Sir William Johnson over the Baron Dieskau, at Fort Edward, on Lake George. It was in this last and successful expedition, that Captain Putnam entered upon that great theatre of honorable strife and hazardous adventure, where he won those enduring laurels, which link his name with the noblest and worthiest of our country.

The object of this expedition was to reduce Crown

Point, and drive the French from their strong holds in and about Lake Champlain. It originated in Massachusetts, and was to be executed by the colonial troops of New England and New York,—General William Johnson, a leading member of the council of the latter colony, being placed in command. The troops from the different sections were to rendezvous at Albany. The greater part of them arrived at that place before the end of June ; but the artillery, *bateaux*, provisions, and other necessaries for the expedition could not be prepared till the 8th of August, at which time the army took up its line of march for the carrying place, between the Hudson and Lake George. General Lyman was already there, and had commenced the erection of a fortification, which was first called Fort Lyman, and afterward changed to Fort Edward.

Toward the end of August, the main body moved forward, and encamped near the southern extremity of Lake George—to which the French had given the name of Lake St. Sacrament. Here it was ascertained, by means of some Indian scouts, who had been sent out to gather intelligence, that a considerable party of French and Indians were stationed at Ticonderoga, on the isthmus between the north end of Lake George, and the southern part of Lake Champlain, about fifteen miles below Crown Point. Their position was admirably selected, as was proved in the subsequent history of the war, when it became a place of great strength and importance. But as yet, no defences were thrown up. Johnson was impatient to bring up his *bateaux* and artillery, intending to proceed with part of his force and seize that important pass. In the meantime, the French furnished him with sufficient employment at his own camp.

Baron Dieskau was in command of the French forces. He had just received intelligence of the commencement of the works at the carrying place by General Lyman, and resolved to give him battle before his entrenchments were completed ; intending, if successful, to desolate the northern settlements, lay Albany and Schenectady in ashes, and cut off all communications with Oswego, and the northern lakes. With this design, he embarked at Crown Point with two thousand men ; and, landing at South Bay, proceeded toward Fort Edward. The troops were ignorant of his purpose of attack until they arrived within two miles of the fort. Then, finding the Canadians and Indians unwilling to face the English cannon, he suddenly changed his route, and moved rapidly northward, hoping to surprise the camp at St. Sacrament, or Lake George.

In the meantime, General Johnson—being apprised by his scouts of the movements of the French Baron—sent messengers to Fort Edward to warn General Lyman of his approach. One of these was intercepted and killed. The others soon returned with the intelligence that they had descried the enemy about four miles northward of the fort.

It was now the 8th of September. A council of war was immediately called, in which it was resolved to send out a detachment, to intercept the enemy on his return. Hendricks, the celebrated Mohawk chief, was present at this council. When the number proposed to be sent out was mentioned to him, he replied: " If they are to fight they are too few ; if they are to be killed they are too many " It was then suggested to send out a larger detachment, in three separate parties. Hendricks took three sticks, and said : " Put these together, and you cannot break them ; take them one by one, and you may do it easily." The Mohawk's advice was taken ; and victory, though dearly bought, was the result.

The detachment was placed under the command of

Colonel Ephraim Williams, a brave officer, who, at the head of one thousand provincials, with about two hundred Indians, met the Baron nearly four miles from the camp. That able commander, apprised of their approach, made an advantageous disposition of his men to receive them. Keeping the main body of the regulars with him in the centre, he ordered the Canadians and Indians to advance on the right and left, in the woods, in such a manner as to enclose their enemy. When the American troops were considerably within the ambuscade, the old Mohawk sachem, who, with his Indians, had been sent out as a flank guard to the detachment, was hailed by a hostile Indian.

" Whence came you ?" said he.

" From the Mohawks. Whence came you ?"

" From Montreal."

The firing, which commenced immediately after this parley, brought on the action sooner than Dieskau intended, and prevented Williams and his party from being entirely surrounded and cut off. The provincials fought bravely, but finding themselves attacked on every side by superior numbers, were compelled to retreat with considerable loss. Colonel Williams was among the slain. Hendricks also was killed, with a number of his Indians, who fought with great intrepidity. The loss of the enemy was also considerable. Among their slain was M. St. Pierre, who commanded all the Indians, and on whom great reliance was placed. The retreating troops joined the main body, and waited the approach of their assailants,—now rendered more sanguine and formidable by their recent success.

A little before noon, the advanced guard of the enemy appeared in sight of the American army, which was encamped in a favorable position on the banks of Lake

George, covered on each flank by a low, thick wooded swamp. General Johnson had just mounted several pieces of cannon, which he had most opportunely received two days before from Fort Edward ; and trees had been felled to form a sort of breastwork, which was his only cover against an attack.

The enemy marched along the road, in very regular order, and in high confidence of victory. When within one hundred and fifty yards of the breastwork they made a momentary halt. A spirited attack was then made by the regulars upon the centre, while the Canadians and Indians fell upon the flanks. The distant platoon fire of the French did but little execution, so that the Americans soon recovered their spirits and determined on a most resolute defence. As soon as their artillery began to play, the Canadian militia and Indians, who were not accustomed to such terrible engines of destruction, fled in confusion and dismay to the swamps. Meeting with a warmer reception than he anticipated, and deserted by his allies, Dieskau was compelled, reluctantly, to order a retreat. His troops retiring in great disorder, were followed briskly by a party from the camp, who fell furiously on their rear, and precipitated their flight.

Baron Dieskau, who had received a wound in his leg, was found leaning against a stump entirely alone. While feeling for his watch, one of the Americans, now supposed to be General Pomeroy, suspecting him to be in search of a pistol, inflicted upon him another wound, which ultimately proved mortal, and conducted him a prisoner to the camp.

The English not continuing their pursuit, the enemy halted about four miles from the camp, at the very place where the engagement took place in the morning, and opened their packs for refreshment. While thus engaged,

5

a detachment of two hundred of the New Hampshire militia, under the brave Captain McGinnes, who had been dispatched from Fort Edward to the assistance of the main body, fell upon them and completely routed them. Captain McGinnes fell in the action. A large number of prisoners were taken. For this victory General Johnson was rewarded with a baronetcy, and a gift of five hundred pounds.

It was in this battle of Lake George, that Thayendanegea, the young Mohawk chief, better known as Joseph Brant, made his first appearance on the field of war. He was only thirteen years old. In relating the particulars of the bloody engagement, some time after, he stated, that " he was seized with such a tremor when the firing commenced, that he was obliged to take hold of a sapling to steady himself; but, after a few volleys, he recovered the use of his limbs, and the composure of his mind, so as to support the character of a brave man." He was born to be a warrior, as his history abundantly proves. " I like," said he, when some one was speaking of music, " I like the harpsichord well, and the organ still better; but I like the drum and trumpet best of all, for they make my heart beat quick."

For the purpose of securing the country from the incursions of the enemy, General Johnson erected a fort at the place of his encampment, which he named Fort William Henry. The remainder of the season was occupied in completing the intrenchments, with an occasional skirmish between reconnoitring and foraging parties, but without any attempt, on either side, to give or provoke a general engagement.

Soon after Putnam's arrival in the camp, he became intimately acquainted with a famous partizan, Captain, afterwards Major, Rogers, whose eminent services, as com-

mander of the corps of New Hampshire Rangers, contributed so much to the success of this expedition. Rogers kept a
journal of his own achievements, and that of his corps,
which was published in London, in 1765. It is full of
stirring interest, though manifestly incorrect in some respects. There is a studied omission of the services, and
even of the name of Putnam, so glaring as to impress the
mind of one acquainted with the facts, that it was the result
of some private pique, which the author was not willing to
acknowledge. In some essential points, which we shall
notice as we proceed, the journal differs entirely from the
orderly books of the army ; and, in others, from the narrative which Mr. Putnam's biographer, Col. David Humphreys, had from his own lips. The discrepancies discovered relate almost exclusively to those matters in which Putnam shared the hardship and the glory. There can be no more
authentic record of such matters than the orderly books of
the army ; and as to Putnam's word, it was always regarded, by all who knew him, as worthy of entire and implicit
credit. The learned Dr. Dwight, afterwards President of
Yale College, was his intimate friend. He was not a man
to " give flattering titles to any," or sacrifice truth to the
mere euphony of a panegyric. It was he who wrote the
epitaph upon Putnam's tomb, in which, after commending
his patriotism and his martial virtues, as above all praise,
he speaks of him as " a man, whose generosity was singular, *whose honesty was proverbial*," &c. Dr. Dwight alludes to him elsewhere in his writings, and always with
the same unlimited confidence. " His word," says he,
" was regarded as ample security for anything for which it
was pledged, and his uprightness commanded absolute confidence."

The omissions in Rogers' journal are the more remarkable, since it was to Putnam that the writer was once in-

debted for the preservation of his life, at the hazard of his own.   Whether it was Putnam's frank, open, republican simplicity of manners, or his bold and successful daring, threatening an eclipse to his own fame as a ranger, that rendered him both ungrateful and oblivious in these cases, it is impossible now to decide.   It is clear, however, that he had little feeling in common with his countrymen, and that, when he performed the remarkable services ascribed to him in " the Seven Years' war," it was not as an American, but as a loyal servant of his majesty.   This loyalty he retained to the end ; and, when the war of the Revolution broke out, he was found in the British service, fighting against the liberties of the land of his birth.   His journal was published in London the same year with the passage of the stamp act, and after the dispute between the colonies and the mother country had begun to wax uncomfortably warm.*

Sometimes in company with Rogers, and sometimes alone, Putnam was employed in reconnoitering the enemy's lines, gaining intelligence of his movements, and taking straggling prisoners, as well as in beating up the quarters, and surprising the advanced picquets of their army.   For these purposes, in addition to the regular corps of Rangers, under Captain Rogers, Putnam and his corps, as we have already stated, though not originally drafted for such a service, were assigned to these difficult and perilous undertakings.   The first time the two Captains went out together, it was the fortune of Putnam to preserve the life of Rogers, by striking down with his own hands a Frenchman, who was about to plunge a dagger into his heart.

The object of the expedition, on which they were detached, was to obtain an accurate knowledge of the position of the enemy, and the state of the fortifications at

* See Appendix, No. 1.

Crown Point.   The fort was so situated that it was impossible to approach it with their whole party, near enough to
effect the purpose of their mission, without being discovered.
To go alone, was to expose themselves to a hazard which
was hardly justifiable, on account of the swarms of hostile
Indians, who infested the woods.   Determined, however,
not to return without an attempt to accomplish their object,
the two leaders left all their men in covert at a convenient
distance, with strict orders to remain carefully concealed
till their return ; and crept stealthily forward, under cover
of the darkness, till they reached the near vicinity of the
fortress.   Here they laid during the night, without making
any satisfactory discoveries.   Early in the morning they
approached nearer, and spent considerable time in examining the defences from several points of view.   Having
completed their observations, and obtained all the information they desired upon the several points to which their
attention had been directed, they were about returning to
their covert, when Rogers, being separated from his comrade a short distance, suddenly encountered a stout Frenchman, who, instantly giving the alarm to a guard near by,
seized his fusee with one hand, and with the other made a
desperate effort to stab him.

A severe struggle ensued.   The guard answered the
call, and there was imminent danger of having the whole
garrison upon them at once.   Perceiving that no time
was to be lost, and that further alarm would be given,
and their danger greatly increased, if he should fire, Putnam sprang upon the Frenchman, administered a heavy
blow upon his head with the butt-end of his musket, and
laid him dead at his feet.   Thus relieved, and expecting
instant pursuit, they flew with the utmost speed to the
mountains, joined their party in ambush, and returned,

5*

without further incident, to the camp. This was in the latter part of October.

The fortress at Crown Point being found too strong, and too ably garrisoned, to justify an attack, and the season being now far advanced, the greater part of the army was discharged, reserving only six hundred men, under the immediate command of General Johnson, to garrison Forts Edward and William Henry. The French, in the mean time, took possession of Ticonderoga, at the northern outlet of Lake George, and fortified it strongly.

The colonial troops having enlisted only for the campaign, Captain Putnam's term of service ended with the season, and he returned home to pass the winter in the quiet enjoyment of domestic life, and to look after the interests of his growing family and his thrifty farm. With a versatility peculiar to a pioneer life, he exchanged the sword for the ploughshare, and the gilded military coat for the homespun frock, equally willing and able to till the soil, as to fight in its defence.

CHAPTER IV.

THE plan of the campaign of 1756, as agreed upon in a
council of the colonial governors, held at Albany in the
early part of the season, was similar to that of the preceding year—having for its object the reduction of Crown
Point, Niagara, and Fort Duquesne. Putnam was re-ap-
pointed to his command, under his old leader—Major-
General Abercrombie being commander-in-chief until the
latter part of July, when he was superseded by the Earl
of Loudoun. The expedition against Crown Point was
committed to Major-General Winslow, which he was to
conduct with the provincial forces alone, without any aid
from the British troops, who were reserved to garrison and
defend the forts.

The astonishing success of Montcalm at Forts Oswego

and George, which he razed to the ground, diverted the British General from his offensive movement towards Crown Point. General Winslow was arrested in his preparations for this service, and ordered to ,fortify his own camp, in anticipation of an attack from the enemy, and an attempt to advance into the country, below the Lake Champlain, by way of South Bay or Wood Creek. General Webb, with fourteen hundred men, was stationed at the great carrying place, near Wood Creek ; and Sir William Johnson, with one thousand, at the German Flats, on the Mohawk, and nearly half way to Oswego. In these precautionary and defensive measures the campaign passed off without another battle.

But, though a season of inactivity to the body of the army, and the commanders, it was full of stirring incident to Putnam and others,—whose task it was to watch the movements, and annoy the outposts of the enemy. Adventures of this kind are sufficiently hazardous in the daytime ; but, when attempted in the night, they are peculiarly liable to accidents. Having been commanded to reconnoitre the enemy's camp, at a place called " The Ovens," near Ticonderoga, Captain Putnam took as a companion in the enterprise, the brave Lieutenant Robert Durkee. In the prosecution of the duties assigned him, he narrowly escaped being made a prisoner himself, in the first instance, and killing his comrade, in the second. It was the custom, with the British and Provincial troops, to arrange their camp fires along the outer lines of their encampment, which gave a great advantage to the enemy's scouts and patrols, laying open the whole extent of the camp to their view, and frequently exposing the sentinels to be picked off by expert marksmen. A contrary, and much more rational practice, prevailed among the French and Indians. They kindled their fires in the centre, lodged

their men circularly at a distance, and posted their sentinels in the surrounding darkness. Ignorant of this arrangement, and supposing that the French sentries were within
the circle of the fires, the bold scouts approached the camp,
creeping upon their hands and knees with the greatest
possible caution, until, to their utter astonishment, they
found themselves in the very thickest of the enemy. The
sentinels, seeing by the light of the fires beyond that some
one had passed stealthily without challenge, gave the
alarm and fired. Durkee was slightly wounded in the
thigh.

There was, of course, no alternative but instant flight.
Putnam, being foremost, and scarcely able, on turning
away from the glare of the fires, to see his hand before
him, soon plunged into a clay-pit. Durkee, limping
briskly along, tumbled, with no gentle fall, into the same
pit. Putnam, not relishing a companion so near, in such
circumstances, and supposing him to be one of the pursuing enemy, was about striking him down, when Durkee,
who had followed so closely as to know what company he
was in, inquired whether he had escaped unhurt. Instantly
recognizing the voice of his friend, and rejoicing to find
him also safe, Putnam dropped his weapon, and both,
springing from the pit, made good their retreat to the
neighboring ledges, amid a shower of random shot. Having reached a place of safety, they found shelter under the
lee of a large log, which afforded them a comfortable lodging for the remainder of the night

Before composing themselves to sleep, Putnam recol-
lected that there was a little rum left in his canteen.
Thinking it could never be more acceptable, or useful,
than at that time, he generously offered to share it with
his comrade, in drinking to the confusion of the sentinel
who had given them so unceremonious a salutation. On

examining the canteen, however, which hung under his arm, it was found perfectly dry, having been pierced by one of the balls that had whistled about him in his flight. The temperance men of the present day, would doubtless regard that ball as having done better service than if it had drawn the blood of an enemy. On inspecting his blanket, the next day, it was found to have been pierced in fourteen places. Whether all this boring was the work of one leaden messenger from the French camp, or of many, it must be regarded as one of those remarkable escapes, which can only be referred to the protecting agency of a special providence, of which so many instances are recorded in the annals of the American wars.

During the continuance of the army at this place, an incident occurred which illustrates, in a very striking manner, the singular courage and ready wit of Mr. Putnam. The garrison had been exceedingly annoyed by a large, powerful, wily Indian, who prowled about the lines under cover of the night, perpetrating all kinds of mischief, and picking off the sentinels apparently at his pleasure, and always eluding the utmost watchfulness of the guards. There was one of the outposts in particular, which had shared more largely than any other in his regards. For several nights in succession, the sentinel on that post was taken off in a most mysterious manner. The commanding officer had given directions, in case any noise should be heard in the vicinity of the station, that the sentinel should call out, " Who goes there ?" three times, and then, if no answer were returned, fire in the direction of the noise. Night after night, these orders had been given, as the post was supplied with a new sentinel, but without any avail. The post was always found deserted in the morning, until it came to be looked upon as certain death to venture upon duty at that place.

As is usual, in well appointed armies, the post of danger was sought for by the best men in the garrison ; and already a number of the bravest and most valuable soldiers had fallen in this hazardous service. It began to be difficult to obtain volunteers. At length the post was utterly declined. The commander was making preparations to supply the place by lot, when Mr. Putnam, whose station as a commissioned officer excused him from all such duties as this, stepped forward, and solicited the honor of standing guard for the night. His offer was promptly accepted. Relying upon the rule he had already laid down, the commander reiterated the instructions he had given to previous sentinels, saying : " If you hear any sound from without the lines, you will call ' *Who goes there* ?' three times, and then, if no answer be given, fire." With these instructions, and a promise to give a good account of himself the next day, Putnam proceeded to his post.

Having examined, with the utmost scrutiny, every tree, and shrub, and rock, in the neighborhood ; measured with accuracy every point in the area around him ; fixed their bearings and distances in his mind, and looked well to the condition of his musket, he commenced his monotonous tramp, to and fro, along his portion of the line. His plan of operations had been fully digested in his own mind, before he volunteered ; and it will be seen, in the sequel, that he perfectly understood the nature of the Indian's artifice, and the manner in which he had taken advantage of the previous sentinels.

For several hours, nothing occurred to attract his notice, or disturb his thoughts. At length, about midnight, his quick ear discerned a slight rustling among the grass, as of an animal stealthily approaching, or passing his post. Presently, this rustling was followed by a crackling sound, like that made by a hog munching acorns. Determined that not even a hog should trespass with impunity upon his premises, he raised his musket to his shoulder, and adjusting his aim with great care toward the spot from which the sounds proceeded, called out, " *Who goes there three times* ?" and instantly discharged his piece. It was followed by a deep groan, and a struggle as of one in the agonies of death. On examining the spot, a huge Indian was found, disguised in a bear-skin, and now just breathing his last. He had been shot through the heart. From that time the sentinels paced their rounds unmolested, and the fatal outpost lost its pre-eminence as the post of danger.*

In the course of the summer, a body of the enemy, consisting of six hundred men, attacked the baggage and provision waggons of the American army, at a place called Half-way Brook—it being equi-distant from Fort Edward and Fort William Henry. Having killed the oxen, and plundered the waggons, they retreated with their booty, experiencing but little interruption from the small body of troops by whom the convoy was escorted. When the tidings of this disaster reached the camp, Captains Putnam and Rogers were ordered to pursue the plunderers, and recover or destroy their booty. They were directed to embark with one hundred volunteers in boats, with two wall-pieces, and as many blunderbusses, and proceed down Lake George to a certain point, there to leave the batteaux under a proper guard, and thence to cross by land, so as to harass, and, if possible, intercept the retreating enemy at the narrows.

* This incident was furnished by a gentleman of the first respectability, to whom it was communicated some thirty years ago, by Jared Scarborough, Esq., of Brooklyn, a neighbor and intimate friend of Putnam, and a sharer in some of his military enterprises.

These orders were executed with so much spirit and punctuality, that the party arrived at the spot designated for the attack a full half hour before the hostile boats came in view. Waiting under cover of the woods until the enemy, wholly unsuspicious of the ambush, entered the narrows, their boats deeply loaded with plunder, the volunteers commenced a brisk and galling fire. They poured in upon them volley after volley, killed many of the oarsmen, sunk a number of the boats, and would have cut off the whole body, encumbered as they were with baggage, had not a strong wind, favoring their desperate exertions to escape, swept a few of them through the narrows into the South Bay, and beyond the reach of the guns of their assailants. This shattered remnant of the little fleet, pushing on with desperate speed to Ticonderoga, reported the disaster, and gave information that Putnam and Rogers were at the narrows, with a large detachment of provincials.

A fresh party, of three hundred French and Indians, was instantly despatched to intercept them on their return to Fort Edward, and cut them in pieces. Anticipating the probability of such an attempt, and being fully twenty miles from their boats, they strained every nerve to reach them before night. With incredible exertion they effected their object, and were soon embarked, and moving briskly down the lake. On the following day, having proceeded as far as Sabbath-day Point, they discovered on shore the pursuing party, who must have passed them unperceived in the night. As soon as the boats came in view, the French embarked with great alacrity, and rowed out into the lake, to give them battle. They advanced in regular line, with a bold and confident air, felicitating themselves upon the certain prospect of an easy victory, from the great superiority of their numbers. Flushed with

6

these expectations, they were permitted to come within pistol shot before a gun was fired. Then, at a signal, the wall pieces and blunderbusses, which had been brought to rake the enemy in their most vulnerable point, were simultaneously discharged. No such broadside reception as this having been anticipated, the assailants were thrown into the utmost disorder. The confusion and dismay was greatly increased by a well-directed and most destructive fire from the small arms. The larger pieces being re-loaded without annoyance, continued, alternately with the musketry, to make such dreadful havoc, that the enemy never recovered from the first surprise and dismay, sufficiently to make one vigorous effort to rally. The rout was complete. The loss of the French was very great. In one of the canoes, containing twenty Indians, only five escaped. From other boats great numbers, both of French and Indians, were seen to fall overboard. The remainder, crippled and shattered, and laden with the wounded and the dying, glad of an opportunity to abandon the scene of so mortifying and terrible a defeat, were driven back to Ticonderoga. Of the American party, only one man was killed, and two slightly wounded. Having dispersed their enemies, they landed on the Point, refreshed themselves at leisure, and then returned in good order and high spirits to the British camp, having inflicted upon an enemy vastly superior in numbers a most mortifying defeat, and an amount of loss scarcely inferior to that of some pitched battles. The loss of the French, in both engagements, could not have been less than five hundred men—a heavy price to pay for their bold reprisals upon the American baggage train.

Another incident occurred soon after, which, though of no great interest in itself, or in its results, will serve to illustrate the nature of the tasks imposed upon a bold and active partisan; the vigilance, fearlessness, enterprise and prudence they demanded of him, and the imminent peril to which his life was constantly exposed. The season was far advanced. It was hardly expected that there would be any active hostilities during the present campaign, but it was very desirable to obtain, if possible, some definite information of the strength and designs of the enemy. For this purpose Captain Putnam was sent out, with five men, to procure a prisoner from some of the straggling parties of the enemy. Approaching the camp with all the circumspection of an Indian scout, he found a place of concealment exactly adapted to his purpose, in a thicket that skirted the road leading from Ticonderoga to the Ovens. His men, whose valor for the moment got the better of their discretion, ascribing the caution of their leader to cowardice, were very unwilling to confine themselves within this covert. It was with difficulty that they were prevented from exposing themselves in such a manner as to defeat entirely the object of their enterprise, and put the lives of the whole party to unnecessary hazard. The issue proved the truth of the common remark, that they who are most bold and boisterous when no danger is near, are the first to shrink from it, when it approaches.

The party had not been long within their covert, when a Frenchman and an Indian passed ; the Indian being considerably in advance. Watching his opportunity, when the Indian was far enough off to render any interference on his part improbable, Putnam sprang from the thicket, ordering his men to follow. After running about thirty rods, he overtook the Frenchman, seized him by the shoulder, and commanded him to surrender. His men, who were lately so bold, now realized the advantage of a place of concealment ; and, disregarding the order of their captain, left him to meet single-handed the danger of a conflict with two of their foes. The Frenchman looking round, and perceiving no other enemy, and knowing that his Indian friend would soon be at hand to assist him, obstinately resisted being made a prisoner. Putnam, finding himself betrayed by his men into a perilous dilemma, and knowing that no time was to be lost, let go his hold, stepped a few paces back, and levelled his piece at the Frenchman's breast. It missed fire ; whereupon the Frenchman, seeing his advantage, gave the alarm to his Indian comrade, and sprung furiously upon his assailant. Putnam thought it prudent to retreat, and thus drew his enemy off in the direction of the place where his men were posted, and where, if they had not shown themselves too soon, he would inevitably have fallen into their hands They played their part so ill, however, that he discovered the ambuscade in season to effect his escape.

It was now a dangerous neighborhood for the American scouts. The alarm had been given, and a diligent and active pursuit was sure to be the consequence. They, therefore, made a precipitate flight, and arrived without accident at their own camp. Mortified with the result of this adventure, Putnam dismissed his men with disgrace, selected another party, on whom he could rely with confidence, and set forth again on the same hazardous errand. Of the incidents of this adventure, we are not informed. It was brief and successful, however, as might have been predicted from the character of its leader, for he never abandoned an enterprise, while there was a reasonable hope of accomplishing it.

To those who are unacquainted with the duties and dangers of the camp, and with the peculiar difficulties to be overcome, in a country covered with thick forests, and with but few roads besides the Indian footpaths, such insignificant feats as the capture of a single prisoner, or a visit of observation to the enemy's lines, will hardly appear of sufficient importance to be recorded; and the services of the bold and able adventurers, by whom they are achieved, will, of course, be lightly appreciated. They may be assured, however, that they were viewed in a very different light by the commanders, for whose benefit they were undertaken. •There were few men in the army, who could not have been better spared than these; and, during the greater part of the campaign, they were the only men who were employed in any active service, or knew anything of the perils and hardships of war.

In this department, no one was more useful, no one stood higher in the estimation of the commanding generals, than Captain Putnam. He was found to be possessed, in happy combination, of all the qualities required for this peculiar service. To a total insensibility to danger, he united prudence, circumspection, sagacity, and uncommon fertility of resources, which was equal to any exigency. The employment of a scout and a ranger was admirably adapted to bring out and display these peculiar qualities, though, unfortunately for their possessor, the sphere in which he operated was too limited, and the duties he performed of too private and confidential a nature, to secure for him a conspicuous place in the history of those times. Such services rarely receive their due award of fame, unless the brave men who render them become their own trumpeters. They come not within the range of the ordinary records of the army. From their very nature, they are concealed from the public gaze at the time of their achievement. They are planned in secret, and executed in secret—their efficiency and success often depending as much upon the fidelity with which their secret character is maintained, as upon any other circumstance. The movements of an army, the fate of a battle—the whole

6*

matter at issue in a war—have often been decided by the information communicated to the commanders by a single scout. Yet his name is not mentioned, nor his agency acknowledged, either by the general in making up his report of the issue, or by the historian in recording it for posterity. The simple phrase—" The general having received information," &c., covers it all ; while the hazards at which that information was obtained are lost sight of, and the boldness of manœuvre, the correctness of observation, the sagacity, and sound judgment, required to render it valuable, are credited to the genius and foresight of the commander.

Putnam kept no journal. A few of his adventures were partially preserved in the orderly books, and some found their way into the newspapers of the day ; while some were transmitted from friend to friend, for many years, without appearing in print. He enjoyed an uncommon popularity in the army. " He was endeared to the soldiers, by the cheerfulness with which he shared their perils and privations, and the gallantry which suffered none to go, where he did not himself lead the way ; to his superior officers, by the energy and promptness with which he executed their commands ; and he began to rise, in the estimation of the public generally, as one who was destined to become distinguished in a broader field of action."

CHAPTER V.

In 1757 the Legislature of Connecticut conferred on Putnam the commission of a Major. Notwithstanding the
many reverses of the Anglo-American forces hitherto, great
exertions were made for opening this campaign with an
army that should make success almost certain. What
might have been the result, had this army been guided by
a competent commander, it is impossible to say. But the
British government, refusing to learn wisdom from the
disasters of past years, persisted in placing the whole control of the affairs of the colonies in the hands of English
officers, who knew nothing of the country, and scorned to
take the smallest advice from the provincials with whom
they were associated. In the present instance, they were
more than usually unfortunate in their selection. Of all
the generals who served at any time in America, Lord
Loudoun was the most incompetent to the arduous service.

He had superseded General Abercrombie about the middle of the previous campaign, and had been frightened, by the success of Montcalm at Oswego, from attempting any other measures than those of mere defence.

During the winter his Lordship made large requisitions upon the colonial Legislatures for the increase of the army. The call was responded to with great alacrity. At the same time, a large fleet and army arrived from Europe, and the colonists began to look upon the speedy downfall of the power of France in America as almost certain.

Their hopes were doomed to a bitter disappointment. Instead of following up, as they expected, the designs of the previous campaigns, by striking a decisive blow in the direction of Canada, and shielding their northern frontier from the continual inroads of the enemy, the commander-in-chief, under pretence of concentrating all his force upon one point, and achieving a certain and brilliant victory there, turned his whole attention upon Louisburg, in the island of Cape Breton. It was midsummer before his preparations for this expedition were completed. When all things were ready, and his forces, both naval and military, assembled at Halifax, he learned that a powerful fleet had arrived at Louisburg from Brest, with a large reinforcement for the garrison. This disconcerted all his plans. The expedition was at once abandoned, and with . it all idea of offensive operations. It required but a single demonstration on the part of the enemy to exhaust the valor of the over-discreet Earl, and throw him upon his defence. Leaving the fleet to watch the motions of the French, he returned to New York to refresh himself for the next year's campaign.

Meanwhile, the French commander, Montcalm, secure with respect to Louisburg, and encouraged by the diversion in that direction of so large a part of the British forces, determined to make a bold push to secure the entire possession of Lake George. The condition of Fort William Henry, the frontier post of the Americans, was such as to invite assault. It was an ill-constructed and ill-appointed fortification, occupying a small eminence, which rose gradually from the waters of the lake, near its southern extremity. It was garrisoned at that time by about three thousand men, under Colonel Munroe, while General Webb, who commanded in the northern department, was stationed at Fort Edward, about fifteen miles below, with a considerably larger force. He was an officer of nearly as much courage and capacity as Lord Loudoun, and a fit representative of that nobleman in any situation where he might be placed.

About the first of August, this valorous commander— who always took especial care to provide for his own safety—proceeded, under the escort of Major Putnam, with two hundred chosen men, to examine in person the state of the defences at Fort William Henry. While there, Putnam proposed to go down the lake, with a party of five men, and reconnoitre the enemy's position at Ticonderoga, and the adjacent posts.

This proposition was rejected by the prudent commander as altogether too hazardous. At length, however, he was permitted to undertake the enterprise with eighteen volunteers. They immediately embarked in three whale-boats, and set forward on their expedition. Before reaching Northwest Bay, the place where they proposed to land, they discovered a large body of the enemy on an island. Satisfied that this indicated a southward movement of the French, preparatory to an attack upon our fortresses, and desirous, in case he and his party should be cut off or taken, to put his commander upon his guard, he immediately directed two of the boats to lie to, as if for the purpose of fishing, while he with the other returned to report progress. The general, seeing him rowing back with great speed, in a single boat, and supposing that the others had fallen into the hands of the enemy, sent out a skiff, with orders for the major alone to come on shore. After making his report to the general, and explaining what he conceived to be the evident design of the enemy, he proposed returning immediately, to rejoin his companions, and prosecute his discoveries still further.

Webb, unwilling to part with his escort in such an alarming emergency, preferred leaving the two boats to their fate, rather than send so brave a man to bring them off. Putnam was urgent, however, and the general yielded a reluctant assent. Pushing vigorously out, he found his men where he had left them, though more intent upon the motions of the men on shore, than upon securing a very large draught of fishes. Passing on a little farther, he presently encountered a large number of boats in motion on the lake—from the foremost of which he was enabled to escape only by the superior fleetness of his own, and the vigorous exertions of his rowers.

Convinced, beyond a doubt, that this formidable armament was destined against Fort William Henry, he hastened his return to that place, and communicated to General Webb all he had seen, and his views of the object of the hostile expedition. That commander, strictly enjoining silence on the subject, directed him to put his men under an oath of secresy, and to prepare, without loss of time, to return to the head-quarters of the army. Major Putnam argued strenuously against such a desertion of the post in the moment of danger, and earnestly pleaded the duty of meeting the enemy on the shore, should he presume to

land.   But General Webb was resolute in his decision.
He would neither remain himself, nor suffer his escort to
remain.   Accordingly, the following day, he returned to
Fort Edward, and sent up a detachment to reinforce the
garrison at Fort William Henry.   The day following its
arrival, Montcalm invested the fortress with a force of
seven thousand French and Canadian soldiers, and two
thousand Indians.

To resist this formidable army, there were only twenty-
five hundred men in the garrison.   Their commander,
Colonel Munroe, was a gallant officer, and worthy of the
post of danger.   It was the third of August, when Montcalm commenced the siege with a summons to surrender.
In his letter to Colonel Munroe, he urged the capitulation
by considerations of humanity; declaring that he had an
engine of such fearful power in his hands, that, when once
set in motion, it would be impossible to check or control
it.   His influence over his Indian allies, to restrain them
from the commission of every atrocity, would be utterly
lost, as soon as the first drop of blood was shed.   No written answer was given to this summons.   A verbal reply
was returned by the bearer, that the fort would be defended to the last extremity.

With this resolution, the garrison held out until the
ninth.   In the meantime, Colonel Munroe had found
means to send several expresses to Fort Edward, soliciting
relief in the most urgent manner, and declaring his intention to hold out till relief should arrive.   But, though the
force at that place had been considerably increased by the
arrival of General Johnson's troops, and the militia, Webb
resolved that no succor could be afforded to the beleaguered fortress.   So urgent, however, were the solicitations
of Sir William Johnson, that, after several days, that
worthy officer, with as many as would volunteer for the

service, marched for its relief. The privilege was eagerly
embraced by the provincials, including Putnam's corps.
They had scarcely been gone an hour, however, when the
general's heart failed him, and a messenger was dispatched, ordering their instant return.

It was this miserable, shameful pusillanimity, on the
part of the commander of the northern department, that
occasioned the loss of Fort William Henry, and the bloody
tragedy that followed its surrender. When, some time
after this, Putnam was a prisoner in Canada, he was assured by Montcalm himself, that the siege would have been
abandoned, if this reinforcement had been suffered to go
forward. He was informed of its approach by one of his
Indian scouts ; who, on being questioned relative to its
numbers, replied, in the figurative style peculiar to that
people : " *If you can count the leaves on the trees, you can
count them.*"

On the receipt of this intelligence, the operations of the
siege were actually suspended, and preparations were
made for embarking ; while it was manifest that a new
spirit was infused into the besieged by the assurance which
these preparations gave, that the siege was about to be
raised. Meanwhile, another runner came in, and reported
that this formidable reinforcement had been recalled. The
siege was, consequently, renewed with more vigor than
ever.

All expectations of relief were now at an end. Two
of the largest guns of the fort had burst ; their ammunition
was almost exhausted ; and further resistance seemed
obviously unavailing. At this juncture, a letter was
received from General Webb, advising a surrender, and
stating, definitively, that no succor could be expected from
Fort Edward. Articles of capitulation were, accordingly,
agreed upon and signed. Honorable terms were granted

to the garrison, " on account of their honorable defence,"
as it was expressed in the articles.   They were to march
out with the honors of war, with their arms and baggage,
and retire under an escort to Fort Edward, with a solemn
pledge of protection against the Indians.   This pledge,
however, was shamefully disregarded.   The scene which
followed is one of the darkest in the bloody annals of war,
and, even at this distant day, can hardly be recited without a thrill of horror.   The troops began their march of
evacuation.   The last files had scarcely issued from the
gates, when the whole body of Indians attached to the
French army fell upon them with the fury of hungry
tigers, and commenced an indiscriminate slaughter.   Great
numbers were killed.   Many were taken prisoners, and
dragged off to a captivity worse than death, in the deep
forests of the west.   A miserable remnant escaped, among
whom was the gallant Munroe, and reached Fort Edward
in a most forlorn condition.

Different writers have taken different views of the conduct of the French general, in relation to this cruel massacre.   Some declare, as the testimony of those who were
eye-witnesses of the scene, that no efforts were made by
the French to arrest these atrocities ; no protection, demanded alike by honor and humanity, was given to those
to whom it had been sacredly pledged.   Others say, that
the utmost exertions of the French commander were used
to restrain his savage allies ; and that he and his officers
did everything, except firing upon the Indians, to put a
stop to the merciless butchery.   For the honor of humanity, it is to be hoped that the latter judgment is correct ;
and charity inclines us to accept it.   There is certainly
something to sustain it, in the caution which accompanied
the original summons to surrender.

The panic-stricken Webb, expecting that this decisive

7

victory would be followed up by a similar demonstration
against Fort Edward, sent out Captain Putnam with his
corps, to watch the motions of the enemy. His previous
conduct leaves us little room to doubt, that he would have
abandoned his post at once, without firing a gun, if Montcalm had turned his face in that direction. With such
men as these to control the movements of the army, it is
no matter of surprise, that the earlier campaigns of the
Seven Years' war presented a continual series of disaster,
defeat and desolation.

Putnam reached the scene of carnage, just as the rear-
guard of the enemy were embarking on the lake. The
fort was dismantled and demolished. The cannon, stores and
water-craft were all carried off. The barracks, outhouses
and sutlers' booths had been fired, and were still burning,
and hundreds of human bodies lay, half consumed, among
the smoking ruins. More than one hundred women were
found among them, some with the brains still oozing from
their battered heads ; others with their hairless sculls in
ghastly baldness, the entire crown having been wrenched
away ; many mangled, lacerated, hacked to pieces, and
violated with all the wanton mutilations of savage ingenuity, lay entirely naked among the heaps of the slain soldiers, as if the last effort of the wife to cling to her husband for protection, and the last wish of the husband to
raise his arm in her defence, had brought down a tenfold
vengeance upon the heads of both. To the generous,
warm-hearted Putnam, whose sympathies were ever alive
to the sufferings of his comrades, and whose constant aim
it was to mitigate, by every means in his power, the horrors of war, the spectacle must have been truly appalling.
We feel, as we shudder over the dreadful account, that
there was some apology for the exterminating retribution,
which our fathers visited upon so merciless a foe.

Not long after this disaster, General Lyman succeeded to the command of Fort Edward. He immediately set himself to strengthening its defences, which the French commander resolved, if possible, to prevent, intending, at an early day, to visit it in the same manner as he had done Fort William Henry. A party of one hundred and fifty men were sent out into the neighboring forest to cut timber for the fort. To protect them in their labors, Captain Little, with fifty British regulars, was posted at the head of a morass, about one hundred rods eastward from the fort. From this station there was a narrow causeway leading to the fort, flanked on one side by the morass, and on the other by a small creek.

One morning, at break of day, the attention of one of the sentinels was arrested, by what he conceived to be birds, coming up from the thicket of the morass, and flying with incredible swiftness over his head. While wondering what species of bird it could be, whose flight was so rapid as to elude observation, he was suddenly enlightened by seeing one of these winged messengers, in the shape of an Indian arrow, quivering in the tree just over his head. A large body of savages had crept stealthily into the morass during the night, and were attempting, in this manner, to pick off the sentinel, without creating an alarm, in order to surprise and cut off the whole party.

The alarm was instantly given. The Indians, finding themselves discovered, rushed from their covert upon the unarmed laborers, shot and tomahawked those who were nearest at hand, and pressed hard on the remainder, as they fled in dismay towards the fort. Captain Little and his band flew to their arms, and pouring in a well-timed and spirited fire, checked the pursuit, and covered the retreat of the fatigue-men, till those who were not wounded in the first onset, were enabled to reach the shelter of the fort. His little party, being almost overpowered by superior numbers, he sent to General Lyman for assistance. But that commander, taken by surprise, ignorant of the extent of the danger, and imagining that this assault was only the precursor of a general attack from the main body of the enemy, called in his outposts, and shut the gates, and left the brave band to their fate.

Major Putnam, with his corps of Rangers, was stationed at one of the outposts, on a small island adjacent to the fort. Hearing the discharge of the musketry, and learning from his runners that his friend, Capt. Little, was in imminent peril of being cut off, he plunged into the river, followed by his men, and waded through the water to the scene of action. Passing near the fort on his way, General Lyman was apprised of his movement. Unwilling that the lives of a few more brave men should be exposed to what he deemed inevitable destruction, he mounted the parapet, and ordered him to proceed no farther. The bold ranger, willing to jeopard not only his life, but, if necessary, his standing, in order to rescue his friend, made a brief apology, and, without waiting to ascertain whether it was satisfactory, hurried on to the scene of conflict. In a few minutes they had opened their way to the little handful of regulars, who maintained their ground with the utmost gallantry. At the suggestion of Putnam, the whole party now rushed impetuously, with shouts and huzzas, into the swamp. The charge was completely successful. The Indians fled in every direction, and were pursued with great slaughter until night-fall. On the part of the chase, only one man was killed during the pursuit; and his death was immediately revenged by that of the Indian who shot him. This Indian was one of that valuable class, called Runners—a chosen body of active young men, whose principal occupation is to procure intelligence, and convey tidings ; but who are sometimes employed in covering the rear on a retreat.

Returning in triumph from the chase, Putnam expected a reprimand, if not something more severe, from his commander. It was the only instance, in the course of his military career, in which he failed to render the strictest obedience to orders. His motive in this case was highly commendable, and his apology was strongly fortified by the brilliant success of his sortie. But neither purity of motive, nor brilliancy of success, can sanction a departure from the rigid rules of discipline, which are absolutely necessary to the maintenance of order and authority in the camp. So seductive is the influence of a brave man's example, particularly when, crowned with new laurels, he returns from some splendid achievement, undertaken in contravention of the positive orders of his superior, that, however elevated the rank of the officer, or however meritorious the service rendered, it would not be well to pass it by unheeded. According to the ordinary usages of war, Putnam should have been subjected to a court-martial, immediately on his return. Why this usage was departed from in his case we are not informed. It is probable, however, that General Lyman, when he recovered from his alarm, and found that no assault was intended, was more ready to admit the apology of his subaltern, than he would otherwise have been, since it saved him from the painful reflection that a brave band of his own men had been unnecessarily exposed to be cut in pieces by a superior force. He chose to treat his order rather as advisatory than peremptory, and commending the good conduct of his men, welcomed them, with a hearty good will, to their quarters.

During the ensuing winter, when the army were comfortably sheltered in their quarters at Fort Edward, a fire

7*

broke out in the barracks, adjacent to the north-western bastion. Within twelve feet of these barracks stood the magazine, containing three hundred barrels of powder. The fire was so far advanced, when it was first discovered, that it raged with great violence, almost bidding defiance to every effort to extinguish it. By the orders of Colonel Haviland, who then commanded at this post, several pieces of heavy artillery were brought to bear upon the barracks, with a view of severing their supporters, and thus levelling them to the ground. The effort was unsuccessful, and the flames continued to spread with great rapidity. Major Putnam, who still occupied his outpost station on the adjacent island, hearing the alarm, and seeing the smoke and flames rising in a dense column to the clouds, hastened to the fort to render what assistance he could. When he arrived, the flames were spreading fiercely in the direction of the magazine, which was now in imminent danger.

By his suggestion, a line of soldiers was formed through a postern gate to the river, from which a constant supply of water was conveyed. Putnam, mounting a ladder to the eaves of the building, received the water, and distributed it upon the burning rafters, with a perseverance that had well nigh cost him his life. Notwithstanding all their efforts, the flames continued to gain upon him, but he stood to his post undaunted, completely enveloped in smoke, and so near the sheet of flame, that a pair of thick blanket mittens was entirely burned from his hands. Calling for another pair, which he dipped in water and kept thoroughly wet, he persevered in his perilous efforts to subdue the devouring element. Colonel Haviland, considering his situation to be too dangerous, urged him to come down, and try some other means that involved less personal exposure. He replied that there was no hope but in resisting the enemy inch by inch, and that a moment's suspension

of their efforts might give it an advantage which would
prove fatal to them all.   He therefore entreated to be suffered to remain, while there was the smallest chance of
accomplishing anything by his endeavors.   The gallant
Colonel, not less astonished than charmed at the coolness
and intrepidity of the Major, was encouraged to renewed
exertions.   He gave orders to arrest the movements of
the men, who were carrying away their valuables from the
fort, and animated them to redoubled diligence in their
efforts to extinguish the flames, exclaiming, with the heroic
enthusiasm of a true soldier, " If we *must* be blown up, we
will all go together."

At length the flames had spread over the whole extent
of the barracks, and began to shoot out fearfully toward
the magazine.   Putnam descended from the tottering building, took his station between it and the magazine, and continued, from an incessant rotation of replenished buckets,
to resist their further progress.   His efforts were bravely
and ably seconded by officers and men.   So near was the
fire, and so intense the heat, that the outside plank sheath-
ing of the magazine was soon consumed, leaving only a
partition of timber between the raging element and a deposit of fifteen tons of powder.   When this partition,
already charred and smoking, was exposed to view, the
consternation became general and extreme.   Had a council of war been convened on the instant, it would undoubtedly have ordered a precipitate retreat.   But the heat and
enthusiasm of the contest left no room for consultation or
reflection.   It was an hour for action, not for debate.   Putnam, still undaunted, covered with a cloud of cinders,
singed and scorched on every side, maintained his position,
pouring an incessant stream of water upon the magazine,
until the rafters of the barracks falling in, the source of the

fire was cut off, and the safety of the remaining works en-
sured.

For an hour and a half he had contended with that terrible element. His face, his hands, his arms, and almost
his whole body were blistered with the intensity of the
heat, to which he had been exposed ; and when he pulled
off his second pair of mittens, the skin from his hands and
fingers followed them.   Several weeks elapsed, before he
recovered from the effects of this exposure.   His sufferings were great, but he was amply rewarded by the warmly
expressed and kind attentions of his commanding officer,
to whom his remarkable merits in the service had already
greatly endeared him, as well as by the consciousness that
he had been instrumental in preserving the fortress, and
saving the lives of many, perhaps all of the garrison

CHAPTER VI.

UP to the commencement of the year 1758, little else than
disaster attended the arms of the British in America. So
humiliating was the result, considering the formidable preparations that had been made for carrying on the war,
and the promptness and efficiency with which the colonies
responded to the requisitions made upon them, that the
king was compelled, by the clamorous voice of the people,
to change his ministers. A new and powerful administration was formed, at the head of which was Mr. Pitt, afterward Lord Chatham, a man whose pre-eminent talents and
commanding energy of character, made, and kept, the name
of his country respected in every quarter of the globe.

He assumed the helm of state in the summer of 1757, and his attention was at once directed to the conduct of the war in this country. The colonies, justly appreciating his vigor and talents, and feeling a perfect confidence in his administration, renewed their generous but exhausting efforts to recruit the army for the next campaign. The extent of their exertions can only be understood, when it is considered that Massachusetts, Connecticut and New Hampshire supplied fifteen thousand men, at a time when their combined resources could hardly have been equal to those of any one of them at the present moment.

The imbecile Lord Loudoun was recalled ; and General Abercrombie resumed the command of the Northern Department. Soon after his arrival at Fort Edward, he ordered Major Putnam to proceed, with sixty men, to South Bay, at the lower end of Lake George, for the purpose of watching the motions of the enemy, and intercepting their straggling parties. In compliance with these orders, the detachment marched to Wood Creek, near the point where it flows into South Bay, and immediately commenced the construction of a parapet for defence, in case of a sudden attack. The position was well chosen, on a bank, which forms a jutting precipice, overhanging the creek ten or twelve feet above the water. The parapet was of stone, thirty feet in length, and was very ingeniously concealed from the view of any one who might be passing, by a considerable number of young pines, brought from a distance, and artfully disposed so as to imitate the natural growth.

The service of a scout requires the utmost caution and silence in all his movements. It is contrary to established rules, and universal practice, to fire a gun, except at an enemy ; or to make any other noise which might expose the party to observation. From this necessary rule of caution, Putnam was obliged for once to deviate, on the fourth day after the completion of his little fortress. Although he had sent back to the camp fifteen of his men who were disabled by sickness, his stock of provisions was quite exhausted. A tempting opportunity to eke out his supply for another day, was offered by the appearance of a fine fat buck, that issued from the wood, with intent to swim across the creek in the vicinity of his camp ; and the prudent scout ventured a single shot to bring him in. It proved in the issue an expensive meal, though it was, fortunately, so conducted by this brave little band, as to throw almost the entire cost upon the enemy.

A large party of hostile Indians and French soldiers, under the celebrated partizan Molang, was, just at that time, on its way down towards the American encampment in quest of plunder. The report of Major Putnam's musket had reached the ear of one of the advanced guard of this party, and created a suspicion that their motions were watched, by those who might be troublesome to them in their further progress. They, therefore, proceeded with more caution, attempting to steal a passage through the creek under cover of the night—hoping thereby either to come upon their opponents by surprise, or to pass by them unnoticed into the country below. Our little fortress was so completely masked, by its artificial cover of fresh pines, as to escape detection even from the practised eye of an Indian.

About ten o'clock in the evening, one of the sentinels stationed at the margin of the Bay, gave notice that a considerable fleet of canoes, filled with men, was making its way toward the mouth of the creek. Putnam immediately called in all his sentinels, and posted his men to the best advantage, to give the strangers a fitting reception. The creek, into which the enemy soon entered, was

about thirty yards wide ; and the bank opposite to the
parapet was twenty feet high.   The moon was at its full,
the sky was clear, and every movement of the canoes was
perfectly in view.   A profound silence prevailed.   It was
intended to permit the van of the little fleet to pass, and
commence the attack upon the centre ; and the major had
given strict orders that every man should reserve his fire
until he gave the signal.   A few of the most advanced of
the canoes had just passed the parapet, when one of the
soldiers behind it accidentally struck his firelock against a
stone.   The commanding officer, who was in the foremost
canoe, alarmed at the noise, checked the advance, repeat-
ing several times, and with earnestness, the Indian watch-
word, "*O-wish !*"   Instantly the canoes crowded together
in a confused mass, with their centre precisely in front of
the works, covering the creek for a considerable distance
above and below.   The officers appeared to be in deep
consultation, and the fleet was apparently on the point of
retreating into the Bay, when Putnam gave the signal to
fire, by discharging his own piece.   It was followed, with
terrible effect, by a volley from his whole party.

Nothing could exceed the apparent consternation occasioned by this well-concerted attack, and the inextricable
confusion into which the fleet was thrown.   Scarcely a
bullet failed to find its victim, amidst the dense mass of the
enemy beneath, whose return fire was little better than
wasted on an invisible foe.   The carnage continued for
some time, when Molang, perceiving, from the fire of his
assailants, that their numbers were small, detached a party
to effect a landing below, and attack them in the rear.
The movement was instantly perceived and frustrated by
Putnam, who sent the brave Lieutenant Durkee, with
twelve men, to prevent their landing.   He arrived in good
time, and drove them back with loss.   Another small

detachment, under Lieutenant Parsons, was ordered up
the creek, to prevent any similar attempt in that direction.

Meanwhile, Major Putnam, whose party, in the absence
of these two detachments, was reduced to twenty, kept up,
through the whole night, an incessant and deadly fire on
the main body of the enemy, without the loss of a single
man on his part. After day-break, he was advised that a
party of the enemy had effected a landing, at a considerable distance below, and were rapidly advancing to cut off
his retreat. His numbers being far inferior to those of the
French, and his ammunition being almost exhausted, he
ordered a hasty retreat, which was successfully accomplished.

During this long-continued action, in which the Americans had slain at least five times their own number, only
two of their party, a Provincial and an Indian, were
wounded. These were sent off for the camp, under cover
of the night, with two men to assist them, and with directions to proceed by way of Wood Creek, as the safest,
though not the shortest route. But, having taken a nearer
way, they were pursued and overtaken by the Indians ;
who judged from the blood on the leaves, that they were
on the trail of the whole party. When they were overtaken, the wounded, despairing of mercy at the hands of
their pursuers, and unable to fly, insisted that their comrades, who were unhurt, should make their escape—
which, on a moment's deliberation, they effected. The
Provincial, whose thigh had been broken by a ball, resolv-
ing to sell his life as dearly as possible, fired his piece
upon the approach of the savages, and killed three of
them ; after which he was quickly despatched. The
Indian, making no resistance, was made a prisoner.

This Indian Major Putnam afterward saw while he was
himself a prisoner in Canada, and learned from him that
8

the number of the enemy in this encounter was five hundred, of whom fully one half were slain.

His brave little band, now reduced to forty, had proceeded along the bank of the creek a few miles, when Major Putnam, who, as usual, was in front of his men, was fired upon by a party near at hand. Not doubting that it was a party of his late antagonists, who had stolen the march upon him and headed him off, and feeling that nothing would be lost in assuming a bold countenance in so critical a position, he ordered his men to rush upon the enemy, promising soon to give as good an account of them, as of those whom they had just encountered at the creek. No sooner was his voice heard in the charge, than an instant reply, " Hold ! we are all friends ! " arrested his hostile movement, and brought his men, with their bayonets poised, and their feet firmly planted for an onset, to a dead halt. A scouting party of Provincials from Fort Edward immediately joined them. " We are friends, Major," exclaimed the leader, " and supposed we were firing upon the French." " Friends or foes," replied Putnam, " you all deserve to be hanged, for not killing more when you had so fair a shot." It was indeed wonderful, when we consider what expert marksmen most of the provincial scouts were, and how completely the unsuspecting Major and his party were exposed to their fire, that only one of their number was mortally wounded in this encounter.

In the meantime, one of the soldiers, whose ammunition had been early exhausted, had made his way back to Fort Edward, conveying tidings of the perilous position of the party ; and General Lyman was immediately dispatched, at the head of five hundred men, to cover their retreat. They met them at the distance of twelve miles from the fort, to which they all returned in safety the next day.

The most active preparations were now made for an assault upon Ticonderoga, which was the strong-hold of the French in this part of America. It was an ill-conducted, ill-starred expedition, which we would fain pass over in silence if we could. The site of this fortress is surrounded on three sides by water. On the fourth it is protected by a loose morass, extending a considerable distance. Beyond this, a line of fortification, eight feet high, was stretched from water to water, and planted with artillery. In front of this line, for the distance of one hundred yards, the plain was covered with large trees, cut for the purpose of defence, and arranged with their interwoven and sharpened branches projecting outwards. These impediments, it would seem, were quite sufficient to prevent any prudent commander from attempting to carry the works by storm. The ground was impracticable for the movement of heavy cannon; and the engineer, who was employed to reconnoitre the position, reported that the defences might be carried with musketry. The adoption of this shallow advice was precipitated by the rumor, that the garrison, consisting of over five thousand men, was on the point of receiving a large reinforcement, by the recall of a party of three thousand who had been detached, on other service, to the Mohawk River.

The expedition was led by General Abercrombie in person. His force consisted of sixteen thousand men, of whom nine thousand were Americans. It was attended by a very formidable train of artillery, and an ample supply of ammunition and military stores. On the morning of the fifth of July, they embarked in one hundred and twenty-five whale-boats, and nine hundred batteaux, and moved slowly, and in admirable order, down Lake George; presenting a brilliant and imposing spectacle, never before seen on those quiet waters. At evening they reached

Sabbath-day Point—a place already rendered memorable by Putnam's successful rencontre with his pursuers. Here they halted a few hours for refreshment, and then resumed their voyage. Being informed that the place where they first proposed to land was in possession of the enemy, they bent their course for another, where they effected a landing without opposition.

It was now noon of the sixth day of July. The place of debarkation was in a cove on the west side of the lake. A short distance from this place, the advanced guard of the enemy, consisting of one battalion, was posted in a logged camp. The troops were immediately formed into four columns, and commenced their march upon the advanced guard of the French, who made a precipitate retreat, after first destroying everything of value in their camp. The march was continued towards Ticonderoga, with the design of investing the place. But the woods being very thick, and some of the guides unskilful, the columns were broken, thrown into confusion, and in some measure entangled with each other. Major Putnam, whose service, as we have before explained, was often independent of the main body of the provincial forces, was at this time with Lord Howe, in the van of the right centre column, assisting to thread the intricacies of the forest. As they were moving slowly onward, they heard a firing on their left.

" Putnam," said Lord Howe, " what means that firing ?"

" I know not," he replied, " but, with your lordship's leave, I will see."

" I will accompany you," rejoined the gallant young nobleman.

In vain did the Major attempt to dissuade him, by saying : " My Lord, if I am killed, the loss of my life will be of little consequence ; but the preservation of yours is of infinite importance to this army." The only answer was :

" Putnam ! your life is as dear to you as mine is to me. I am determined to go."

One hundred of the van, under Major Putnam, filed off with Lord Howe. They soon fell in with the left flank of the enemy's advanced guard, which, in retreating from its late position on the lake, had lost its way in the woods, and were now skirmishing with our left. An engagement immediately took place. Though it issued in great loss to the French, its commencement was attended with an irreparable disaster to the British and American cause, which was ominous of the fate of the expedition. Lord Howe fell at the first charge.

The army could not have sustained a heavier loss. He was in the prime of manhood, of a fine person, and a winning address, eminent for manly virtue, and distinguished for every amiable accomplishment. He had already acquired an enviable military fame, which gave the most brilliant promise for the future. No British officer was ever employed in America, who had, in so short a time, endeared himself so universally to the Provincial troops, or won so extensively the esteem and confidence of the people. From his first arrival in the country, he had accommodated himself, in all respects, to the peculiar nature of the service, and to the customs of his New England friends. An example to the officer, a friend of the soldier, a model of military order and discipline, he had freely encountered every hazard, and shared in all the hardships of the campaign. His death was bewailed as a public loss.

His fall was immediately avenged by his exasperated troops, with Putnam at their head, who charged the enemy with desperate intrepidity, broke through their ranks,

8*

where they were joined by several small parties of the
Provincials, and attacked them again furiously in the rear.
Three hundred of the enemy were killed, and one hundred
and forty-eight made prisoners, among whom were five
officers and three cadets. This retrograde movement
brought them directly upon the front of the left wing of
their own army, who, seeing them advancing rapidly over
the bodies of the slain, supposed them to be French, and
opened upon them a brisk and heavy fire, by which one
sergeant and several privates were killed. They might
thus have been cut in pieces by their own friends, had not
Putnam, hazarding his own life, to save those of his comrades, rushed in the face of the flying balls, and showing
himself to his friends, put a stop to their work of slaughter.

No farther progress was made on this day. The advanced parties of the American army were called in, and
the French kept themselves closely within their entrenchments.

Putnam remained on the field while the light lasted,
employed in administering to the comfort of such of the
wounded among the enemy, as could not be immediately
removed. He furnished them with such refreshments as
he could procure, supplied them with blankets, and offering them a soldier's sympathy, assured them they should
be taken to the camp on the following day, and be cared
for as friends, for an enemy disarmed and disabled is an
enemy no longer.

On the morning of the seventh, the Americans were again
in motion, and, pushing forward, encamped at the Saw
Mills, about two miles from the fort. They were nearly four
times in number to that of the enemy. There can be little
doubt, if they had proceeded at once to the assault, without giving time for the extension of the formidable *abattis*,
by which Montcalm had now bristled the entire space in

front of his lines, they would have brought the campaign
to a successful issue. Instead of this, however, they delayed their movements till these works were completed ;
which, while they rendered useless the heavy train of
English artillery, formed impenetrable barriers to the orderly advance of the infantry.

The eighth was the fatal day fixed for the assault. Sir
William Johnson, with a re-inforcement of four hundred
and forty Indians, arrived in the camp at sunrise. At
seven o'clock, the movement of the army commenced,
being slightly impeded by a brief and unfruitful skirmish,
between the rangers and a party of the enemy in ambush.
These being dispersed, and the advance-guard driven in, a
general assault was made upon the works, soon after ten.
Notwithstanding the height of the breast-work, and the
obstacles arising from the peculiar character of the defences, an attempt was made to scale it. This perilous
service was led by Major Proby, who fell, in the first
onset, within a few yards of the works. The attempt to
carry them by storm was repeated several times during
four hours, attended with a tremendous loss on the part
of the assailants. The enemy, securely entrenched behind their fortifications, suffered comparatively little.

Finding that the works could not be carried by light-
armed troops, and the nature of the ground precluding the
possibility of bringing the heavy artillery to bear, a retreat
was ordered, and further operations against this post abandoned. Major Putnam, who had acted as Aid in bringing
the Provincial regiments successively to action, assisted,
with his usual coolness and intrepidity, in covering the
retreat, that being the post of danger, and the one to which
he was generally assigned.

Considering all the circumstances, this defeat was as
disgraceful to General Abercrombie, as it was disastrous

to his army. The attack, though bravely attempted and
boldly sustained by the soldiers, was ill-concerted and ill-
timed.   It was delayed until the French defences were
completed ; and then abandoned, when the numbers of the
assailants were more than double those of the enemy, and
amply provided with all the means for investing the fortress,
cutting off all communication with the surrounding country, and so reducing it by famine, without the necessity of
hazarding a battle on such unequal terms.   Had the conduct of this expedition been committed to American officers, it would probably have terminated as fatally to Montcalm, as his own assault upon Fort William Henry, in the
previous campaign, had done to the English ; though it
would not, like that, have been followed by a treacherous
massacre of an unarmed and surrendered garrison.

   There fell in this disastrous assault, of the British regulars, four hundred and sixty-four killed, and eleven hundred and seventeen wounded ; of the Provincials, eighty-
seven killed, and two hundred and thirty-nine wounded ;
thirty-seven more were missing—making a total of nine-
teen hundred and forty-four.   The loss of the French
did not much exceed five hundred.

CHAPTER VII.

In the course of this season several remarkable adventures
occurred to our hero, in which the public interests were
little concerned, but which are still worthy of record, as
illustrating the character of the man, and the vicissitudes
of the service.

One day, as Major Putnam chanced to be with a few
men in his boat, on the eastern shore of the Hudson, very
near the head of the rapids at Fort Miller, he was suddenly
warned from the opposite shore, that a large number of
Indians were close in his rear, and would be upon him in
an instant. To remain where he was and be sacrificed—
to attempt crossing the river exposed to the almost unerring rifles of the Indians—or to go down the falls, with an

almost certainty of being dashed on the rocks and drowned —were the only alternatives left to his choice. The Indians arrived at the shore, in season to fire a number of balls at the *bateau*, before it could be fairly got under way. One man, who, being at a little distance from his party on shore, had not time to reach the boat, was instantly seized and killed. No sooner had the *bateau* men, by favor of the rapidity of the current, escaped beyond the reach of musket shot, than death seemed only to have been avoided in one form, to be encountered in another no less terrible. Prominent rocks, latent shelves, and abrupt descents, for near a quarter of a mile, afforded scarcely the smallest chance of escaping without a miracle.

Putnam trusting himself to a Providence, whose kindness he had often experienced, rather than to men, whose tender mercy is cruelty, was now seen to place himself calmly at the helm, affording an astonishing spectacle of serenity. His companions, with a mixture of terror, admiration, and wonder, saw him incessantly changing his course, to avoid the jaws of ruin that seemed to expand to swallow the whirling boat. Twice he turned it quite round to shun the rifts of rocks. Amidst those eddies in which there was the greatest danger of its foundering, at one moment the sides were exposed to the fury of the waves ; then the stern, and next the bow glanced obliquely onward, with inconceivable velocity. With no less amazement, the gazing savages beheld him sometimes mounting the billows, then plunging abruptly down ; at other times dexterously veering from the rocks, and shooting through the only narrow passage ; until at last they viewed the boat safely gliding on the smooth surface of the stream below ! At this extraordinary sight, it is said that these rude sons of nature were affected with the same kind of superstitious veneration which the Europeans in

Escape down the Rapids of the Hudson.　PAGE 94.

the dark ages entertained for some of their most valiant
champions.   They regarded him as possessed of " a
charmed life," and conceived it would be a sin against the
Great Spirit to attempt to kill him with powder and ball,
if they should ever recognise him at a future period.
It will be seen, in the sequel, that some others of the same
race were not affected by their impressions, or not disposed to push these superstitious scruples so far, as to deny
themselves the satisfaction of trying the efficacy of the
tomahawk, and subjecting him to the ordeal of fire.

In the month of August, Major Putnam was deserted by
the good fortune which had hitherto attended him, and
made the subject of a series of adventures and perils,
which seem, in many particulars, more like romance, than
a sober tale of real life.   A train of baggage teams having
been cut off by a large party of the enemy's rangers, a
corps of about eight hundred men, under the command of
Majors Rogers and Putnam,* was dispatched to head the
party, and cut it off.   So rapid was the retreat, however,
that the enemy had reached their canoes, and embarked,
before their pursuers could come up with them ; though
they were not so far in advance but that their shouting
was heard in the distance.

Defeated in this expedition, the party was now separated into two equal divisions, Rogers taking his station with
one half, at South Bay, and Putnam, with the other, at
Wood Creek, twelve miles distant.   It was their hope to
surprise some straggling party of the enemy, or in some
other way retaliate upon them the loss they had just experienced.   But, being discovered by the enemy's scouts,
they deemed it expedient to re-unite their forces at Wood
Creek, and return without delay to head-quarters, at Fort
Edward.   Their march was a difficult one, through thick

* Holmes' Orderly Book.

woods rendered almost impassable by fallen trees, and a thrifty undergrowth. They were obliged to advance in Indian file, Putnam in the van, Captain Dalyell in the centre, and Rogers bringing up the rear. The first night, they encamped on the bank of Clear River, not far from the site of the old Fort Anne.

The next morning, before resuming their march, Major Rogers, with a singular forgetfulness of those precautions to which rangers are often indebted, for success in their enterprises, and security to their persons, amused himself by a trial of skill with a British officer, in firing at a mark, —an act of fool-hardy imprudence, which was followed by the loss of many valuable lives.

Immediately on the discovery of the two parties at South Bay and Wood Creek, the celebrated French partizan, Molang, was detached from Ticonderoga, with five hundred men, to intercept them. He was now so near their encampment, that the report of this firing reached his ears, and guided him at once to their position. Availing himself skilfully of this gratuitous information, he hastened to lay an ambuscade in that part of the wood through which his enemy was to pass, where he could do the most damage to them, with the least damage to himself.

The march having proceeded about a mile from their encampment, Major Putnam was about emerging from the thicket into the common forest, when the enemy, starting up from his ambush, with horrid yells and discordant whoops, commenced a furious attack upon the right of his division.* Putnam was surprised, but not dismayed. He returned the fire of his assailants, with his accustomed spirit, and immediately passed the word for the other

* The incidents of this engagement, and of the captivity of Putnam, are given, with a few verbal alterations, in the language of Colonel Humphreys.

divisions to advance to his support. Dalyell moved rapidly up, and a brisk engagement commenced. Though the action was widely scattered, and principally between man and man, it soon grew general and intensely warm. Rogers did not come up with Dalyell, but, as he afterward declared, formed a circular file between the other two divisions and the creek, so as to prevent their being taken in the rear, or *enfiladed*. It was a singular movement in one, who, according to his own journal, was the master-spirit of the expedition ; and, though not censured by his superiors, did not escape the imputation, in the army, of being instigated by an unworthy motive.

Putnam, finding that it would be impracticable to cross the creek, determined to maintain his ground. Inspired by his example, the officers and men behaved with great bravery, sometimes fighting in masses, in open view, with as much order as the nature of the ground would allow, and then individually and under cover, after the Indian fashion, each one sheltering himself behind a tree, and acting in a manner independent of his party. For himself, having discharged his *fusee* several times, it at length missed fire, while the muzzle was pressed against the breast of a large and powerful Indian. This warrior, availing himself of the unprotected attitude of his adversary, with a tremendous war-whoop, sprang forward, with his lifted hatchet, and compelled him to surrender. He was immediately disarmed and bound to a tree, while his captor returned to the battle.

Notwithstanding the capture of their bravest officer, the engagement was continued by the resolute men under Captains Dalyell and Harman. But their numbers being greatly inferior to their adversaries, they were forced to give ground for a few moments. The savages, conceiving this to be the commencement of a retreat, immediately

9

made a new and impetuous onset, with redoubled cries, as
if sure of victory. It was a momentary advantage which
they gained. Our intrepid partizans having collected
together a handful of brave men, gave their pursuers such
a warm reception, that they, in their turn, were forced
back beyond the ground upon which the action commenced. This movement brought the tree to which
Putnam was bound directly between the fire of the two
parties. It is scarcely possible to imagine a more desperate situation; a mark alike for every random shot of
friends or foes. The balls flew incessantly from either
side. Many struck the tree, while some passed through
the sleeves and skirts of his coat. So equally balanced
and so obstinate was the fight, that he was kept in this
trying situation more than an hour. During this time, he
was twice exposed to the mischievous malice of his un-
feeling enemies. A young Indian warrior coming up, and
seeing the white chief confined in that awkward position,
hurled a tomahawk several times at his head; rather
as if he were amusing himself with a mark, than with any
settled purpose to despatch his victim. So unerring was
the savage's aim, that the weapon several times grazed
his skin, and stuck in the tree by the side of his head.

When the young savage had satisfied himself with this
amusement, one of the inferior French officers came up,
and levelling his musket at his breast, attempted to discharge it. It missed fire. In vain did the intended victim
of his malice solicit the treatment due to his situation, by
declaring that he was a prisoner of war. The degenerate
Frenchman did not understand the language of honor or
of nature. Deaf to their voice, and dead to sensibility, he
violently and repeatedly pushed the muzzle of his gun
against Putnam's ribs, and finally gave him a cruel blow
on the jaw with the butt-end of his piece, and left him.

At length the active intrepidity of Dalyell and Harman, seconded by the persevering valor of their followers, prevailed. They drove from the field the enemy, who left about ninety dead behind him. As they were retiring, Putnam was untied by the Indian who had made him prisoner, and whom he sometimes called master. Having been conducted a considerable distance from the place of action, he was stripped of his coat, vest, stockings and shoes ; loaded with as many of the packs of the wounded as could be piled upon him, strongly pinioned, and his wrists held together as closely as they could be pulled by a cord. After he had marched in this painful manner for many tedious miles, through unpleasant paths, the fatigued party halted to breathe. His hands were now immoderately swelled from the tightness of the ligature, and the pain had become intolerable. His feet were severely scratched, so that the blood flowed freely from them. Exhausted with bearing a burden above his strength, and frantic with torments exquisite beyond endurance, he entreated the Irish interpreter to implore, as the last and only grace he desired of his captors, that they would knock him on the head and take his scalp at once, or loose his hands. A French officer, instantly interposing, ordered his hands to be unbound, and some of the packs to be taken off. By this time the Indian who captured him, and who had been absent with the wounded, coming up, gave him a pair of moccasins, and expressed great indignation at the unworthy treatment his prisoner had received.

That chief, being obliged again to return to the care of the wounded, the Indians, about two hundred in number, went on before the rest of the party to the place where the whole were that night to encamp. They took with them Major Putnam, on whom, besides innumerable other outrages, they had the barbarity to inflict a deep wound with a tomahawk in the left cheek.* His sufferings were in this place to be consummated. A scene of horror, infinitely greater than had ever met his eyes before, was preparing. It was determined to roast him alive. For this purpose they led him into a dark forest, stripped him naked, bound him to a tree, and piled dry brush, with other fuel, at a small distance in a circle around him. They accompanied their labors, as if for his funeral dirge, with screams and sounds inimitable but by savage voices. Then they set the pile on fire. A sudden shower damped the rising flames. Still they strove to kindle it, until at last the blaze ran fiercely round the circle. Major Putnam soon began to feel the scorching heat. His hands were so tied that he could move his body. He often shifted sides as the fire approached. This sight, at the very idea of which all but savages must shudder, afforded the highest diversion to his inhuman tormentors, who demonstrated the delirium of their joy by correspondent yells, dances and gesticulations. He saw that his final hour was inevitably come. He summoned all his resolution, and composed his mind, as far as the circumstances would admit, to bid an eternal farewell to all he held most dear. To quit the world would scarcely have cost a single pang, but for the idea of home—but for the remembrance of domestic endearments, of the affectionate partner of his soul, and of their beloved offspring. His thought was ultimately fixed on a happier state of existence, beyond the tortures he was beginning to endure. The bitterness of death, even of that death, which is accompanied with the keenest agonies, was, in a manner, past—and all the concerns of time seemed

* Rev. Dr. Holmes, in his Annals of America, speaking of this incident, says: "A deep scar on the cheek of that veteran warrior (Putnam) is well remembered by the writer, who believes it was from the wound inflicted by the tomahawk."—*Annals*, Vol. ii., p. 523.

as nothing in the near view of eternity—when a French
officer rushed through the crowd, opened a way by scattering the brands, and unbound the victim.   It was Molang himself; to whom an Indian, unwilling to witness the
immolation of another human sacrifice, had run and communicated the tidings.   That commandant spurned and
severely reprimanded the barbarians, whose nocturnal
pow-wows and hellish orgies he suddenly ended.   Putnam did not want for feeling or gratitude.   The French
commander, fearing to trust him alone with them, remained until he could deliver him in safety into the hands of
his master.

The savage approached his prisoner kindly, and seemed
to treat him with particular affection.   He offered him
some hard biscuits, but finding that he could not chew
them, on account of the blow he had received from the
Frenchman, and the wound of the tomahawk, this more
humane savage soaked some of the biscuit in water, till
it was sufficiently soft to be swallowed without effort.
Determined, however, not to loose his captive, though he
was willing to treat him kindly, he took the moccasins
from his feet, and tied them to one of his wrists; then directing him to lie down upon his back on the bare ground,
he stretched one arm to its full length, and bound it fast to
a young tree; the other arm was extended and bound in
the same manner; his legs were stretched apart, and fastened to two saplings.   Then a number of tall but slender
poles were cut down, which, with some long bushes, were
laid across his body from head to foot; on each side lay
as many Indians as could conveniently find lodging, in
order to prevent the possibility of his escape.   In this disagreeable and painful posture he remained until morning.
During this night, the longest and most dreary conceivable,
our hero used to relate that he felt a ray of cheerfulness
9*

come casually across his mind, and could not even refrain
from smiling, when he reflected on this ludicrous group
for a painter, of which he himself was the principal figure.

The next day he was allowed his blanket and moccasins,
and permitted to march without carrying any pack, or
receiving any insult.   To allay his extreme hunger, a little
bear's meat was given, which he sucked through his teeth.
At night, the party arrived at Ticonderoga, and the prisoner was placed under the care of a French guard.   The
savages, who had been prevented from glutting their diabo-
lical thirst for blood, took other opportunity of manifesting
their malevolence for the disappointment, by horrid gri-
maces and angry gestures ; but they were suffered no more
to offer violence or personal indignity to him.

After having been examined by the Marquis de Montcalm, Major Putnam was conducted to Montreal by a
French officer, who treated him with the greatest indulgence and humanity.

At this place there were at this time several prisoners. Colonel Schuyler, remarkable for his philanthropy,
generosity and friendship, was one of the number. No
sooner had he heard of Major Putnam's arrival, than he
went to the interpreter's quarters, and inquired whether
he had a Provincial Major in his custody. He found
Major Putnam in a comfortless condition—without coat,
waistcoat or hose ; the remnant of his clothing miserably
dirty and ragged ; his beard long and squalid ; his legs
torn by thorns and briars ; his face gashed with wounds,
and swollen with bruises. Colonel Schuyler, irritated
beyond all sufferance at such a sight, could scarcely restrain his speech within limits, consistent with the prudence of a prisoner, and the meekness of a Christian. On
his remonstrance, Major Putnam was immediately treated
according to his rank. He was also clothed in a decent

manner, and supplied with money, by that liberal and sympathizing patron of the distressed.

While on this dismal journey an attempt was made to try the strength of Putnam's nerves. Exhausted with the tedious march of the previous day, he was sleeping soundly on the bare earth, some time after the remainder of the party had shaken off their slumbers, and were preparing for a new start. A proposition was made to frighten the Major. Accordingly a musket was loaded with a double charge, faithfully rammed home, placed within an inch of his head as he lay, and discharged. Instead, however, of starting suddenly up, and staring wildly round, to see what might be the matter, he just muttered out, " That's a good one," turned on the other side, and adjusted himself for another nap.

The capture of Frontenac, by Colonel Bradstreet, afforded occasion for an exchange of prisoners. Colonel Schuyler was comprehended in the cartel. A generous spirit can never be satisfied with imposing tasks for its generosity to accomplish. Apprehensive, if it should be known that Putnam was a distinguished partisan, that his liberation might be retarded, and knowing that there were officers who, from the greater length of their captivity, had claims of priority to exchange, he had, by his happy address, induced the governor to offer, that whatever officer he might think proper to nominate should be included in the present cartel. With great politeness in manner, but seeming indifference as to objects, he expressed his warmest acknowledgments to the governor, and said, " There is an old man here, who is a Provincial Major. He is very desirous to be at home with his wife and children. He can do no good here, or anywhere else. I believe your Excellency had better keep some of the young men, who have no wives or children to care for, and let this old fellow go home with me." It was a well-managed artifice, and had the desired effect. Putnam was immediately released, and left Montreal, in company with his generous friend, who procured his enlargement.

At the house of Colonel Schuyler, in Montreal, Major Putnam became acquainted with Mrs. Howe, the story of whose captivity and sufferings among the Indians, full of the most thrilling romance, is familiar to American readers. By the payment of a considerable sum of money, Colonel Schuyler obtained the release of this lady, and undertook to escort her in safety to her friends in New England. He also interested himself in behalf of her children, who were also in captivity, and did not remit his exertions, until they were all at liberty. Business having made it necessary that Colonel Schuyler should entrust his charge to other hands, he committed her to the protection of his friend Putnam, from whom she received those kind attentions by the way, which her forlorn condition, and the difficult character of the roads, rendered necessary and acceptable.

CHAPTER VIII.

THE campaign of 1759 was distinguished by the memorable achievement of General Wolfe, who fell in the arms
of victory, in his daring attack upon Quebec. Ticonderoga and Crown Point were successively evacuated by
the French, on the approach of General Amherst.   In
these advances, there was no opportunity for the usual
stirring detail of partizan adventure.   There is, therefore,
little to relate of the subject of this work.   He was raised,
during this year, to the rank of Lieutenant-Colonel ; was
present at the occupation of both the above named fortresses ; and was afterward   employed in superintending
the parties, which were detached to procure timber, and
other materials, for strengthening the defences at Crown
Point.

In opening the campaign of 1760, General Amherst found himself in possession of the most important posts which the French had hitherto occupied in America ; and resolved, in obedience to instructions, to attempt the immediate and entire annihilation of that power in Canada. The Marquis de Vaudreuil, who was in command at Montreal, applied himself diligently to strengthen the fortifications of that place ; and determined, if possible, to make a final stand against the further progress of the English. For this purpose, he called in all his detachments, and collected around him the entire force of the colony.   His resolution was vain.   The British general, having but one point on which to concentrate his forces, very wisely and humanely prepared to collect them all at that point, in hopes, by compelling an immediate surrender, to secure a bloodless victory.   For this purpose, three armies were directed to proceed by different routes, and appear at the same moment before Montreal.   General Murray, with the corps which had been commanded by the victorious Wolfe, was ordered to ascend the St. Lawrence from Quebec.   Colonel Haviland, at the head of another division, sailed from Crown Point, by way of Isle-aux-Noix—which was evacuated by the enemy on his approach. General Amherst, with the remainder of the forces, consisting of about ten thousand regulars and provincials, passing up the valley of the Mohawk, and down the Oneida, advanced to Oswego, where he was joined by one thousand Indians of the Six Nations, under Sir William Johnson.   Embarking, with his entire army, on Lake Ontario, and taking in his way the Fort of Isle Royale, he arrived at Montreal, after a difficult and dangerous passage, on the same day that General Murray landed at the same place from Quebec.   The two generals met with no opposition in disembarking their troops ; and by a happy concurrence in the execution of a well-concerted plan, Colonel Haviland joined them with his detachment the next day.

Lieutenant-Colonel Putnam's regiment formed a part of the main division under the general-in-chief. During their progress, several incidents occurred, in which his peculiar ingenuity, as well as his intrepidity, was put to the test. Having entered the St. Lawrence, it was necessary, in order not to leave an enemy in their rear, to dislodge the garrison at Fort Oswegatchie—situated on Isle Royale, at the mouth of the Oswegatchie river.

The approach to this place was guarded by two armed vessels of twelve guns each, that kept possession of the stream, and rendered it impossible for the British army to proceed, as one broadside from these ships would demolish their whole fleet of boats. General Amherst was somewhat disconcerted; as he must either abandon his boats altogether, and proceed by land, or contrive some extraordinary means to get rid of this formidable adversary. While he was pondering what should be done, Colonel Putnam came to him, and, pointing to one of them, said : " General, that ship must be taken."

" Ay," replied Amherst, " I would give the world if she *were* taken."

" I'll take her, Sir," said Putnam, coolly.

" How ?" asked Amherst, smiling incredulously.

" Give me some wedges, a beetle, and a few men of my own choosing, and I will soon put her out of your way."

Amherst could not conceive how an armed vessel was to be taken by four or five men, with no other arms than a beetle and wedges. But he had known something of the ingenuity and daring of the provincial Colonel, and his skill in executing feats of peculiar difficulty. He was,

accordingly, authorized to proceed ; and furnished with
everything that he desired for his experiment.

In the darkness of the night, Putnam and his chosen
few, in a light boat, with muffled oars, stole unperceived
under the vessel's stern, and drove the wedges so firmly
between the rudder and the stern-post, as to render the
rudder quite immovable.   They then effected their
escape, in the same stealthy manner as they had come.
Deprived of her helm, the ship was left at the mercy of
the winds and the stream, and was soon driven ashore.
In this condition she offered no resistance to the British
arms, but struck her colors at the first summons.   Her
companion followed her example without delay, so that
this victory was won without the loss of a man, or the
firing of a gun, on either side.

This incident is found in *"Almon's Impartial Remembrancer,"* published in London in 1775, thirteen years before
the appearance of Colonel Humphreys' Life of Putnam.
That work represents the French as voluntarily running
one of their vessels ashore on the approach of the British.
Other historians* of the day have said, that one of the
vessels having accidentally run ashore, the other was
easily overcome, &c.   While Knox, and after him, Mante,
give all the credit of the adventure to a Col. Williamson,
of the British army.   From the incident of the wedging
of the rudder being published at so early a date, and on
British authority, it is most probable that the anecdote is
true in all its particulars—that Putnam first procured one
of the vessels to be disabled, and that then the thousand
men, under the command of Col. Williamson, joined him,
and followed up the work.   No man in his senses would
think of approaching an armed vessel by daylight, with a
view to get under her stern, and unship or otherwise

* Marshall, and others.

destroy her rudder. The probable truth, therefore, is, that one vessel being disabled, the other yielded readily, as all accounts agree in stating. In this manner they are all easily reconciled, and the whole credit of the success placed where it belongs, to the ingenuity and daring of Putnam—as Humphreys understood and intended it should be; while he completely defeats that intention, by running the two parts of the story into one, and so leaving the main incident out of sight. It affords another illustration of the modesty of Putnam, and the little account he made of his own acts, in detailing to his biographer the movements of the army. The following is Colonel Humphreys' account of the matter; which briefly describes the onset of the boats, and the sudden surrender of the panic-struck enemy, without detailing the circumstances, which made that surrender unavoidable.

"Two armed vessels obstructed the passage, and prevented the attack. Putnam, with one thousand men, undertook to board them. This dauntless officer, ever sparing of the blood of others, as prodigal of his own, to accomplish it with less loss, put himself, with a chosen crew, a beetle and wedges, in the van, with a design to wedge the rudders, so that the vessels should not be able to turn their broadsides, or perform any other manœuvre. All the men in his little fleet were ordered to strip to their waistcoats, and advance at the same time. He promised, if he lived, to join them, and show the way up the sides. Animated by so daring an example, they moved swiftly, and in profound silence, as to certain victory or death. The people on board the ships, beholding the good countenance with which they approached, ran one of the vessels on shore, and struck the colors of the other. Had it not been for the dastardly conduct of the ship's company in the latter, who compelled the captain to haul down his ensign, he
10

would have given the assailants a bloody reception ; for
the vessels were well provided with spars, nettings, and
every customary instrument of annoyance as well as
defence."

It was now determined to attack the fortress, which
the enemy supposed they had rendered inaccessible by a
high *abattis* of black-ash, that everywhere projected over
the water.   Lieutenant-Colonel Putnam proposed a mode
of attack, and offered his services to carry it into effect.
The proposal was approved of by the general ; and Putnam, accordingly, caused a sufficient number of boats to
be fitted for the enterprise.   The sides of each boat were
surrounded with fascines, musket proof, which covered
the men completely.   A wide plank, twenty feet long,
was then fitted to every boat in such a manner, by having
an angular piece sawed from one extremity, that, when
fastened by ropes on both sides of the boat, it might be
raised or lowered at pleasure.   The design was, that the
plank should be held erect while the oarsmen forced the
bow, with the utmost exertion, against the *abattis ;* and
that afterwards being dropped on the pointed brush, it
should serve as a kind of bridge to assist the men in passing over them.   Lieutenant-Colonel Putnam, having made
his dispositions to attempt the *escalade* in many places at
the same moment, advanced with his boats in admirable
order.   The garrison, perceiving these extraordinary and
unexpected machines, did not wait the assault, but capitu-
lated.   Putnam was particularly honored by General
Amherst, for his ingenuity in this invention, and for his
promptitude in its execution.

The three armies arrived at Montreal within two days
of each other.   The Marquis de Vaudreuil, seeing that
resistance to forces so far superior to his own would be
worse than useless, proposed an instant capitulation.   With

Montreal, Detroit, Michilimakinak, and all other French posts on the lakes, were surrendered to the English ; and the conquest of Canada was thus completed, without the loss of a single drop of blood.

At the Indian village called Cochnawaga, a short distance from Montreal, Putnam saw the savage who had made him prisoner in the previous campaign. The Indian was highly delighted to see his old acquaintance, whom he entertained in his own well-built stone house with great friendship and hospitality ; while his guest showed no less satisfaction in having an opportunity of shaking the brave savage by the hand, and proffering him protection in this reverse of his military fortunes.

The year 1762 found England in rather a gloomy situation. The previous campaign had left her much exhausted, and Spain, as well as the majority of the other powers of Europe, combined against her and Prussia. In the event that she should be much farther reduced, the Americans could apprehend nothing less than a speedy and energetic attempt by France to recover the lands which she had lost during the past years of the war. The colonies, therefore, were called upon to raise supplies, and prepare for a desperate struggle. Large bounties were offered by England to those who would enlist under her standard—which were doubled by the continental authorities.

In the meantime, a large army of British and provincials, under Admiral Rodney and General Monckton, had sailed for Martinique, an island in the West Indies, belonging to the French. On the 14th of February, 1762, that island was captured. This success was soon followed by the subjugation of all the Caribbees. Another powerful expedition was also sent, the same season, against Havana. It consisted of 10,000 men, thirty-seven ships of war, and nearly 150 transports, under the command of Admiral Pococke and Lord Albemarle. These landed safely on the 17th of June ; but being foiled in all their attempts against the fortresses, the climate destroyed a great number of them, so that, in less than two months, their numbers were reduced about one half.

At this gloomy crisis aid arrived from the colonies. A body of Provincials, composed of five hundred men from the Jerseys, eight hundred from New York, and one thousand from Connecticut, were sent to reinforce his Lordship. General Lyman, who raised this regiment of one thousand men in Connecticut, being the senior officer, was appointed to the command of the whole, consequently the immediate command of his regiment devolved upon Lieutenant-Colonel Putnam. The fleet, in which these men embarked, sailed from New York, and ultimately arrived safely in Cuba, though not without perilous accidents by the way.

While on the coast of that island a terrible storm arose, and the transport, in which Lieutenant-Colonel Putnam had embarked with five hundred men, was wrecked on a reef of craggy rocks. The weather was so tempestuous, and the surf, which ran mountain-high, dashed with such violence against the ship, that the most experienced seamen expected she would go to pieces. The rest of the fleet, so far from being able to afford assistance, with difficulty rode out the gale.

In this situation, strict military order was maintained, and all those people, who best understood the use of tools, were instantly employed in constructing rafts from spars, planks, and whatever other materials could be procured. Strong lines were secured to each of these rafts, and run out from the ship, as they put off towards the land. When the first had, with inconceivable hazard and difficulty, reached the shore, these lines proved of infinite service, in preventing the others from driving out to sea, as well as in dragging them athwart the billows to the beach, and keeping up a constant communication with the ship. By these means every man was finally saved.

As soon as all were landed, Lieutenant-Colonel Putnam fortified his camp, that he might not be exposed to injury or insult from the inhabitants of the neighboring districts. Here the party remained unmolested several days, until the storm had so much abated as to permit the convoy to take them off. They soon joined the troops before Havana, who, having been several weeks in that unhealthy climate, began to feel its effects severely in the gradual reduction of their numbers, and the transformation of their camp into a hospital. The opportune arrival of the Provincial reinforcement, in perfect health, contributed not a little to forward the works which were in progress, and to hasten the reduction of that important place. But the Provincials suffered so miserably by sickness afterwards, that very few of their number ever found their way home again.

The entrance into the harbor of Havana is by a narrow channel, the east side of which is secured by a fort of great strength, and deemed quite impregnable, called *El Moro*. The west is protected by another, called *El Punto*. Lord Albemarle, having command of the land forces, amounting to fourteen thousand men, of whom four thousand were Provincials, commenced the siege of the Moro. After suffering incredible hardships, and surmounting the most appalling obstacles, the besiegers obtained possession of the covered way, which led to the fortress, made a lodgment before the right bastion, and sprung a mine, which threw down a part of the works, and left open a small breach. The soldiers, now ordered to storm the place,

10*

mounted the breach, under command of Lieutenant Forbes, supported by Lieutenant-Colonel Stuart, and entered the fort with such order and intrepidity, as entirely disconcerted the garrison. Four hundred Spaniards were either cut in pieces, or perished in attempting to escape by water to the city. The remainder threw down their arms, and received quarter.

The British troops, now in possession of the castle, and having completed their own batteries, on an eminence that commanded the city, were enabled to plant sixty pieces of cannon in position to play effectively on the place. Thus fortified, Lord Albemarle sent a flag of truce, with a summons to the governor to surrender. The haughty Spaniard replied that he should hold out to the last extremity. The batteries, however, were opened with such effect the next morning, both against the city and the Puntal, that a deputy was sent out about noon, to settle the terms of capitulation. A cessation of arms immediately ensued, and the city of Havana, with a district extending one hundred and eighty miles westward, and embracing about one fourth part of the island, with the fortresses and the ships in the harbor, were surrendered to His Britannic Majesty.

Soon after this event, the combined powers, finding that war with Great Britain, whether by land or sea, was only a losing game, proposed terms of peace, which removed the dark cloud that had so long hung over the prospects of the colonies.

CHAPTER IX.

THE PONTIAC WAR.

Results of the late contest between England and France—Condition, character, and hopes of the Indians—Pontiac, the Otoway chief—His first successes and plan of Union—Movements of General Amherst—Captain Dalyell ordered to Detroit—His bold sortie from the fort—His glorious death—Putnam, now a Colonel, accompanies Col. Bradstreet to Detroit—Supplies thrown into the fortress—Pontiac, overawed by the superior numbers of his enemy, proposes conditions of peace—Colonel Putnam's letter from the camp—Enlarged views and bravery of Pontiac—Review of Colonel Putnam's military career—His high reputation as an officer—Retires to his farm—Honorable testimonials of public confidence—Domestic affliction.

TILL the year 1758 or 1759, it seemed doubtful whether France or England would have the ascendency in the New World; and in particular, whether the British should not be confined to a narrow slip of land on the shores of the Atlantic. The superior population and wealth of the English colonies, and the immense superiority of the British navy over that of France, and particularly the energy of Pitt's Administration, turned the scale in favor of England. Great joy was diffused throughout the British dominions; but in no place was it felt, in a higher degree, or with greater reason, than in America. For one hundred and fifty years France and England had been contending for American territory; and for the last half of that period there had been but little intermission of active hostilities, or of those irregular border difficulties, which are scarcely less annoying or destructive than actual war. There were no precise, well-defined boundaries to the possessions of the two nations ; but both were willing to enlarge them in any direction. They possessed much, but coveted more. Neither was backward to make encroachments on the other ; and both were prompt to repel them when made, or supposed to be made, on themselves. Throughout this period, especially the last half of it, in addition to the unavoidable calamities of war, indiscriminate massacres had been so frequently and extensively committed on numerous settlers, dispersed over many hundred miles of exposed frontier, that it has been supposed the British colonies lost in this way not less than twenty thousand inhabitants. War assumed a most terrific aspect among the colonists. Not confined to men in arms, as is common in Europe, aged persons, women, and children, were frequently its victims. The tomahawk and scalping knife, carried to the fire-sides of peaceable, helpless families, were applied promiscuously to every age and sex.

It was hoped that the reduction of Canada would close these horrid scenes for ever, with respect to the northern and middle colonies. As the Indians could in future derive supplies from none but the English, and as they would be no longer exposed to the seductiveness of French influence, it was confidently expected that they would desist from their depredations, and leave the colonies to pursue the advantages gained in this long and expensive contest. In this expectation they were disappointed. Some of the Indians laid down their arms, but many of the tribes on the western frontiers still continued hostilities—not, as before, to sustain or restore the French dominion, but apparently with a view to regain, for themselves, some of that ancient power which both the contending parties had combined to wrest from their hands. It is not improbable, indeed, that they were instigated in a great measure by the catholic priests who still remained among them, and who possessed unbounded influence over their minds.

Even at that early day, however, they seem to have had a prophetic intimation of the fate that awaited them, from the continual influx and rapid increase of the European race. The most sagacious of their leaders saw, even then, as in a vision, that they had nothing to expect from the pale-faced intruders upon their territories but perpetual encroachment, treacherous, over-reaching negotiation and diplomacy, and the ultimate extermination of their whole race. In a conference between some of the American governors and the Six Nations, soon after the peace of 1761, a warm dispute arose concerning certain lands, which—the Indians asserted—had been seized by some English settlers under a fraudulent conveyance. Population, too, augmented so rapidly during the interval of peace, after England had acquired the mastery of the continent, that the colonists soon overran their prescribed limits ; and, as a chain of forts had been constructed round the most important lands of the Indians, they perceived that the English, by fate or by design, were about to extirpate them, or drive them back upon the distant mountains of the west. Under these impressions, the truth of which has been so signally realized, the Shawanese, the Delawares, and the tribes along the Ohio, this side Mississippi, and about Detroit, concerted a plan, in 1763, to attack, at one and the same time, all the English posts and settlements in their neighborhood.

Under Pontiac, the celebrated Otoway chief, and other highly gifted leaders—thirty-six of whom were now united under this confederacy—they succeeded in getting possession of several important posts, which the French had

surrendered, and were proceeding to concentrate a formidable power on the northern lakes. General Amherst,
who still remained in command, immediately ordered strong
reinforcements to forts Pitt, Detroit and Niagara—those
of Le Boeuf, Venango, Presque Isle and Michilimacki-
nack, being already in possession of the Indians. Captain
Dalyell, of whom we have had occasion to speak in another place as the faithful friend and intrepid fellow-soldier
of Colonel Putnam, commanded the first party destined for
Detroit, with orders from General Amherst to raise the
siege, by dispersing the Indians. On his arrival, he succeeded in effecting an entrance into the fortress, without a
conflict with the enemy who invested it. Major Glad-
wine, who commanded the garrison, satisfied that with
this reinforcement the place could hold out against the
besiegers, while they were still too few to hazard an open
encounter, would fain have dissuaded Captain Dalyell from
offering them battle. But the latter, relying on the discipline and courage of his men, replied : " God forbid that I
should ever disobey the orders of my general," and immediately disposed them for action. His force consisted of
only two hundred and fifty men. Those of Pontiac were
vastly superior in numbers. The conflict, which. commenced at two o'clock in the morning, was obstinate and
bloody. The Indians, on every side, kept up a galling
fire from behind trees and fences, and threatening to surround and enclose Captain Dalyell and his party, compelled
him reluctantly to retreat. Having gained a temporary
shelter, and halted to breathe, he saw one of his bravest
sergeants lying on the ground at a little distance, wallow-
ing in his blood from a severe wound in his thigh, and
desired some of his men to run to his relief. They declined the service, as too hazardous. Dalyell, declaring
" that he would never leave so brave a soldier in the field,

to be tortured by the savages," went alone to his rescue. As he was endeavoring to raise the wounded man from the ground, a volley from the enemy was poured in upon them, and they both fell dead together. How do such acts of heroic disinterestedness and self-sacrifice, elevate the character of the true soldier, and eclipse the proudest laurels of the mere conqueror !

The Indians still maintaining their position, Colonel Bradstreet was sent the following year, 1764, with a force sufficient to reduce them. To this force Connecticut contributed a regiment of four hundred men, under the command of Putnam—who had now received the commission of a colonel. The old Indian chief, who has been before mentioned as his captor, and whom in that relation he had called master, was also on this expedition, at the head of a hundred Cochnawaga warriors. He had made peace with the English, and was now marching side by side with his former prisoner, to fight with the ancient enemy of his tribe. Joseph Brant, the celebrated Mohawk chief, took part also in this expedition.

Meanwhile, Detroit continued to be closely blockaded, and the garrison suffered extremely from fatigue and the want of provisions. On the third of September, a schooner, dispatched from Niagara with twelve men and six Mohawk Indians, with provisions for the relief of the garrison, arrived in the river. She was immediately attacked by three hundred and fifty Indians in boats, but, by the admirable skill and bravery of the little band on board, she was carried safely into the fort, with the loss of the master and one man killed, and four wounded.

Saved from certain death by this seasonable supply of provisions, the garrison held out till the arrival of the forces under Colonel Bradstreet. Overawed by the superior numbers now arrayed against them, and feeling that all farther efforts would be worse than vain, the Indians withdrew, without battle, and proposed conditions of peace ; which, after long delays and frequent changes of terms, were duly arranged and ratified in the course of the following season.

As this expedition afforded little opportunity for brilliant services, or daring achievements, we have nothing to say for Colonel Putnam—save that, as usual, he was always at his post, ready for any service that might be required of him, and weary of nothing so much as inaction. The following letter, supposed to be the longest he ever wrote, will give some idea of the state of the frontier settlements at that time, and of the difficulties they had to encounter in dealing with the Indians. It was addressed to Major Drake, of Norwich, Connecticut, and was published in the Boston Gazette, of December 24th, 1764.

> *"Camp Sandusky, near the Carrying Place,*
> *October* 7, 1764.

" DEAR SIR :—

" I can tell you the land here is good enough, and suppose you will think it strange if I should tell you, that in many places in this country, there are ten or twenty thousand acres of land in a place, that have not a bush or twig on them, but all covered with grass, so big and high that it is very difficult to travel—and all as good plough-land as ever you saw ; any of it fit for hemp ; but there are too many *hemp birds* among it, which will make it very unhealthy to live among.

" Detroit is a very beautiful place, and the country around it. We sent out an officer, and three Indians, to the Delawares and Shawanese from Presque Isle, who returned and were illy used. We sent the like number from Sandusky, but all before any one returned.

" From Sandusky we sent Captain Montieur and Captain Peters, from Maumee we sent Captain Morris of the 17th, and one Thomas King with three Indians. Captain Morris returned some time ago, and was much abused, and stripped, and whipped, and threatened to be tomahawked, but had his life spared in case he would return. Captain Thomas King and three of the Kanawawas proceeded. This Captain King is one of the chiefs of the Oneida Castle ; and about ten days ago King came into Detroit, and had left all the Kanawawas, who gave out for want of provisions, and could not travel ; he supposed they all perished in the woods. And three days ago he arrived here, and yesterday he had a conference with the Indians ; and when all assembled, he made a speech to them. After some talk with them, he expressed himself in this manner :

" ' Friends and Brothers : I am now about to acquaint you with facts, too obvious to deny. I have been, since I left you, to Monsieur Pontuck's (Pontiac's) camp, and waited on him to see if he was willing to come in, and make peace with our brothers, the English. He asked me what I meant by all that, saying, " You have always encouraged me to carry on the war against the English, and said, the only reason you did not join me last year was the want of ammunition, and as soon as you could get ammunition, you would join me." '

" King said there was nothing in it, at which Pontuck produced six belts of wampum, that he had had the last year from the Six Nations, and said, ' The English are so exhausted, they can do no more, and one year's war, well pushed, will drive them into the sea.'

" King then made a stop for some time (when he added), ' Brothers, you know this to be true, and you have always deceived me.' At which the Six Nations were all angry,

11

and this day they are all packing up to go off; and what will be the event I don't know, nor don't care, for I have no faith in an Indian peace, patched up by presents.

" Yesterday, Captain Peters. arrived, which is the last party we had out.   Capt. Peters says the Wyandots are all coming in ; but the Delawares and the Shawanese are not coming, nor durst they come, for they are afraid that, if they should come here, Colonel Bouquet will be on their towns and castles.   For he has sent to them to come and make peace, and, on the contrary, if they should go to him we should be on them.   They intend to be still until Bouquet first comes to them, and then send out and make peace, if possible ; if not, to fight him as long as they have a man left.   But, believe me, they wait to get some advantage of us before they try for peace.   Capt. Peters says Bouquet is within thirty miles of their towns, and believes he is to make peace with them ; for Colonel Bradstreet had orders from General Gage, eight days ago, to make no peace with them, but to march and meet Bouquet.   But, on calling a council of war, and examining the Indians and Frenchmen, who were acquainted with the road, it was found to be thirty leagues to travel by land, and nothing to carry any provisions but on men's back, which, allowing for hindrances, must take forty days to go and come.   There are four large rivers to pass, two of which must be crossed with rafts, and that very difficult. Considering the season of the year it was judged impracticable.   And here we are, and for what I know. not, nor when we are to leave it.

" I am, &c.

" ISRAEL PUTNAM."

It gives us an exalted view of the conscious power and fearless courage of the brave chiefs, who, at this time, commanded the Indian tribes on the frontier, to find them boldly meditating the utter annihilation of the British power in America, or to use the expressive language of Pontiac, hoping " by one year's war, well pushed, to drive them into the sea." The colonies, at this time, numbered probably more than two millions of inhabitants, and were rapidly increasing. They had powerful armies, backed by others still more powerful, sent from Europe for their protection. They had numerous well-appointed fortresses, with all the terrible engines of war, which civilized science had invented. They had numberless large towns and populous cities, and their millions were all banded together, as one, for the common defence ; while the Indian tribes, divided among themselves, and inflamed against each other by the never-ceasing feuds of a hundred ages, knew no bond of union, and acknowledged no common head, who could harmonize their councils, or concentrate their power toward one point. They realized the prophetic character of the father of the wandering tribes of Arabia, " His hand shall be against every man, and every man's hand against him."

Ten years had now elapsed, since Putnam, at the call of his country, relinquished the peaceful pursuits of rural life, for the stirring scenes and perilous duties of the camp. He entered the service without experience, but with a high reputation for personal bravery. He had risen regularly through every grade, from the command of a company to that of a regiment. He had won the confidence of his superiors, and the affectionate regards of his men ; and now, the great object of the war being accomplished, and peace secured to the colonies on every side, he returned to the bosom of his family, and to the shades of private life, his brows crowned with enduring laurels, and his name, encircled with the halo of fame, associated with the best and bravest in the land.

The part he had acted in "The Seven Years' War," was one of peculiar hardship and peril. Always in the van, when charging the enemy, and in the rear, when a retreat was ordered—stationed among the outposts when the army was in camp—scouring the woods or the lakes with a handful of men, or creeping stealthily alone into the enemy's lines—his was ever the post of danger. But he encountered and achieved it all with a chivalrous indifference to personal danger, and an inexhaustible fruitfulness of resources, which, while it excited the envy of a few, commanded the admiration of all. His military knowledge was all the fruit of his own experience and observation, the result of that strong common sense, that ready ingenuity in adapting himself to the circumstances in which he was placed, and that perfect coolness and self-possession in seasons of danger, for which he was eminently distinguished, and which qualified him, without the previous advantages of education, for the important stations he was called upon to fill.

"Personal bravery," says Mr. Peabody, "is perhaps the cheapest of the military virtues ; but there was something cool, daring and unostentatious in that of Putnam, which attracted equally the wonder of the cultivated and the rude. In the words, recorded by a personal friend* upon his monument, he had always 'dared to lead where any dared to follow.' His disposition was full of the frankness of the soldier, united with a kindness and generosity, not always found in union with the sterner qualities, demanded by the life of camps ; an extended intercourse with others had refined the asperity of his manners,

* Dr. Dwight

without impairing the simplicity of his genuine New England character."

In laying aside his uniform, and returning to his plough, and to the pleasures of domestic life, he lost nothing of that respect and esteem, with which the brave soldier and the accomplished officer had been regarded. Success had not inflated him with pride, or made him forgetful of his old connections. He possessed the entire good will and confidence of his neighbors and fellow-citizens, and stood very high in the public estimation, throughout the country, for integrity, courage and patriotism. No sooner was the sword laid away in its scabbard, then he was called, by the united voice of his fellow-citizens, to counsel and aid them in the management of their civil affairs. And, during the entire interval of repose, between the French war and that of the Revolution, he was employed, by their choice, to fill the higher municipal offices, and to represent the town in the General Assembly of the colony.

But who ever enjoyed sunshine in this life, which clouds did not darken? Or found repose, which affliction did not mar? Returning in peace to the bosom of his family, after so long a period of toil and danger, from so many vicissitudes of fortune, by land and sea, from weary marches and perilous adventures, from conflicts, single-handed, with a lurking foe, and the terrible *melée* of the battle-field, and " the imminent deadly breach,"—the veteran soldier might have promised himself, at least a *brief* interval of pure enjoyment, amid the loving and loved ones that clustered about his fireside, and graced and cheered his table. But he had scarcely returned to his home, when it was visited by the severest of earthly bereavements. The wife of his youth, the mother of his children, was smitten by the shaft of death. After ten years of exposure to danger in almost every form, he came

11*

back, in full health and vigor, and with a heart yearning for the bliss which can only be found at home, to witness the dying struggle, and receive the dying blessing, of her who had been his counsellor and his comforter, and the chief joy of his existence, for a quarter of a century. It was a heavy stroke, and deeply and bitterly was it felt, though he murmured not against Him who dealt the blow.

After a considerable period of widowhood, Colonel Putnam married again. His second wife was Mrs. Deborah Gardner, the widow of John Gardner, Esq., the fifth proprietor of Gardner's Island. She was a native of Pomfret, the daughter of Mr. Avery, one of Putnam's neighbors. She accompanied him in most of the campaigns of the Revolutionary War, and died at his Head Quarters, in the Highlands, in 1777. Her youngest son, Septimus Gardner, entered the army, under his step-father, and died at Peekskill, about the same time with his mother. Mr. Putnam had no children by his second marriage.

CHAPTER X.

THE causes which led to the Revolutionary War, and the
establishment of American Independence, are too generally understood to require detailed explanation here.
The oppressive enactments of the mother-country, on the
one hand, and the bold and spirited resistance of the colonies on the other, had already awakened feelings of no
amiable character on both sides of the water. And, while
the heroes and patriots of the provincial army were fighting bravely, side by side with the officers and soldiers of
the crown, and learning the art of war in their campaigns
against their French neighbors, the contest had already
begun which was to divide them into separate armies, and
array them in deadly hostility to each other.

The Navigation Acts of 1651 and 1660, and others of a
still later date, placing severe restrictions upon American
commerce, had been the subject of frequent remonstrance,

and had often been either quietly evaded or openly violated. The "writs of assistance," or general warrants,
ordered in 1761, for the discovery of contraband articles,
which had been imported into the country without the
payment of the established duties, were met by the bold
and spirited denunciations of Thatcher, Otis, and the
Adamses, nobly seconded by the voice of the people, so
far as it could be heard through the press. The actual
enforcement of the laws, by the confiscation of smuggled
goods, in 1763, increased the excitement, and alarmed the
staunch lovers of liberty in the colonies.

The first formal declaration of a settled purpose on the
part of the ministers to tax the colonies directly was made
by Mr. Grenville, prime minister of George III., in 1764.
It was not only received with a burst of indignation in
America, but met by an able and talented opposition in the
British Parliament. The consequences were foreseen by
those who best understood the American character, and
valued the privileges of the British Constitution. But the
ministers, backed by the obstinacy of the king, were not
to be diverted from their purpose. The Stamp Act was
passed in March, 1765, by a large majority of both
houses of Parliament.

When the news of the passage of this Act reached
America, a general indignation spread throughout the
country, breaking forth, in some places, in acts of outrage
and violence, and in others assuming the spirit of calm but
determined resistance. At Boston and Philadelphia the
bells were muffled, and rung a funeral knell. At New
York the Act was carried through the streets, with a
death's head affixed to it, and styled " The Folly of England and the Ruin of America." When the stamped
papers arrived in the country they were, in many places,
seized and destroyed ; the houses of those who sided with

the government were violently entered and plundered ; the stamp officers were compelled to resign their commissions ; and the doctrine was openly asserted, on every side, that England had no right whatever to tax America, or to claim a dollar of her money without her own free consent.

Among those who entered most zealously into these measures of remonstrance and open resistance, was Colonel Putnam. With his accustomed fearlessness and impetuosity, he set his face against every movement toward putting this hateful system of oppression into execution. By a concert of action throughout the colonies, the people had determined, in order to prevent the stamped paper from being distributed, that the stamp-masters should not enter upon the execution of their offices. That appointment, in Connecticut, had been conferred upon a Mr. Ingersol, of New Haven, a very dignified, sensible, and learned native of the colony ; who, upon being solicited to resign the trust, did not, in the first instance, give a satisfactory answer. He, probably, did not like the bold and peremptory style in which the application was made to him ; preferring rather to show his patriotism by his own free act, than by the dictation or compulsion of his fellow-citizens.

The people, however, were resolute, and would not allow a moment's hesitation or delay. At the instigation of Colonel Putnam—who was prevented from joining the party in person by an accident which had recently befallen him—a large number of the substantial yeomanry of the province assembled at a convenient rendezvous in one of the eastern counties, and proceeded in a body towards New Haven, to demand and receive the resignation of Mr. Ingersol. Another similar body of self-constituted rulers was to have formed a junction with them in Branford. On the arrival of the eastern company at Hartford, they were informed that Mr. Ingersol was on his way to that place, where he was expected to arrive the next day, to claim the protection of the assembly. They, accordingly, took up their quarters there for the night—having first posted their patrols on the southern and western avenues, to prevent the possibility of his arrival without their knowledge. The next morning they resumed their line of march, and met Mr. Ingersol in Weathersfield. They immediately made known to him the errand on which they had come, giving him to understand that the people were resolute in their purpose, and not to be trifled with. After a little dignified hesitation, the worthy man yielded to the law of necessity, and, mounting on a round table, in the midst of his judges, read aloud the following paper :

"*Weathersfield, Sept. 9th*, 1765.·

" I do hereby promise, that I never will receive any stamped papers which may arrive from Europe, in consequence of an Act lately passed in the Parliament of Great Britain ; nor officiate as stamp master or Distributor of Stamps, within the colony of Connecticut, either directly or indirectly. And I do hereby notify to all the Inhabitants of his Majesty's colony of Connecticut (notwithstanding the said office or trust has been committed to me) not to apply to me, ever after, for any stamped paper ; *hereby declaring that I do resign the said office, and execute these Presents of my own* FREE WILL AND ACCORD, without any equivocation or mental reservation.

" In witness whereof, I have hereunto set my hand.
" J. INGERSOL."

Having finished the reading, he was desired to shout three times, " Liberty and property," which was responded to by three loud and hearty huzzas from the assembled

Mr. Ingersol's Resignation of the Stamp Office.   PAGE 130.

multitude. He was then invited to dine with some of the principal men of the party and the place, by whom he was treated with the greatest respect and politeness. After this, he was escorted by about five hundred horse to Hartford, where he again read his resignation, amid the unbounded acclamations of the people. All this was done in that quiet and orderly manner, which distinguished the lawful assemblages of *the people*, for purposes of counsel and the common defence, from the turbulent and ill-considered outbreaks of an excited, irresponsible mob. The utmost urbanity and good humor prevailed, and jokes were freely exchanged, and kindly received, by both parties. During the progress of the cavalcade to Hartford, Mr. Ingersol, who rode a white horse, was asked what he thought, to find himself attended by such a numerous and motley retinue. He immediately replied, with a smile, " that he had now a clearer idea, than he had ever before conceived, of that passage in the Revelations, which describes *Death on the pale horse, and hell following him.*"

Soon after this, Putnam, having so far recovered as to be able to attend to his ordinary duties, was deputed, with two other gentlemen, to wait on the Governor of the colony, in relation to the same subject, and with the same resolute purpose of preventing the introduction of the hated papers into any part of the colony. The conversation that took place between Governor Fitch and Colonel Putnam on this occasion, will serve well to illustrate the spirit of the times, and the resolute character of the men, on whom the duty devolved of representing and leading the people. The object of the conference having been explained, and the Governor satisfied that the people were immovable in their determination to resist the slightest encroachment upon their rights, he asked, in some concern, addressing himself to Colonel Putnam—

" What shall I do, if the stamped paper should oe sent to me by the King's authority ?"

" Lock it up," replied Putnam, " until we shall visit you again."

" And what will you do then ?"

" We shall expect you to give us the key of the room, in which it is deposited ; and, if you think proper, in order to screen yourself from blame, you may forewarn us, upon our peril, not to enter that room."

" And what will you do afterwards ?"

" Send it safely back again."

" But if I should refuse you admission ?"

" In such a case your house will be levelled with the dust in five minutes."

Such interviews and scenes as this, could not fail to produce a deep impression of the difficulty of enforcing the obnoxious law. In some of the colonies it was never attempted. The stamped paper was never sent into Connecticut ; and it was supposed, at the time, that a report of Putnam's plain talk with the Governor, and the constrained resignation of the stamp-officer at Hartford, deterred them from trying the experiment in that quarter.

The same spirit prevailed on every side. The Provincial assemblies were unanimous in their reprobation of the measure, and one long, loud note, not of remonstrance only, but of defiance, was heard from the masses of the people from north to south. Its echoes reached the ears of the infatuated legislators on the other side of the Atlantic, and convinced them of the futility of attempting to rivet paper chains upon a people born to freedom, and jealous of the slightest encroachment upon their rights. The Revenue System was accordingly abandoned for a season. The Stamp Act was repealed on the 18th of March, 1766. The news was received in America with lively expressions of joy and gratitude. Public thanksgivings were held. Trade with England, which had been suspended, was renewed, and the importation of British goods encouraged, and a general calm, without a parallel in history, immediately succeeded the storm, which had raged with such threatening violence.

During this short season of tranquillity, Putnam resumed his agricultural employments, which he pursued with his accustomed vigor, though slightly interrupted by two accidents, one of which deprived him of the first joint of the thumb of his right hand, while the other was attended with a compound fracture of his right thigh, which shortened that leg nearly an inch, and made him slightly lame during the remainder of his life. He also, at this time, threw open his house for the accommodation of the public. The old sign, which swung before his door, as a token of rest and good cheer for the weary wayfarer, is now to be seen in the Museum of the Historical Society of Connecticut, at Hartford. It represents General Wolfe, in full uniform, his eye fixed, in an expression of fiery earnestness, upon some distant object, and his right arm extended, in emphatic gesture, as if charging on the foe, or directing some other important movement of his army. The sign seems to have fared hardly in one respect, being plentifully sprinkled with shot-holes, which gives the young hero the appearance of having been deeply pitted with the small-pox.

The Provincial officers and soldiers, who survived the expedition to Havana, having deputed General Lyman to receive their portion of prize-money, he repaired to England for that purpose. He was charged, at the same time, with a commission from a company in America, called " Military Adventurers," to solicit from the crown a grant of land on the Mississippi.

12

The delays, vexations and disappointments, attending
this business, so chafed the spirit, and wounded the
manly pride of General Lyman, that he sunk into a state
of despondency and mental imbecility, and retiring to a
solitary place, resolved never more to expose himself to
the indignities and disappointments of public life, and determined never more to return to his native land, lest he
should be reproached with the failure of· his mission. In
this state of morbid depression, he was visited by some of
his own family, who crossed the Atlantic in quest of him,
and succeeded in finding his place of retreat. By their
kindness, sympathy, and good nursing, he was soon restored to his wonted health and activity, and once more repaired to London, to prosecute the object of his mission.

After several years, thus consumed in attendance upon
court, the grant was obtained, and General Lyman returned home, comparatively successful. Colonel Putnam,
with several other gentlemen, accompanied his old commander, in 1774, in a tour to ·the far west, to explore the
tract, and make preparation for settling it. Such an expedition was not accomplished with as much ease, seventy-
five years ago, as at the present day. The steamboat was
not known. The railroad had not been dreamed of. A
trip to Oregon is not more difficult now, than was the pioneer jaunt to the Mississippi, then. After a tedious voyage
to the Balize, and a laborious passage up the river, and
weeks of toilsome engineering, they succeeded in establishing the metes and bounds of their grant, and locating
the portions of the several grantees. This done, they all
returned to Connecticut, with the intention of encouraging emigration, and planting a colony of industrious thriving Yankees on the banks of the Great River. General
Lyman returned thither in the course of the following
season, and formed an establishment at Natchez, where

he remained till his death. Colonel Putnam placed some laborers, with provisions and farming utensils, on his section of the grant ; and, from his well-known enterprise and energy of character, would no doubt have pushed the speculation to a successful issue, had not the clouds, which began to gather anew over his devoted country, thrown a deep shade over all such prospects, and diverted his thoughts from enterprises of private gain, to devising and executing measures for the public weal.

It was now manifest to every observer, that the affairs of the colonies had reached a crisis—that, in the language of Washington, " the once happy and peaceful plains of America were either to be drenched in blood, or inhabited by slaves." The season for petition and remonstrance was gone by. The time for action had arrived. The future was big with events of immeasurable importance to the interests, not of the American colonies merely, but of humanity. The present was destined to be an epoch in the history of human progress. And the men, to whom Providence had assigned the task of directing the great struggle, by which it was to be achieved, were equipped for the service, and ready to take their posts. Under these men, as councillors and leaders, the people instinctively ranged themselves. The athletic frame, the bold and active mind, the prompt, determined air, and tried courage of Colonel Putnam, added to his large experience in military affairs, his ardent patriotism and untiring zeal, marked him out as one of the leaders, and gave him a conspicuous rank among them. By his advice and assistance, measures were extensively taken, in his own province, to prepare for the worst that might come. New life was infused into the militia. The men, and even the boys, who were capable of bearing arms, were urged, and assisted, to devote themselves diligently to systematic exercise in the military art. Voluntary associations were formed among them, for regular practice in military manœuvres and drilling, and the execution of all the varied evolutions of the camp and the field. The militia trainings of that period bore no resemblance to the spiritless and purposeless farces of our day. They had an object, lofty, solemn, momentous, and were conducted with a spirit that made every soldier feel himself a man, and gave to every officer the aspect and bearing of a hero. Every village had its military school, and its miniature camp, where children learned the art of war from their fathers, and where the scarred veteran acted over again the scenes of his youth, and taught the striplings to emulate them. Such were the notes of preparation that indicated the coming crisis.

CHAPTER XI.

THE repeal of the Stamp Act was accompanied by another
declaratory Act, designed as a sort of salvo to the national
pride of British Legislators, affirming that the Parliament
had power to bind the colonies in all cases whatever
—a sufficient warning, it would seem, that the repeal was
but a temporary truce, in the war against American rights.
That truce was shorter than was at first anticipated.   Taking advantage of the absence of Mr. Pitt, who was confined
by sickness in the country, Mr. Townshend, then chancellor of the Exchequer, introduced a bill into Parliament,
in 1767, imposing duties on glass, paper, painters' colors,
and tea, which was immediately passed, and approved by
the king.   A bill was also passed, establishing a board of
trade in the colonies, independent of colonial legislation ;
and others equally at variance with the known views of
the Americans, as well as with the fundamental principles
of the British constitution.

On the revival of this scheme of oppression, the old
12*

spirit of resistance revived in all its force.   The colonial Assemblies protested earnestly against it.   The columns of the public papers were filled with spirited essays from the ablest political writers of the day, setting forth, in the clearest manner, the fallacy of the principles, and the injustice of these measures of the ministry ; and appealing earnestly to the people to resist them, even to the last extremity.   Otis, the Adamses, Patrick Henry, and many others, stepped boldly forth to the defence of American liberty, and kindled a flame which was not to be quenched, but by the entire independence of the colonies from the domination of their unnatural step-mother.   Some of them, by their fearless denunciation of British oppression, and their uncompromising advocacy of the doctrine of resistance and independence, rendered themselves so peculiarly obnoxious to the crown, as to be honored with a special exemption from the promise of pardon, which was subsequently offered to all who would return to their allegiance, and quietly submit to any burden which royalty, moved and instigated by a tyrannical ministry, might be pleased to lay upon them.

Associations were immediately formed, and agreements entered into, to abstain entirely from the use of the articles enumerated in the bill, and to suspend, as far as possible, all commercial intercourse with the mother-country, till the policy of colonial taxation should be utterly and for ever abandoned.   All foreign luxuries were dispensed with ; domestic manufactures of every kind were freely encouraged ; and other measures adopted, to show to their British taskmasters, that all the advantages and conveniences of a lucrative commerce would be sacrificed in a moment, sooner than they would forego one jot or tittle of their birthright, as free born Englishmen.   The excitement grew warmer and warmer.   Difficulties thickened on every side. The colonial Assemblies were repeatedly threatened, dissolved, and broken up, only to meet again, with a sterner purpose of resistance, and bolder resolves than before. Soldiers were quartered upon the citizens, and stationed about the legislative halls, to overawe the people, and intimidate their advisers ; who only became the more bold and unyielding, at every new demonstration of the power that was destined to enslave them.

It was in the midst of these excitements, that Colonel Putnam made his exploring tour to the banks of the Mis sissippi. The season of his absence was one of pecu liar agitation and ferment, and he returned to find the storm of civil discord raging violently, and ready to burst over his devoted land. The first blood of the American Revolution had been spilt, in the massacre of the fifth of March, at Boston ; and other scenes of agitation had been enacted, which portended the coming conflict, and warned every patriot citizen to be ready at his post, to meet the impending crisis. It was clearly foreseen that it would not terminate but in blood. It was a time to try men's souls. America was thinly populated, divided into thirteen separate governments, with many conflicting interests, and sectional jealousies, to distract her councils, and divide and weaken her strength ; without a head, without an army, without a treasury, and without credit. The odds against them were fearful, in case of actual outbreak, their antagonist being by far the most powerful nation on earth, both by sea and land, and capable of commanding the resources of nearly all Europe. She had also a tremendous advantage, in having the reins of government, in all the colonies, in her own hands ; and holding possession of the fortified posts, with a large part of the arms and ammunition of the country. Besides this, the people of America were as truly loyal as any in the wide spread

dominions of the king. They were proud of their ances-
tors and their father-land. They prized highly the privileges of the British constitution ; and nothing short of a
melancholy persuasion, that the principles involved in
these measures of the ministry were subversive of every
hope of liberty, guaranteed to them by that constitution,
could have induced them to raise the standard of revolt.

There were still many Americans, and among them
some of the ablest and most intelligent men in the country,
who held fast their allegiance to the king, and discoun-
tenanced every act of resistance as arrant rebellion. Some,
too, of the most experienced officers, who had served in
the French War, and who well understood the military
power of England, shrank from so unequal a contest, and
frowned upon every measure which seemed calculated to
widen the breach, and provoke an ultimate recourse to
arms. In such circumstances, it required more than ordinary decision and courage to become a leader ; for though
success would win for them enduring laurels, a failure
would consign them all to the ignominious fate of rebels.
Fortunately for us and the world, the crisis produced the
men who were equal to its utmost exigency. Counsellors
and statesmen, bold, sagacious, and far-seeing, resolved to
hazard everything dear, sooner than relinquish one of the
principles of liberty, for which alone they contended,
were found in every province. Brave soldiers, and competent officers, men of ample military experience were
not wanting, who were ready at a word, to leap into the
breach, and lead their undisciplined fellow-citizens to battle with the veteran troops and well-trained legions of the
old world ; preferring the prospect of an early grave, or a
prison and a halter, to the certainty of chains worse than
those of iron, which can only enslave the body.

Among the foremost and most conspicuous of the latter

class, was Colonel Putnam, whose courage and patriotic
zeal was well and widely known, and who possessed the
entire confidence of the people, not only of Connecticut,
but of the sister provinces. He entered at once, and heartily, into the preparatory measures, which signalized the
trying interval between the first blood-shedding at Boston,
and the actual opening of the grand drama at Lexington.
By reference to the papers, and official documents of that
period, we find him an active and zealous partizan in the
affairs of the colonies, watching, as a sentinel at his post,
the signs of the times, and urging, with all his accustomed
impetuosity and energy, every expedient to rouse and keep
alive the spirit of resistance, and evade or prevent the execution of those hateful laws, which threatened to enslave
them. Boston was, at that time, the head-quarters of
what the English were pleased to term "the rebellion,"
and the point upon which they concentrated their severest
enactments, and their first military preparations to subdue
the refractory colonies. Putnam was often there. He
was familiarly known to General Gage, the British commander-in-chief, Lord Percy, Colonel Small, and many
others, with whom he had formerly served, in the "Seven
Years' War." His character, for all that constitutes a
brave soldier and an able commander, was well known
and highly appreciated among them ; while his personal
qualities had endeared him greatly to those who had been
most familiar with him, in war and in peace.

As the crisis approached, and the storm of war seemed
inevitable, the conversation often turned, from a warm discussion of general principles, to matters of more personal
concern. But Putnam was not a man to hesitate about
consequences, when his mind was settled, and his resolution fixed upon principles. When, therefore, he was
questioned, by his British friends, as to the part he should

take, in case the dispute should proceed to actual hostilities, he always replied, and with an energy that left no
doubt of the sincerity and heartiness of his determination—
" I shall take part with my country in any event ; and,
whatever may happen, I am prepared to abide the consequences."

When asked whether he, who had witnessed the prowess of the British arms, and their repeated victories by sea
and land, did not believe them equal to the immediate conquest of a people, who did not own a single ship, and who
had neither armies, nor commanders, nor munitions of war
—he replied, with equal confidence, " I can only say, justice would be on our side, and the event with Providence.
And, if the combined forces of Great Britain and her colonies, required six full years to drive the French out of Canada, I apprehend it will be no easy task, for British
troops alone, to enslave a country, much more extensive
and populous than Canada.   Besides, men fighting on their
own soil, in defence of their altars, their hearths and their
liberties, have an advantage, in the sacredness of their
cause, over the mere mercenaries, who fight only for pay,
with nothing at stake on the issue, but the idle breath of
fame.   For my part, I fully believe you will find it no
easy matter to conquer these American provinces, poor as
they are."

On one occasion, he was asked, with an expressive
sneer, if a well-appointed army of five thousand British
veterans might not march, without serious molestation,
from one end of the continent to the other.   " No doubt
they could," he replied, with animation, " if they behaved
themselves civilly, and paid well for everything they
wanted.   But," he added, after a moment's pause, " if
they should attempt it in a hostile manner, the American
women, if the men were out of the way, would meet them

with their ladles and broomsticks, and put them to rout, before they had measured half the breadth of the land."

Such was the substance of frequent amicable discussions, which took place between the advocates of the crown on the one part, and the bold American leaders on the other, indicating clearly the nature of the contest, in which they were soon to engage, but never resulting in conviction in the minds of the disputants.

Among the measures of preparation and precaution, which were generally adopted, and ably sustained, in all the colonies, was the appointment of committees of vigilance and correspondence, whose duty it was, to keep the whole people informed of whatever occurred in any part of the land, that should alarm the fears, or awaken the jealousy of the most sensitive defenders of liberty. Colonel Putnam was chairman of such a committee, for the district in which he resided, and, as such, incurred a large share of the displeasure of the British party, for his sleepless vigilance, and prompt, untiring zeal.

A gentleman, in New York, writing to a friend in Annapolis, under date of September 6th, 1774, says: " Two days ago, we were alarmed by the arrival of an express from Colonel Putnam, of Connecticut, to the committee of this city, with the intelligence that a certain person was just come to his house from Boston, to acquaint him that an affray had happened between the people and the troops in Boston. Colonel Putnam, upon this advice, alarmed the whole country, moving them to arm themselves, and take the road to Boston—which they actually did, insomuch that, the postman says, that the roads were covered with people."

This proved to be a false alarm, and the part which Colonel Putnam took in it, was the subject of no little comment in those papers of the time, that were still in the

British interest.   One of General Gage's defenders, in a letter to Peyton Randolph, of Virginia, written at this juncture, says : " Colonel Putnam, of Connecticut, with a zeal, not according to knowledge, alarmed that and all the southern provinces, and the whole country was in motion."

To show the spirit of the man, and the excited state of the country at this time, we give the following extract from Colonel Putnam's letter, explaining and justifying the part he took in the affair.   After stating how the story came to him, by a Captain Keys, purporting to be an authorised messenger from Boston, he adds : " Now I submit it to the determination of every candid and unprejudiced reader, whether my conduct, in writing the above-mentioned letter, merits the imputation of imprudence, as asserted by said writer, or whether they would have me tamely sit down, a spectator of the inhuman sacrifice of my friends and fellow-countrymen.   *   *   *   And pray, what easier way could I have proceeded, than in writing to one of the militia captains, whom I desired to forward the intelligence to the adjacent towns, when I really believed the story to be true ?   Which having done, I mounted my horse, and made the best of my way towards Boston, having only four gentlemen to accompany me.   Having proceeded as far as Douglass, which is about thirty miles from my house, I met Captain Hill, of that town, with his company, who had been down within about thirty miles from Boston, and had just returned.   He informed me that the alarm was false, and that the forces of Worcester and Sutton were on their return.   I then turned my course homewards, without loss of time, and reached my house about sun-rising on Sunday morning, taking care to acquaint the people on the road, that they need not proceed any further.

" I believe the alarm was first occasioned by Mr. Benjamin Hallowell, who, going into Boston in a great fright, informed the army that he had killed one man, and wounded another, while they were pursuing him from Cambridge, and the country were all in arms, marching towards Boston, which threw the military into great consternation. * * * In the midst of this hurry and confusion, a post was dispatched into the country, but by whom, or to answer what purpose, I cannot tell. But what took place in consequence of it, is evident. General Gage's apprehensions of danger were so great, that he speedily began to fortify the entrance to the town, to prevent a surprise from the enemy without."*

The agitation, here referred to, was that which resulted from General Gage's taking possession of the powder in the Arsenal, at Charlestown. The Arsenal was situated in the north-west part of the town, between Medford and Cambridge. About two hundred of the British troops, in thirteen boats, passed silently up the Mystic River, during the night of the 1st of September; and, disembarking at a convenient place, proceeded to the powder-house, and carried off the entire quantity of powder deposited there, amounting to nearly three hundred barrels. Intelligence of this transaction was rapidly circulated ; and, in the morning, several thousand inhabitants of the neighboring towns assembled at Cambridge, principally. in arms, and were with difficulty restrained from marching into Boston, to demand a delivery of the powder, and, in case of refusal, to attack the troops. Amidst the noise and confusion attending this affair, there sprang up a rumor, that the fleet and troops were firing on the town of Boston. It flew through New England with such rapidity, that, in less than twenty-four hours, there were between thirty and

* Am. Arch., 4th Series. Vol. i., p. 942.
13

forty thousand men in arms. The roads to Boston were thronged in all directions. And there can be no doubt, that, if the report which caused all this excitement had proved true, General Gage would, at that time, have been attacked in his citadel, and his whole military force annihilated at a blow. At that date, his force was comparatively small, and the fortifications, which he afterwards relied on to protect him from incursions from the country, were not yet erected. It was the serious aspect of this occasion, and the determined air of the people — who gathered by thousands from all sides, at the first tap of the drum—that suggested the necessity of such defences.

CHAPTER XII.

It was in this state of general excitement, and individual alarm and watchfulness, that the war of the Revolution broke upon the colonies. They were, in a great measure, unprepared for any serious conflict, but were unanimously resolved to submit to extermination at the point of the bayonet, rather than yield to oppression under the forms of law. They had no army, though almost every man and boy in the land was ready to step into the ranks, at a moment's warning. Their legislative assemblies were forcibly dissolved; the inhabitants were formally declared rebels; and an army sent to Boston to subdue them.

On the dissolution of the Assembly of Massachusetts, its members met again, and resolved themselves into a Provincial Congress. They appointed committees of "safety," and "supplies," and voted to raise and organize an army of twelve thousand men. They also made arrangements for the immediate enlistment of one fourth part of the militia, as minute-men, to be ready for action at a moment's warning. Similar preparations, proportioned in extent to the population of each, were made in the other colonies. Military stores and ammunition were purchased, and magazines provided, in suitable places, for their reception. Meanwhile, the Americans carefully abstained from all offensive acts. The first aggression was on the part of General Gage. Having previously seized, and conveyed to Boston, the ammunition and military stores in the provincial arsenals at Cambridge and Charlestown, he proceeded, on the night of the 18th of April, 1775, to dispatch a force of eight hundred men, under the command of Colonel Smith and Major Pitcairn, to destroy those at Concord.

This expedition was planned in profound secrecy ; and the greatest precautions were taken to prevent the intelligence of it from going out in advance, to alarm the people. But the Yankees were too wakeful to be taken by surprise. The patriots of Boston, by some means, became acquainted with the Governor's design, and Dr. Warren immediately dispatched confidential messengers along the supposed route, to prepare for their reception. At Lexington, a little more than half way to Concord, where they arrived about daylight, on the morning of the 19th, the British troops met with the first appearance of hostile resistance. About seventy men, under command of Captain Parker, were drawn up on the green. Major Pitcairn, supposing the voice of a British officer, backed by such a force as he had at his feet, would be quite sufficient to subdue a single company of raw militia, rode up to their line, and cried out, in an insolent tone, "Disperse, you rebels, throw down your arms and disperse." Not being obeyed, he discharged his pistol, and ordered his soldiers to fire. Several of the militia were killed, and the rest, feeling it was useless to contend with numbers so greatly superior, retreated and dispersed, but only to gather again, with large reinforcements from every quarter.

The detachment proceeded, without further interruption, to Concord, destroyed a part of the stores deposited there, and made a hasty retreat. But the militia of all the surrounding country, having been alarmed, assembled in great numbers. A smart skirmish ensued, and several were killed on both sides. To retreat through such a country, where every man was an enemy, if not a disciplined soldier, and where every house, and tree, and fence, sheltered one or more expert marksmen, each capable of picking off his man at any reasonable distance, was no easy matter. The Americans hung upon their rear, and harassed them on every side, and would inevitably have cut the whole detachment in pieces, had not Lord Percy, with a reinforcement of nine hundred men and two field pieces, met them at Lexington.

Lord Percy formed his detachment into a square, in which he enclosed Colonel Smith's party, who, according to Stedman, " were so much exhausted with fatigue, that they were obliged to lie down for rest on the ground, their tongues hanging out of their mouths, like those of dogs after a chase."

The enemy, now amounting to about seventeen hundred men, having halted an hour or two at Lexington, recommenced their march, but the attack from the Provincials was renewed at the same time, and an irregular, yet very galling fire was kept up on each flank, as well as in front and rear. The close firing from behind stone walls, by good marksmen, put them in no small confusion ; but they, on their part, kept up a brisk retreating fire on the militia and

13*

minute-men.   A little after sunset, they reached Bunker's Hill, where, exhausted with excessive fatigue, they remained during the night, protected from further annoyance by the guns of the Somerset man-of-war, which was so situated as to rake the neck, and so prevent their pursuers from gaining access to Charlestown.   The following day, they crossed over to Boston, carrying with them ample evidence to satisfy General Gage, that the work of enslaving the colonies would be no farce.

The British lost, during this expedition, in killed, wounded, and missing, nearly three hundred men ; the loss of the Provincials being less than one third that number.

During the retreat from Lexington, Major Pitcairn's horse was shot under him.   The Major fell with him, and only escaped being made a prisoner, by feigning himself dead.   His pursuers, coming up, pulled his pistols from his holsters, and leaving him unmolested, kept on their march.   When they had passed out of sight, he took to nis feet, and, by a singular good fortune, succeeded in escaping their vigilance, and overtaking his friends.   His pistols were presented to General Putnam, on his arrival at Cambridge, and were his constant companions through all his subsequent military career.   They are still in the possession of one of his grandsons, John P. Putnam, Esq., of Western New York.   They are represented as being of exquisite workmanship.*

* There was another relic of the old hero, the remains of which may, perhaps, at some future day, become the property of one of the bold watermen on the Ohio.   We refer to the good old musket that killed the wolf, and accompanied its owner through all the perils of the Seven Years' War.   It is said to have been dropped overboard, in the Ohio, as the General, in one of his western expeditions, was crossing that river in a boat.

The Alarm.—Putnam, leaving his Plough, hastens to Cambridge.   PAGE 151.

With the rapidity of lightning, the intelligence spread on every side, that American blood had been shed by the British troops at Lexington. It was the signal and declaration of war. The country was all in motion. The militia, on all sides, seized their arms, which had been kept in constant readiness, and rushed to the scene of action. In the course of a few days, a line of encampment was formed from Dorchester, through Roxbury, Brookline, Cambridge and Charlestown, to the Mystic River, thus completely environing the British troops in Boston, with an army of twenty thousand men.

The alarm, which was carried by a man with a drum on horseback, found Putnam ploughing in the field. Captain Hubbard, afterwards a quarter-master in the army, was in the adjoining field. They were both ready for action in their own way. Hubbard was a cool, systematic, orderly man. He walked quietly home, put things in order, filled his knapsack, and took his way to the camp. Putnam merely unyoked his team from his plough, and bidding his boy to go home, and tell his mother where he was gone, mounted his horse, and dashed away down the road towards Boston. In twenty-four hours he was there, a distance, in those days, of nearly one hundred miles. He attended a council of war at Cambridge, on the 21st, where the parole, in honor of his arrival, was " Putnam."*

Finding the British confined to Boston, and invested with a sufficient force to watch their movements, and being especially requested by the Legislature of Connecticut, then in session, to meet them for the purpose of consultation, he returned at once to Hartford. Having assisted in levying and organizing a regiment, under authority of the Legislature, by whom he was promoted to be Brigadier-General, he hastened back to Cambridge, from which

* Orderly Book.

place he was absent only one week, leaving orders for the troops to follow as speedily as possible. Among those troops, Knowlton, Durkee, and many others, who had served with him in the French and Indian Wars, were foremost to enlist under the banner of so able and tried a commander.

Collected, as the American forces were, from different and independent provinces, they were without a common head, and liable to all the difficulties arising from personal jealousy and military pride, in arranging their respective stations and commands. Some of the best officers took offence at the position to which they were assigned ; and some absolutely refused obedience to those who were ranked above them. For the most part, however, the utmost harmony and good feeling prevailed. To remedy, on their part, the difficulties arising from this cause the Council of Connecticut passed a resolution, advising the Governor " to order the officers and soldiers of the province to be subordinate, and yield obedience to the General and commanding officer of Massachusetts Bay, while acting in that province, and until the Governor should see fit to order otherwise."* Whatever may have been the case with other officers, it appears that General Putnam's established reputation, and universal popularity, secured for him the confidence of all, and raised him at once to the post of honor and of danger. The supreme command, by the above resolution, was vested in Major-General Ward. Putnam, as appears, among other evidences, from the following extracts from letters of the time, held a separate command under him, at an advanced post, which it was deemed of great importance to defend ; and was regarded, at the time, as but little inferior to the commander-in-chief. The first is from Jedediah Huntington to Jonathan

* Am. Archives, 4th Series, vol. ii., page 1039.

Trumbull, jr., Governor of Connecticut, dated Cambridge, April 27th, 1775, and says: "General Ward is at Roxbury. General Putnam is commander-in-chief at this place. They have both of them too much business upon their hands."

The second is from an intercepted letter of one of the British soldiers in Boston, to his friends in England, dated April 30, 1775 : " The whole country is in arms against us, and they are headed by two of the Generals that headed our army in the last war.—Their names are Ward and Putnam." * They were both distinguished in the French War, and bore an active part, the former as a Lieutenant-Colonel, the latter as a Major, in the disastrous storming of Ticonderoga, under the command of General Abercrombie ; and now, by a singular concurrence of events, were associated in the direction of an army, in open hostility to their old commanders, and comrades in arms. Ward, as Major-General, and commander-in-chief of the Massachusetts troops, was first. His head-quarters were at Cambridge, and Putnam was his principal executive officer in that wing of the army ; his immediate command being a central and advanced position, on the northern bank of Charles River, in Cambridge, and the same spot where Smith and Pitcairn's detachment landed, on the night of the 17th of April, in their stealthy march to Lexington. Wooster and Spencer, who were his superiors in rank in his own province, were stationed at Roxbury, with the right wing of the army under the command of Lieutenant-General Thomas.

One of the measures resorted to by the British commanders, to weaken the forces of their adversaries, was an attempt to win over to the king, by bribes of gold and offices of distinction, some of the ablest and bravest of our

* Am. Archives, 4th Series, vol. ii., page 423.

military leaders. With some, among whom were Rogers, William Stark, &c., they were successful. But Putnam, John Stark, Henry Lee, and many others, spurned the proposal with a contempt and dignity becoming their true-hearted patriotism, and the claims of their injured country. In the case of Putnam, the bait held out was a Major-General's commission in the British establishment, and a large pecuniary compensation for his services, as well as a handsome provision for his sons.

"These facts," as Mr. Everett happily remarks, in his memoir of General Stark, "show that the course pursued by the gallant and patriotic officers, who had distinguished themselves in the Seven Years' War, and who hastened to range themselves on the side of the Revolution, was not a hasty and unreflecting adhesion to the popular cause. They prove that the question was presented to the mind of (Putnam) as one to be weighed deliberately, and that he decided for his country, against the influence of authority and temptation, to which many a mind would have yielded. His mind, however, was made up from the first." And he never wavered or hesitated in the choice he had made.

The inhabitants of Boston, finding their commerce broken up, and themselves cut off from all communication with the country, began to be 'seriously distressed for provisions. General Gage, taking advantage of this distress, promised to allow them all to leave the town, if they would first deliver up their arms. The terms were readily complied with. But the General, having received their arms, basely refused to let the people go. It would seem that he wished to hold them for his own security, to guard against an attack from their friends without. At least, such was the charitable construction put upon his

breach of faith, by the poet Trumbull, in the first canto of
McFingal :

> " So Gage, of late agreed, you know,
> To let the Boston people go ;
> Yet, when he saw, 'gainst troops that brav'd him,
> They were the only guards that saved him,
> Kept off that satan of a Putnam
> From breaking in to maul and mutt'n him,
> He'd too much wit such leagues to observe,
> And shut them in again to starve."

The first object of the besieging Generals was to construct
a line of intrenchments, which, if not a sufficient protection against actual assault, would serve to inspire an undisciplined and inexperienced army with confidence in their
position. In devising and completing these defences, the
ingenuity, industry, and fine humor of General Putnam
were of the greatest service. The lines went up with
astonishing rapidity ; and, in less than a month, the extended camp of the American army, stretching from Dorchester to Chelsea, a circuit of not less than twelve miles,
was so fortified in every assailable part, as to secure every
practicable pass from Boston to the country. The remains
of those simple, impromptu redoubts are still to be seen
in many places along the line of the encampment.

Having completed their intrenchments, the next care of
the American commanders was to cut off, as far as possible, such sources of supply as lay within the reach of the
enemy. For this purpose, an expedition was set on foot
to drive off the live stock from the islands in Boston Bay.
Those nearest the encampment, and the most important,
were Hog-Island, and Noddle-Island—the latter being now
known as East Boston. From Chelsea to the former of
these, the water is scarcely two feet deep, at low tide.
It, therefore, required neither bridges nor boats to effect

the passage. The space between the two islands is also fordable at low water.

On Saturday, the 27th of May, at eleven o'clock in the morning, a party, consisting of between twenty and thirty men, passed over to Hog-Island, and commenced driving off the stock that was there. They were interrupted in their operations, and drawn into a skirmish with a party of marines—who were stationed there to protect the stock —asssisted by another party in a schooner and sloop, that were instantly dispatched to their aid from the fleet in Boston harbor. They succeeded, however, in securing and killing a considerable number of horses and cows, as well as in bringing down several of the British marines, upon whom they kept up a steady and well-directed firing during their retreat.

Having cleared Hog-Island, notwithstanding the opposition of the marines, and effected their retreat to Chelsea, without the loss of a man, they drew up on the neck, and sent for a reinforcement, to complete the object of their expedition. This was immediately furnished. It consisted of three hundred men, with two field pieces (four pounders), under the command of General Putnam. Warren, who had not then received his appointment in the army, accompanied him as a volunteer. Being obliged to wait the time of the tide, it was near nine o'clock in the evening before they reached the island. General Putnam then went down to the beach, and hailed the schooner, demanding an immediate surrender, and promising good quarters in case of a quiet submission. This demand was answered by two cannon shot from the schooner; which was immediately returned by a discharge of the American field-pieces. From this time, a heavy fire was kept up on both sides, till near eleven o'clock, when the firing from the schooner ceased. Her decks had been

completely swept by the pieces and small arms of the
Americans, and her crew was now obliged to abandon her
and take to the boats—a considerable number of which had
been sent from the ships to their assistance, with a reinforcement of marines.

The schooner being thus deserted, drifted on shore.
About break of day, the provincials, having first stripped
her, carried some hay under her stern, and set her on fire
—the men in the sloop, meanwhile, keeping up a small
fire upon them.   About the same time, a heavy cannonading was commenced at Noddle-Island (East Boston) Hill,
by a fresh party of marines from the British fleet; notwithstanding which, Putnam plied the sloop so briskly, that
she was soon entirely disabled.   To prevent her from
sharing the fate of the schooner, she was towed off by the
boats, and thus the conflict ceased.   The expedition was
entirely successful, having been effected by the loss of one
man only killed, and four slightly wounded—one by the
bursting of his own gun, and another losing only his little
finger.   The loss of the British was twenty killed, and
fifty wounded, besides four double fortified four pounders,
twelve swivels, and a quantity of rigging, sails, clothes and
money, taken from the schooner.*   It also brought away
from the keeping and use of the British, several hundred
sheep and cattle, and secured them for the benefit of the
Americans.

A number of prisoners having been taken on both sides,
in the various skirmishes since the battle of Lexington,
arrangements were made for an exchange to take place on
the 6th of June.   General Putnam and Dr. Warren were
appointed to conduct the prisoners, on their part, to the
place of meeting.   Entering Charlestown about noon,
under the escort of Captain Chester's company of Wea-

* Am. Archives, 4th Series, vol. ii., pages 719 and 874.
      14

thersfield infantry — the élite corps of. the army — and marching slowly through it, they halted at the ferry ; where, upon a signal being given, Majors Moncrief and Small landed from the Lively, to receive the prisoners, and to see their old friend, and comrade in arms, General Putnam. They had served together in the Seven Years' War ; had shared the dangers and hardships of the camp, in a common cause ; and had learned to regard each other with that peculiar respect and affection, which brave men and good soldiers always feel for their comrades, and which they are ever as ready to recognize in a foe, as in a friend. Their meeting was truly cordial and affectionate.* Their present differences were forgotten for the moment, and, when the wounded privates had been sent on board the Lively, Major Small, Major Moncrief, and the captive officers, repaired with General Putnam and Dr. Warren to the house of Dr. Foster, where an entertainment was provided for them.

About three o'clock, a signal was made from the Lively, that the exchange prisoners were ready to come on shore ; upon which General Putnam and Major Moncrief went down to the ferry to receive them. They then returned to their company at Dr. Foster's, and spent an hour or two in a very agreeable manner. Between five and six o'clock they parted ; Major Moncrief, with his released officers, going on board the Lively, and Putnam and Warren, with their new found friends, returning, under the same escort as before, to Cambridge. The whole affair was conducted with the utmost decency and good humor

* The late Governor Brooks, of Massachusetts, who was present at this interview, stated, that when Putnam and his British friends met at Charlestown, they ran into each other's arms, and kissed each other, to the great diversion and astonishment of the country people of the army.

—neither party realizing at all, that in ten short days they would be arranged in bloody conflict, each using his utmost endeavor to maim, capture, or destroy, the other. To those who have not been trained to arms, it seems impossible that men who truly love, admire, and respect each other, should be capable of being excited, by the beat of a drum, the blast of a trumpet, or the voice of a commander, to such desperate and savage exertions for mutual destruction. But such is war.

It is greatly to the credit of the American army, at this period, which they maintained throughout the whole war, that the British officers, on parting with their captors, expressed the most grateful acknowledgments for the kind and generous treatment they had received during the term of their captivity. The privates, who were all wounded men, did the same in the strongest terms—some of them with tears, expressing their grateful sense of the tenderness which had been shown to them in their miserable situation. A writer of that day, in describing the scene, and contrasting the treatment of American prisoners among the British, with that of their prisoners in our camp, concludes with the following sensible remarks : " Compassion is as essential a part of the character of a truly brave man, as daring ; and an insult offered to a person entirely in the power of the insulter, savors as strongly of cowardice, as it does of cruelty." In this quality of compassion and generosity to his foes, General Putnam was not excelled by any officer in the army. He was sometimes reproached, by those of a sterner character, for carrying this virtue too far, and showing too much lenity to the enemies of his country. He was incapable of a lasting resentment, and never regarded a foe unarmed as any longer a foe, or a prisoner as other than an unfortunate friend.

The position of the contending parties was peculiar,

The Americans greatly outnumbered the British, but were, at the same time, altogether inferior to them in arms, ammunition, and all the other means of active warfare. They had full knowledge of the force and equipments of the enemy, and of most of their plans and designs. The British General, on the other hand, was ignorant of the real strength of his antagonist. He, therefore, quietly suffered himself to be shut up, for several weeks, in his narrow quarters in Boston; looking down upon an enemy whom he affected to despise, but whom he did not dare to invite to a general engagement. That enemy, too sensible of his own weakness to provoke an engagement, yet daily acquiring the means and the power to meet it, when it should become inevitable, was calmly, hopefully awaiting the issue; equally resolved to yield nothing to fear, and to hazard nothing by presumption.

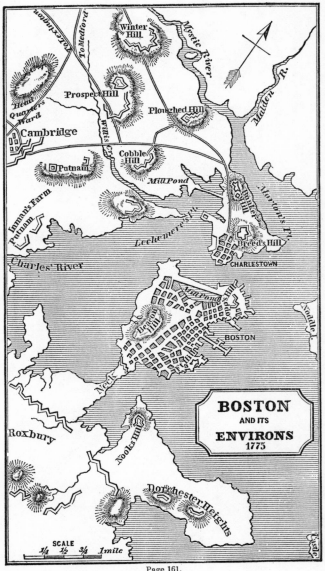

BOSTON
AND ITS
ENVIRONS
1775

SCALE
1/4 1/2 3/4 1 mile

Page 161.

CHAPTER XIII.

THE BATTLE OF BUNKER HILL.

An intrenchment ordered on Bunker Hill—Divisions in the Council respecting this measure—The detachment—The Peninsula of Charlestown—Detachment pauses at the foot of the Hill—A discussion—Breed's Hill selected for a redoubt—Colonel Gridley—Description of the redoubt—Industry and spirit of the men—Surprise of the British—Severe cannonade—Preparations for a battle—Putnam goes to Cambridge for reinforcements—General Ward's opinion—Putnam's position—His desire to fortify on Bunker Hill—Landing of the British—"The Breastwork"—The rail fence—Accessions to the American force—Warren, Pomeroy, Stark, Reed, &c.—Putnam's activity—Terrible slaughter among the British—They retreat—Captain Callender—British compelled to retreat again and again—Burning of Charlestown—Putnam's reception of the incendiaries—Arrival of Captain Foster with a wagon-load of powder—Heavy loss of the British—Storming the redoubt—The retreat—Putnam bringing up the rear—Intrenchment on Prospect and Winter Hills.

THE American commanders, having ascertained that the British intended to take possession of the heights of Charlestown, as a vantage ground from which to dislodge them from some of their intrenchments, and thus make a way into the country, resolved, by a sudden and secret movement, to defeat the project, by advancing to that position a portion of the left wing of their own camp.

Putnam, who had already carefully examined the ground, was strenuously in favor of this movement, and had urged it again and again in council, with all the arguments at his command. In common with Prescott, and

14*

other veterans, who understood the character of the American soldiery, and knew the immense advantage to the order and discipline of the army, which would be derived from active and hazardous service, he had repeatedly proposed to lead a party which should invite an engagement with the enemy. Nothing short of this, it was held, would satisfy the army, or the country, who were growing weary of their fruitless inaction. It was with peculiar satisfaction, therefore, that they hailed the decision of the Council, to occupy the heights of Charlestown, and show a bold front to the enemy.

The measure was ably opposed by some of the best and bravest men in the Council, and there were obstacles in the way of its accomplishment, which would have appalled any other men, than those who planned and achieved it. One of these was the want of powder. There were, at that time, only eleven barrels in the public depots, and sixty-seven barrels in all Massachusetts—scarcely enough, under the most prudent management, for one day's fighting. To this objection, General Pomeroy answered that he was ready to lead his men to battle with but five cartridges a-piece. They were all experienced marksmen, and would fire no random shots; and if every American killed his five, they would have but little occasion for more powder.

Ward and Warren objected, that the enterprise would bring on a general engagement, for which they were by no means prepared. To this Putnam replied, " We will risk only two thousand men. We will go on with these, and defend ourselves as long as possible ; and, if driven to retreat, we are more active than the enemy, and every stone-wall shall be lined with their dead. And, at the worst, suppose us surrounded, and no retreat, we will set our country an example, of which it shall not be ashamed, and teach mercenaries what men can do, who are determined to live or die free."

Warren walked the floor, then paused, and leaned on his chair. "Almost thou persuadest me, General Putnam," he said, "but I must still think the project rash ; if you execute it, however, you will not be surprised to find me at your side."

"I hope not," replied Putnam, "you are young, and your country has much to hope from you, in council and in the field.   Let us, who are old, and can be spared, begin the fray.   There will be time enough for you hereafter, for it will not soon be over."*

The bolder counsels prevailed, and orders were issued to Colonels Prescott and Bridge, and the regiment of Colonel Frye, to be prepared for an expedition with all their men, who were fit for service, and with one day's provision.   The same order was issued to one hundred and twenty men of General Putnam's regiment, under the command of the brave Captain Knowlton, and one company of artillery, with two field pieces.   Putnam having the general superintendence of the expedition, and Colonel Gridley, the chief Engineer, accompanied the troops.

Putnam's eldest son was a Captain under him.   His youngest, only sixteen, was a volunteer.   At sunset his father said to him, " You will go to Mrs. Inman's to-night as usual ; stay there to-morrow, and if they find it necessary to leave town, you must go with them."   From this order, and the attending circumstances, the young man knew there was to be a military movement of some importance, in which his father would participate.   " My imagination," says he, " figured him as mangled with wounds, and no one near to aid him.   I earnestly entreated permis-

* Statement of Colonel Daniel Putnam, as given by Colonel Swett.

sion to accompany him. ' You, my dear father, may need
assistance, much more than Mrs. Inman'; pray, let me go
where you are going.' ' No, no, Daniel, do as I bid you,'
was the reply, which he affected to give sternly, while his
voice faltered, and his eyes filled, as if entering into my
feelings.   He added, ' You can do little, my son, where I
am going, and there will be enough to take care of me."

The peninsula of Charlestown is a mile and one-eighth
in length, from east to west, and two-thirds of a mile across,
from north to south.   The Mystic River forms its northern, and the Charles River its southern border—the distance between them, at the Neck, being only one hundred
and thirty yards.   A narrow channel separates it from
Boston on the east.   Bunker's Hill commences at the
Neck, and rises abruptly to the height of one hundred and
thirteen feet, and then, falling off in a gentle slope towards
the east, stretches, in a low ridge, for a considerable distance along the shore of the Mystic, and parallel with
Breed's Hill.   Breed's Hill, which is eighty-seven feet
high, commences near the southern extremity of Bunker
Hill, and extends towards the south and east, the two
summits being distant from each other one hundred and
thirty rods.

The ground on the east of Breed's Hill, as well as on
the north, between that and the village before mentioned,
is low and marshy, constituting what was called *the
slough*.   The village of Charlestown was on the south side
of the hill, and had begun already to extend itself a little
upon its slope.   Morton's Point, where the ground was
also somewhat elevated, the hill being thirty-five feet
above the level of the water, forms the north-eastern extremity of the peninsula, with a narrow channel between
that and Noddle Island.   It is now the site of the Charlestown Navy Yard, the hill having been levelled for the

mutual accommodation of the town and the Navy Yard. The peninsula was traversed, on its northern side, by a narrow road, which, branching off at the Neck from the main avenue to the village, ran over Bunker's, and swept entirely around Breed's Hill, approaching very near the summit of the latter on its southern side.

The detachment, drafted for this expedition, consisting of about one thousand men, under the immediate command of Colonel Prescott, were assembled on the common at Cambridge, at an early hour on the evening of the 16th of June, where prayers were offered by Rev. President Langdon, of Harvard College. Immediately after dark they commenced their silent march through Cambridge and across the Neck, Colonel Prescott leading the way. He was attended only by two sergeants, carrying dark lanterns, open only in the rear.

Arrived at the base of Bunker's Hill, they found the wagons laden with intrenching tools, and then only were the men made acquainted with the nature and purpose of their expedition. A serious question now arose among the leaders. The order, directing the expedition, designated Bunker's Hill as the position to be taken and fortified. But it was perceived at once, by the experienced eye of the sagacious men, who influenced that little council, that intrenchments upon that elevation would be of little avail, unless the advance post on Breed's Hill was first secured. The water in the adjacent channel being very deep, the Neck and the Hill were completely commanded by the ships-of-war on either side, while the distance was too great to render the place of any advantage, in restraining and annoying the enemy in Boston, which, as well as the ships in the harbor, was easily commanded by Breed's. Much time was consumed in deliberation, before they could decide upon taking the responsibility of

deviating from the letter of their orders, and acting upon
their own judgments. It was only after repeated and
urgent warnings from Colonel Gridley, that longer delay
would defeat their plans altogether, not leaving them time
enough to complete their fortifications, that they came to a
decision. They then yielded to the bolder counsels of
Putnam, to occupy first the position nearest the enemy,
with a view to erecting the principal work there, and a
subsidiary one on Bunker's Hill, for the protection of the
rear, and as a rallying point in the event of their being
driven from the other.

Having arrived at this decision, Colonel Gridley proceeded immediately to lay out the works, which he planned with a genius and skill, that would have done honor to
the most experienced engineer in the veteran armies of
the old world. The redoubt on the summit of the hill
was about eight rods square. The southern face, looking
towards Charlestown, was deemed the most important,
and consequently was furnished with the strongest defence.
The eastern side commanded a very extensive field,
stretching down towards Morton's point. In a line with
this, running down the northern declivity of the hill to *the
slough*, a breastwork was thrown up, separated from the
redoubt, at its southern extremity, by a narrow passage-
way, or sally port, protected in front by a blind. In the
rear of the redoubt, was a passage, or gate-way, opening
toward *the slough*.

It was midnight, before the first spade entered the
ground. It was then within four days of the Summer
Solstice. They had, consequently, but about four hours
to work, before the dawning light would disclose their
operations to the enemy, and expose them to an immediate cannonading from the batteries in Boston, and the
ships in the harbor. But, such was the spirit and resolu-

tion of the whole party, officers and men, that the work
was effected in that brief space. Instructed and stimulated
by Putnam and Prescott, who did not fear a spade, or a
pick-axe, any more than a sword or a musket ; and feeling that life and liberty alike depended on their success,
they performed prodigies of labor, during that notable
night—surpassed only by the prodigies of valor, by which
they signalized the following day. The works being in a
state of promising forwardness, and every man cheerfully
doing his whole duty, Putnam repaired to his camp, at an
early hour, to make all necessary preparations for the
coming crisis.

The crisis came with the dawning light. When the
British officers, aroused at peep of day by their startled
sentinels, beheld their daring foes above them, overlooking
their whole position with formidable entrenchments, which
had sprung up as by enchantment in the night, they could
scarcely credit the evidence of their own senses. It was
instantly perceived, that, if the Americans were not driven
from their bold position at once, Boston would be no longer
tenable by the British. A council of war was called,
which directed an immediate assault.

. Meanwhile, as preparations for the assault were going
on, a brisk but unavailing fire was opened upon the Americans, from the armed vessels and floating batteries, and
from the battery on Copp's Hill. No sooner did the report
of this cannonade reach the ear of Putnam, than he hastened back to the scene of action. The streets of Boston
were in full view ; and the busy preparations of the British were easily discerned and understood. It was manifest that they were soon to come to the trial of strength
with the veteran troops of the old world. The prospect
inspired Prescott with new ardor ; but some of his officers,
fearing that men, who were exhausted by the unintermit-

ted toils of the night, and who were now entirely without water and provisions, would be incapable of performing the service required of them, earnestly desired that a request should be sent to the camp for their relief. Prescott refused to admit the proposition, declaring that the men who had raised the works were best able to defend them, and best entitled to the honors of victory. After much persuasion, however, he consented to despatch a messenger to General Ward for refreshments. This messenger was Major Brooks, afterwards distinguished by his faithful services in war, as well as by the highest civil honors in the State.

General Putnam, on discovering the design of the enemy, returned immediately to Cambridge, and urgently advised that a reinforcement should be sent to Colonel Prescott's aid, and that his men should be supplied with suitable refreshment, before the action should commence. His application for reinforcements was unsuccessful. General Ward was strongly impressed with the idea that the British would land on Lechemere's Point, or Inman's farm, in Cambridge, and make an assault upon the camp, and so cut off the rear of the party in Charlestown. He was the more convinced of this, as the scanty depots of ammunition and military stores, on which the salvation of the American army depended, were at Cambridge and Watertown, and the British could in no way gain so decided an advantage over them, as by securing or destroying *them*. And this had been the direct object of all their active operations hitherto. It appears, also, that a formidable party in General Gage's council of war, among whom were Generals Clinton and Grant, were urgently in favor of making their attack at this place. Ward, therefore, thought it unsafe to weaken his own force, as that would not only invite an attack, but render it difficult to repel it. On the same grounds, he resisted the earnest solicitation of Putnam's troops to follow their commander to the battle, assuring them that theirs was the post of danger, and, consequently, of honor.

Such being the position of the army, it is manifest that Putnam, though he superintended the expedition to fortify the hill, had no definite command in the battle which ensued. His camp and his men, with the exception of Captain Knowlton's company, were at Inman's Farm, a point which General Ward regarded as most liable to attack, and most important to be defended. On that point, it was necessary that General Putnam should keep a watchful eye, in order to prevent a surprise. His attention was, consequently, divided between his own post—which it was his first duty to defend—and the scene of the battle, from which he could not persuade himself to be absent. And it was not until the British had landed, and the fight commenced, that he was relieved from all apprehension in relation to the expected attack upon his own camp, and at liberty to give his undivided attention to the enemy.

The cannonading from the British ships and floating batteries, though kept up incessantly during all the morning, effected nothing. The Americans kept on steadily at their works, suffering more from hunger and fatigue, than from the fire or the fear of the enemy. Putnam was very anxious to avail himself of the time required for the British troops to prepare for engagement, to throw up another redoubt, according to the original plan, and in obedience to orders, on Bunker Hill. He, accordingly, with a handful of men, commenced an intrenchment on that summit, which, if it could have been completed so far as to afford a tolerable protection to his troops, would have enabled him to check the advance of the British, and prevent them

15

from occupying the redoubt on Breed's Hill. The .two summits were within gun-shot of each other, the former, which was nearly thirty feet higher, having complete command of the latter.

It was late before this intrenchment was begun, and other and warmer work soon required its abandonment. A little after noon, a large detachment of British soldiers, under command of General Howe, supported by General Pigot, Colonels Nesbit, Abercrombie and Clarke, and other distinguished officers, landed on Morton's Point. The breastwork, extending from Prescott's Redoubt to *the slough*, still left an undefended pass over the " ridge," towards Bunker's Hill. Putnam instantly ordered Captain Knowlton to cover that pass, for which purpose an extempore and perfectly original defence was constructed. A rail fence, which traversed " the ridge," was pulled up and placed a few feet from another of the same kind, and the intermediate space filled in with new mown hay. Behind this shadowy parapet, they watched the movements of the enemy, prepared and resolved to give him a worthy reception, as soon as he should be ready to advance.

The rumor of a probable engagement spread rapidly on every side ; and many private citizens, as well as some brave officers not on duty, flew to arms, and volunteered their services. Of the latter were Generals Warren and Pomeroy, each with his musket and cartridges, prepared for the hardest service, and inspiring, with their presence and their words, a new courage into the hearts of the brave men, whose deeds of valor and self-sacrifice were to consecrate that day to the cause of liberty.

When Warren came upon the field, he was met by Putnam, who said to him : " I am sorry to see you here, General Warren. I wish you had left the day to us, as I advised you. From appearances, we shall have a sharp time of it. But, since you are here, I will receive your orders with pleasure." Warren replied : " I came only as a volunteer ; I know nothing of your dispositions, and will not interfere with them ; tell me where I can be most useful."

Putnam, intent on his safety, directed him to the redoubt, observing, " You will be covered there." " Do not think," replied Warren, " I come here to seek a place of safety ; but tell me where the onset will be most furious." Putnam again pointed to the redoubt ; " That," said he, " is the enemy's object. Prescott is there, and will do his duty. If that can be defended, the day is ours ; but, from long experience of the character of the enemy, I think they will ultimately succeed, and drive us from the works ; though, from the mode of attack which they have chosen, we shall be able to do them infinite injury ; and we must be prepared for a brave and orderly retreat, when we can maintain our ground no longer."

Warren assented to his opinions, and, promising to be governed by them, went on to the redoubt. The soldiers, to many of whom he was well known, received him with loud huzzas. Prescott offered him the command, which he declined ; saying, that he had come only as a volunteer, and " was happy to learn service from a soldier of experience."*

The veteran General Pomeroy, on hearing the distant roar of the artillery, borrowed a horse to carry him to the field. On approaching the neck, which was swept by a tremendous firing from the British ships, he became alarmed, not for his own safety, but for that of the horse he had borrowed. He, accordingly, left his charger in charge of a sentinel, and coolly walked over, mounted the hill, and

* Colonel Swett.

advanced to the rail fence. He was received with the highest exultation, and the name of Pomeroy rang through the line.*

While these accessions were making to the American forces, and the British, already landed, were waiting for reinforcements, Putnam had twice ridden to head-quarters, to represent the absolute necessity of a competent force to resist the superior numbers of the enemy. His representations were at last effectual, and General Ward ordered the New Hampshire troops at Medford, under Colonels Stark and Reed, to repair to the scene of action. Colonels Little, Brewer and Gardner, with their respective commands, were successively brought into the field; and these were ultimately followed by Putnam's Connecticut troops, under Captains Coit, Chester and Clarke, and the heroic Major Durkee. Before the action commenced, Putnam was employed in assigning these successive parties to their posts, and giving a general direction to the arrangements of the forces, not under the immediate command of Prescott. Warren and Pomeroy were with that officer in the redoubt, but each declined taking the command, affirming that it was justly due to him who had constructed the defences. Putnam was the only general officer on the field without, and was drawn into the hottest of the engagement, as soon as it was ascertained that the whole force of the British was to be concentrated against Charlestown. Until the drums beat to arms, he did not wholly abandon the prosecution of his works of intrenchment. At that signal he hastened to the lines.

The British van soon appeared in view. The Americans, eager to salute them, were with difficulty restrained from firing too soon. General Putnam rode along the line, giving strict orders that no one should fire till the

* Colonel Swett.

enemy had arrived within eight rods, nor then, till the word of command should be given. " Powder is scarce," said he, " and must not be wasted. Do not fire at the enemy till you see the whites of their eyes—then fire low—take aim at their waistbands—aim at the handsome coats—pick off the commanders." The same orders were given by Prescott, Pomeroy, Stark, and all the veteran officers.

The effect of these orders was tremendous. With a bold and confident front, assured of an easy victory over the raw, undisciplined troops of the Provinces, the British troops advanced to the fatal line, eight rods in advance of the defences, when a well-aimed volley from the deadly muskets within, swept away the whole front rank, and laid many a gallant officer in the dust. Rank succeeded rank, and volley following volley mowed them down, till at length they were compelled to retreat.

The American army was somewhat deficient of artillery, and the pieces they had on the field were neither well provided, nor well manned. Captain Callender carried his pieces into the action, but, finding that his cartridges required adjusting, was retiring, in violation of orders, to the cover of the hill, to put them in order for use. Putnam observed this movement, and instantly ordered him to his post. Callender remonstrated, but Putnam threatened him with instant death, if he hesitated, and thus forced him back to his post. His men, however, who had not been trained to the use of artillery, were disgusted with a service which they did not understand ; and, as most of them had muskets, they mingled with the infantry, deserting their pieces altogether.*

* This story of Callender should never be told without its sequel. It illustrates the truth of the remark, which an old writer has made, that " unquestioned circumstances, and even the verdict of an impar-

15*

Three times did the brave veterans of the British retreat before the deadly fire of the American militia, with the loss of whole ranks of men, and the very élite of their officers ; and three times, in the face of this almost certain death, they returned to the charge. They had expected an easy victory, and promised themselves that, at the first approach of a regular army, the raw, undisciplined Americans would fly like frightened sheep. They now found, no less to their cost than to their surprise, that they had

tial jury, *may* misrepresent a man's real character, and affix a stigma to his name, to which every other act of his life, before and after, shall give the lie direct." Callender was tried before a court-martial, on a charge of cowardice, and cashiered. He bore his disgrace with that moral fortitude, which is generally of a higher character than personal bravery. He instantly enlisted as a common soldier in the company he had commanded, and followed the fortunes of the war. The soldiers treated him with the greatest respect, as did the officers of the company also, believing him to be a brave and an honorable man. It was not long before he had an opportunity to show the spirit that was in him. He distinguished himself in several skirmishes ; and, on one occasion, when his commanders were all killed, and his comrades had retreated, he alone, in the face of the advancing enemy, loaded and fired his piece, and continued to do so, while his ammunition lasted. When that failed, he mounted his piece, resolved to be found there, and there only, and thus give the lie to the unjust sentence under which he was suffering. His gallant conduct attracted the notice of the British officer, who was opposed to him, and so commanded his admiration, that he ordered his men not to fire upon the unarmed and solitary hero. He took him under his immediate protection, gave him a letter to General Washington, stating the facts relative to his capture, and dismissed him without an exchange. That noble-hearted chieftain received Callender with open arms, and with tears of joy, restored his commission, allowing him to take rank from its original date before the Battle of Bunker Hill, at the same time ordering his sentence to be erased from the Orderly Book. Callender remained in the army after the peace, being one of the few whom the old Congress retained, and he died in the service on the peace establishment.

men to deal with, and that courage, daring, and the highest heroism, were less a matter of training than of principle. As Colonel Abercrombie led up his men to the charge, he was saluted by a familiar stentorian voice from the redoubt, reminding him, probably, of a reproachful epithet he had applied to his enemies, " Colonel Abercrombie, are the Yankees cowards ?"*

Hitherto the British had neglected the only manœuvre, by which they could possibly defeat their enemy, so long as their ammunition should last. This was to charge with the bayonet. The Americans were wholly unprovided with bayonets, and therefore could not resist or withstand a charge. But this the assailants did not know. They relied upon their fire, which was for the most part aimless and ineffectual, while every shot from the redoubt, the breast-work, and the rail-fence, being reserved and deliberate, found its victim.

While these terrible scenes were enacting, several reinforcements arrived from Boston, to the aid of the British, till their whole number amounted to not less than eight thousand. To add new horrors to the scene, vast columns of smoke were observed over Charlestown, and the village was seen to be on fire in several places. General Howe, on his first advance, had sent word to Generals Burgoyne and Clinton, that his left flank was much annoyed by an incessant discharge of musketry from Charlestown, and ordered them to burn it down. A carcass was accordingly fired from Copp's Hill, but it fell short. A second, with better aim, took effect. The conflagration was completed by a detachment of men, who landed from the

* See an intercepted letter from an officer in the British army in Boston to his friend in England, dated June 25, 1775. Am. Arch., 4th Series, Vol. ii., p. 1092. This speaker was supposed to be Captain McClary, of the New Hampshire regiment.

Somerset man-of-war.   Under cover of the smoke, the enemy hoped to be able to gain the rear of the Americans, unperceived.   But a sudden change of wind revealed their movements, and defeated their purpose.

Putnam, who had been active in every part of the field, now encouraging and stimulating his men to do their whole duty, now seeking and bringing up the reinforcements, and directing them where their services were most needed, undertook, with his usual promptness, to arrest this new movement of the enemy.   Callender's deserted cannon were near the foot of Bunker's Hill, when Captain Ford appeared with his company, marching over the hill.   Putnam, delighted with so opportune an accession to his strength, ordered them to man the cannon, and draw them into the line.   After a brief remonstrance, on the score of their ignorance of the discipline and employment of artillery, they obeyed the order, and moved with the cannon, and the General himself, first to the rail-fence, and then to the brow of the hill, overlooking Charlestown.   Here he opened a deadly fire upon the detachment of incendiaries. Their cartridges were few and soon expended ; but the pieces were well-aimed, General Putnam dismounting and pointing them himself, and every ball took effect.   One cannister was so well directed that it made a complete lane through the columns of the enemy, and threw them into momentary confusion.   With wonderful courage, however, they closed their ranks, and advanced again to the charge.   The Americans, their cartridges being spent, resorted to their muskets, and suffering their assailants to approach still nearer than before, poured in a volley with such deliberate aim, that the front rank was swept wholly away, and officers and men fell in promiscuous heaps.

The pieces belonging to Captain Gridley's company, having been furnished with some cartridges that were too large for use in the ordinary way, the pieces were deserted, and the company scattered. Putnam coming up, angrily demanded where the officers were. On being informed of the difficulty, he protested it was no difficulty at all, and that the pieces could and *should* be loaded. Dismounting, and taking one of the condemned cartridges, he broke it open, loaded the piece with a ladle, and fired it. This he did several times, and with good effect.

In the midst of this thunder of artillery and rattling of musketry, the sulphurous smoke rolling up in heavy volumes, and the balls whistling by on every side, Captain Foster, of Colonel Mansfield's regiment, arrived with a supply of powder from the American camp. It was brought in casks in wagons, and distributed loose to the soldiers, as they were able to take it; some receiving it in their *horns*, some in their *pockets*, and some in their *hats*, or whatever else they had that would hold it.*

More than a thousand of the best of the British troops had now fallen before the murderous fire of an enemy, whom they affected to despise as peasants and rebels. Among these, was a large number of their bravest and most accomplished officers. Major Small, an old acquaintance and friend of General Putnam, was left standing alone, every one having been shot down about him, and he a prominent mark for the next shaft of death. The

* General Gideon Foster, of Danvers, Massachusetts, who died November 1, 1845, aged 97. The above is from his manuscript copy of an address made by him on Bunker Hill, June 17, 1843. He proceeds to say: "I well remember the blackened appearance of those busy in this work, not unlike those engaged in the delivery of coal in a hot summer's day. At the same time we were thus occupied, the enemy's shot were constantly whistling by; but we had no time to examine their character or dimensions. I have often thought what might have been our condition, had one of their *hot shot* unceremoniously come in contact with our wagons."

never-erring muskets were already levelled at him, and a
certain death seemed instantly to await him; when Putnam, coming up, immediately recognized him as an old
friend and fellow-soldier, and making a sign to his men to
spare him, suffered him to escape unharmed.*

In the same spirit of generous chivalry, the brave and
distinguished Colonel Abercrombie, who received his
death-wound in front of the redoubt, remembered his old
friend and comrade, General Putnam, to whom he was
devotedly attached, and, with his dying breath, enjoined
it upon his surrounding countrymen to treat him with
kindness and respect, on his account.   " If you take General Putnam alive," said he, " do not hang him, for he is a
brave fellow."†   A striking comment upon the characters
of the two heroes, as well as upon the summary mode of
treatment which the British then designed to adopt with
their principal captives.

Meanwhile, the Americans, protected by their entrenchments, had sustained but little loss.   But now the crisis,
was to come.   Their ammunition was exhausted, and
there was no alternative but to retreat.   General Howe
had learned, by a terrible experience, that it was vain to
think of frightening the " undisciplined rebels " from their
defences, by the mere smell of gunpowder.   With the
advice of the accomplished and chivalrous General Clinton, who had just come to his aid, he commanded the
works to be scaled, and the enemy driven out at the point
of the bayonet.   He led the charge in person, as he had
done before.   General Clinton joined General Pigot, with

* This incident is established by the joint testimony of Colonel
Small, who related it to Colonel Trumbull, in London, and of Colonel Daniel Putnam, to whom his father related it, a few days after
the battle.

† From a London paper of 1775.

a view to turn the right flank of the enemy. The artillery were ordered to advance, at the same time, turn the left of the breast-work, and rake the line. This was the most vulnerable point in the American defences, and had hitherto been wholly overlooked.

The brave, and so far victorious, defenders of the soil, made every possible preparation to repel this last desperate effort of the assailants. Putnam hastened again to the rear, and made every possible effort to bring on further reinforcements. In this, he was but partially successful; but, with such as he could command, he returned to his charge. It was of little avail, however, for their powder was exhausted. They had sent in vain to the camp for a further supply. The magazine there was reduced to less than two barrels. The few who had a charge remaining, reserved their last fire till the artillery, now advancing to turn the flank of their breast-work, had approached within the prescribed distance. Then, every shot took effect. The gallant Howe, who had escaped unhurt hitherto, received one of the last of the American balls in his foot.

The fire of the Americans gradually diminished, and then ceased. Instantly their muskets were clubbed, and the stones of their defences were seized, and hurled at the advancing foe. This only served to betray their weakness, and infused a new energy into their assailants. No longer exposed to that destructive fire, which had so fearfully thinned their ranks, they now marched forward, scaled the redoubt, and began the work of retribution. The artillery, advancing at the same instant to the open space on the north, between the breast-work and the rail fence, enfiladed the line, and sent their balls through the open gateway, or sally port, directly into the redoubt—under cover of which the troops at the breast-work were compelled to retire.

The heroic but diminutive Pigot was the first to scale the works. He was instantly followed by his men, now confident of an easy victory. Troops succeeded troops over the parapet, till that little arena, where the first great effort of American prowess was put forth, was filled with combatants, prepared to contest its possession.

To contend, without a bayonet in his company, with such a superior force, would have been worse than madness. Prescott saw this, and reluctantly ordered a retreat. He and Warren were the last to leave the redoubt. The latter seemed to disdain to fly, even when nothing else remained to him. With sullen reluctance he followed his countrymen to the port, which he had scarcely passed, when a ball from the enemy arrested him. Major Small, as a personal friend, and in return for the generous protection he had just received from Putnam, endeavored to save him. But Warren would neither yield nor fly. He fell between the retreat and the pursuit, having won the respect of his enemies, and the everlasting gratitude of his countrymen, and leaving his name as one of the watchwords of liberty throughout the world. His death was deeply felt, and long lamented, by General Putnam, who was often heard to remark upon the similarity of his fate, to that of the gallant Lord Howe, who fell at his side, in the old French War. Both of them were intimate friends, and with both he had earnestly remonstrated against the exposure of their persons to the danger, by which they were destined to fall.

The retreating Americans were now between the two wings of the British army, so that they could not fire, without endangering the lives of each other. A brave and orderly retreat was effected. Putnam was exceedingly efficient and daring in assisting to bring up and protect the rear. He had confidently hoped, a short time

Bunker Hill.—The Retreat.   PAGE 181.

before, that they would be able at least to maintain the ground, if not to secure the victory, and was now most unwilling to abandon it. The left wing, where his troops were stationed, was, from its position, the last to retreat, its flank being exposed by the retreat of the right wing. He threw himself between the retreating force and the enemy, who were but twelve rods from him, and seemed to brave their utmost fury. Not fully aware that their ammunition was quite exhausted, he entreated his countrymen to rally, and renew the fight. He urged them to finish his works on Bunker's Hill, and again give the enemy battle on that unassailable position, and pledged his honor to restore to them an easy victory. He was the more encouraged to urge these propositions, as a new reinforcement arrived from the camp, under command of Captain Smith. The retreat was inevitable, however, and the most these fresh troops could do, was to assist in keeping the enemy at bay, and defending from their fire, those who had neither powder nor bayonets to defend themselves.

Putnam, though the balls fell around him like hail, was wholly insensible of danger. Coming to one of the deserted field-pieces, he dismounted, took his stand by its side, and seemed resolved to brave the foe alone. One sergeant only dared to stand by him in this perilous position. *He* was soon shot down, and the General himself retired only when the British bayonets were close upon him, and he was in imminent danger of being made a prisoner. It is in this attitude of protecting the rear of our retreating troops, that General Putnam is represented by Trumbull, in his celebrated picture of this great battle. His figure is conspicuous, dressed in a light blue and scarlet uniform, with his head uncovered, and his sword waving towards the enemy, as if to arrest their impetuous pursuit, or defy
16

their further advance.   In nearly the same attitude he is
exhibited by Barlow in " The Vision of Columbus :"

> " There strides bold Putnam, and from all the plains,
> Calls the third host, the tardy rear sustains,
> And, 'mid the whizzing deaths that fill the air,
> Waves back his sword, and dares the following war."

The Americans had retreated about twenty rods, before
the enemy had time to rally.   They were then suddenly
exposed to a destructive fire, which proved more fatal to
them than all the previous contest.   Some of the best and
bravest men were left on this part of the field, and several
officers, whose behavior that day had given promise of the
highest military distinction.   The retreat was maintained
in good order, over the Neck, to Prospect and Winter
Hills, where they took up their position for the night,
throwing up hasty intrenchments, which were soon
strengthened and fortified, so as to present to the enemy
another line of defence, equally formidable with that
which they had just purchased at the expense of so much
blood.

In presenting this brief sketch of the Battle of Bunker
Hill, that fulness and completeness of detail has not been
aimed at, which is essential to a perfect historical narrative, and which alone can do justice to all the actors in
this opening scene in the drama of the Revolution.   Our
special business is with General Putnam, and the details
of the battle are gone into only so far as is necessary to
exhibit, in its true light, the part which *he* bore in the conflict.*   It would, however, be doing unnecessary violence
to the common sentiment of patriotic gratitude, on the part
both of writer and reader, to leave the glorious field without bearing testimony to the heroism, valor, and endurance, of the many brave compeers of our hero, who will

* Some further remarks upon this point will be found in Appendix No. 2.

continue, to the end of time, to share with him the glory of one of the hardest fought, and most unequal, battles recorded on the page of history.   The names of Prescott, of Warren, of Pomeroy, of Gridley, of Stark, of Frye, of Bridge, of Gardiner, of Knowlton, of Durkee, and many others, will be held in grateful and honored remembrance, while the cause of freedom is dear to the heart of man. It is true, they lost *the field*—but they gained *the day*, and made it a marked day in the calendar of the nations They were dislodged from their defences, but not defeated They were driven back, but not vanquished.   And though the proud Briton claimed to himself a victory, in gaining possession of the ground, he was himself compelled to acknowledge, that a few more such victories would ruin him, and leave his rebel antagonist master of the whole field.

It appears, from General Gage's official account of the battle, that the numbers of the Americans engaged in it were greatly overrated by the British ; unless, indeed, the statement is to be regarded as a convenient fiction, to cover his own chagrin at the result.   " This action," he says, " has shown the superiority of the king's troops, who, under every disadvantage, attacked and defeated above three times their own number, strongly posted and covered by breast-works."

In his letter to Lord Dartmouth, accompanying this account, he somewhat inconsistently observes, " The success, of which I send your Lordship an account by the present opportunity, was very necessary in our present situation, and I wish most sincerely that it had not cost us so dear.   The number of killed and wounded is greater than our forces can afford to lose.   The trials we have had show the rebels are not the despicable rabble too many supposed them to be.   When they find cover, they make a good stand, and the country, naturally strong, affords it to them ; and they are taught to assist its natural strength by art, for they intrench, and raise batteries. Your Lordship will perceive that the conquest of this country is not easy, and can be effected only by time and perseverance, and strong armies attacking it in various quarters, and dividing their forces."

In the account transmitted to the Continental Congress, by the Congress of Massachusetts, are the following remarks : " With a ridiculous parade of triumph, the ministerial generals again took possession of the hill, which had served them as a retreat, in their flight from the battle of Concord. It was expected that they would prosecute the supposed advantage they had gained, by marching directly to Cambridge, which was not then in a state of defence. This they failed to do. The wonder, excited by such conduct, soon ceased, when we were told, that of three thousand men,* who marched out upon this expedition, no less than fifteen hundred were killed or wounded, and about twelve hundred of them either killed or mortally wounded. Such a slaughter was perhaps never before made upon British troops, by about fifteen hundred men, which were the most that were at any time engaged on the American side."

* It was afterwards ascertained, upon good authority, that the number of the British was five thousand. That of the Americans fluctuated. There were probably as many as thirty-five hundred on the hill, during the day, though numbers of them took no active part in the battle, and a considerable detachment arrived only in season to cover the retreat.

CHAPTER XIV.

THE war had now commenced in serious earnest ; and
there was no amicable retreat from the positions mutually
taken, without such concessions of principle, as neither of
the contending parties could be reasonably expected to
make.   The appeal to arms, forced upon the colonies by
the stringent and unyielding policy of the mother-country,
and hurried to a crisis by the rash and ill-advised measures of the representatives of royal power, was solemnly
accepted, and the issue fearlessly referred to the decision
of that all-wise Providence, that guides and controls the
affairs of nations, and of men.

The colonies were as yet distinct Provinces, having
many common interests and sympathies, but no common
16*

bond of union. There were different shades and degrees of attachment to the crown, and widely varying convictions of the " divine right " of kings. But there was an almost universal sentiment of the injustice and inequality of the ministerial policy, and a general and determined resolution to maintain the divine rights of the subject, at whatever cost to themselves, or to the assumed and unconstitutional prerogatives of the throne. This had been boldly, but respectfully expressed in all the colonies. But, hitherto, there had been no concert of action, with a view to forcible resistance. A Congress of the several colonies was now in session at Philadelphia, but without any certain and well defined powers to bind the colonies to any measures which they might recommend. The Provincial Congress of Massachusetts had proposed a definitive alliance, and "the establishment of such a form of federal government, as should promote the union and interests of all America ;" declaring, at the same time, their own readiness to " submit to such general plan as the Congress might direct." This was the voice of New England, now involved in actual war. It demanded immediate action on the part of the sister colonies. Nor did their delegates in Congress hesitate a moment what course to pursue. They determined immediately and unanimously, that, as hostilities had actually commenced, and large reinforcements to the British army were instantly expected, they should be immediately put in a state of defence. They assumed command of the army, made provision for its increase and support, and appointed George Washington, then a Colonel in the Provincial ranks of Virginia, to be Commander-in-chief of all the American forces.

General Washington arrived in the camp, at Cambridge, and took command of the army on the 2d of July. He brought with him commissions from the Continental Congress for four Major-Generals, and for other officers of inferior grade. The four superior stations were assigned to Ward, Lee, Schuyler, and Putnam. Pomeroy, Montgomery, Wooster, Heath, Spencer, Thomas, Sullivan, and Greene, were made Brigadiers; and Gates an Adjutant-General, with the rank of Brigadier.

These appointments, as they disturbed the relative position of some of the officers then in the service, occasioned much dissatisfaction, and called for all the wisdom and prudence of Washington, to adjust and harmonise their differences. Putnam's commission he handed to him immediately on his arrival at Head Quarters. The others he took the responsibility of withholding, till he could have time to consult Congress further upon the subject. Meanwhile, these appointments had been publicly announced in the newspapers, and commented upon in private correspondence. The pride of military rank was touched in its most sensitive point. Personal honor, which always divides, with the glory and interest of his country, the soldier's heart, was deeply aggrieved, and demanded to be heard in its own defence. This is a worthy principle, and should not be lightly overlooked. It is not always purely selfish. A strict regard to its claims is absolutely essential to the maintenance of that profound respect and prompt subordination, without which there can be no such thing as discipline, order, or efficiency in the military establishment. It should never, therefore, be looked upon as a matter of mere personal etiquette, or a question of form. It has higher and more extended relations, whose delicacy and intrinsic importance can be duly estimated only by those who have had large experience in the service of the camp and the field.

Some of the most valuable officers in the provincial service left the camp in disgust—among whom were Thomas,

Wooster, and Spencer. The two last named officers were superseded by the promotion of General Putnam, who was of a lower grade in the provincial establishment. Spencer retired from his post, without waiting the arrival of the commander-in-chief, or leaving any formal announcement of his resignation. The officers under his immediate command addressed a letter to the President of the Provincial Congress, speaking in the highest terms of respect, admiration and confidence towards their General, and deprecating his resignation, as not only a source of grief and solicitude to themselves, but a calamity to the high and holy cause, in whose defence they were all enlisted. A similar representation was made on the part of those more immediately interested in the reputation and services of General Wooster.

A Committee was immediately appointed by that body,* with instructions to write to the Continental Congress in relation to the matter, acquainting them with the high estimation in which Wooster and Spencer were universally held, " at the same time testifying their sense of the singular merit of General Putnam ;" and expressing their earnest hope and desire, that some mode might be devised to reconcile these differences, without wounding the honor, or jeoparding the invaluable services, of any of those able and experienced officers, on whose cordial co-operation their hopes, under Providence, mainly depended.

It is highly creditable to General Spencer's patriotism, as well as a proof of his high sense of General Putnam's extraordinary merit as an officer, that he soon returned to the army, and consented to serve under him whom he had formerly commanded. Thomas, also, after much persuasion, returned to his post ; from which he was soon after promoted to a higher grade, with the distinguished honor

* Am. Archives, 4th Series, vol. ii., page 1586.

of succeeding Montgomery in the command of the American forces before Quebec. Wooster, from his advanced age, declined any appointment on the continental establishment, though he rendered some service, as a provincial officer, in some of the subsequent campaigns ; and ultimately fell, April 27, 1777, in a gallant attempt to repel a strong party of royalists, who, under command of General Tryon, made a descent upon Connecticut, to destroy the American stores at Danbury.

General Putnam had now arrived at the highest grade of distinction, recognized in the American army. Widely known, and universally respected by his own countrymen, and equally respected and feared by the enemy, to whom he had been long and favorably known, as an officer of eminent courage and ability, his position was one well calculated to stimulate the enthusiastic ardor and emulation of the younger officers, and awaken the natural jealousy and discontent of those of equal age and experience, who were aspiring to the same honor, and whose long and arduous services were recognized and appreciated by the army and the country, as a just title to the best awards of fame. But his popularity was universal. Even those, who might then have envied him, did not presume to detract from his well-earned fame, or to breathe a whisper to his discredit, either as a citizen or as a soldier. He passed the ordeal of an eventful life, without a reproach. It was reserved for a malice, that could rankle, unseen and unheard, in the heart, till almost thirty years had passed over nis honored grave, and till his original biographer and the natural protector of his fame had followed him to his long home, to attempt the work of detraction. The utter failure of that attempt, and the ample proof which it called forth, of the clear and indisputable title of its victim to the glorious name he had won among the worthies of the olden time, " speaks volumes of comfort to the illustrious, yet slandered living, showing how true merit outlives calumny, and receives its sure reward in the admiration of after ages."

The case of Captain Callender has already been alluded to. His was by no means a solitary one. Probably no conflict in the history of the world, ever gave rise to so many charges of cowardice, and dereliction of duty, or was followed by a more severe and searching scrutiny into the conduct of those engaged in it, than that of Bunker Hill. The Colonists had not yet absolutely thrown off the yoke of England. There was still a great diversity of opinion, whether or not it would be necessary, or expedient, ultimately to do so. There were, consequently, among the supporters of the American cause, very different degrees of hostility to the king, and of military ardor and zeal, in opposing his unjust exactions. It was, therefore, oftentimes difficult to distinguish, with absolute certainty, between friends and foes. In such circumstances, the conduct of every individual was watched with the strictest scrutiny ; and every man, against whom the shadow of a charge could be raised by the most jealous defender of liberty, was arraigned before a court-martial, and subjected to a formal and severe trial. Even Colonel Bridge, notwithstanding the severity of his labors, and the dangerous and honorable wounds he had received, did not escape this ordeal. These trials were continued, without intermission, from the 7th of July to the 5th of October,† and so rigorously was the discipline of the camp sustained by the court, that offences, which would now be overlooked, or visited with a slight reprimand, were then punished with severity. In view of these facts, it is no small praise to the spirit of

† Hubley, pp. 352, 390, 416, 470, 498, 507, 511, 525, 528, 537, 546, 558, 577, 588, 592. See also the Orderly Books of the day, passim.

the men engaged in that conflict, that two only of the commissioned officers were degraded from their rank, on the
charge of cowardice, and that one of them, by nobly dis-
proving, in his after-life, the charge which deprived him
of his commission, compelled even his enemies to plead
for its restoration. The other was regarded, by many of
those who knew him best, as too harshly treated. Three
others were found guilty of misconduct, and dismissed
from the service, with an acknowledgment on the part of
the court, that their errors were those of inexperience,
rather than of cowardice.

The British, having gained possession of the peninsula
of Charlestown, proceeded to erect a strong fortification
upon the summit of Bunker Hill, where Putnam had already broken ground for them, and where, had he succeeded in his plan of intrenchments, he would undoubtedly
have kept them at bay. The fortifications in Boston were
also greatly strengthened, while the Provincial, now adopted as the Continental army, was so posted in the circum-
jacent country, as to form a complete blockade, except on
the side of the sea. The Colonists, having no fleet, and
the Castle being in the hands of the enemy, the British
had free access to the port.

Immediately on the arrival of Washington, the army
was formed into three grand divisions, each consisting of
about twelve regiments. Major-General Ward was appointed to the command of the right wing, stationed at
Roxbury and Dorchester. Major-General Lee commanded
the left wing, stretching to the Mystic River; and Major-
General Putnam occupied an advanced post in the centre,
within a few miles of the head-quarters of the commander-
in-chief.

Washington and Putnam were personally unknown to
each other, until they met at Cambridge. The open, undis-

guised frankness of the Yankee General, together with his great activity and personal industry, in everything pertaining to the army, soon attracted the attention, and won the approving smile, of his commander. An early intimacy was formed between them, and a firm friendship established, which continued undisturbed, during the whole period of their eventful military service. It was not in Putnam's nature to be idle. Inured to habits of industry himself, he was an able and efficient director of the labors of others. He was as single-hearted, frank and generous, as he was bold and energetic. The men, under his direction, worked with such hearty good will, and the works, on which they were engaged, advanced with such unusual rapidity and success, as to excite the admiration of Washington, who, addressing General Putnam, as he passed around to inspect the works, remarked, " You seem to have the faculty, sir, of infusing your own industrious spirit into all the workmen you employ." In one of his letters from Cambridge, written about the same time, and addressed to the President of Congress, he speaks of Putnam as " a most valuable man, and a fine executive officer." The commendation of Washington was never thoughtlessly bestowed, and his confidence was so rarely misplaced, as to invest his judgment, and his penetration into the character of those about him, with an almost unerring precision.

Soon after the arrival of Washington, Putnam received an urgent invitation from his friend, Major Small, of the British army, to hold a conference with him, under the protection of a flag. By Washington's advice, he accepted the invitation, and, to his surprise, found that its principal object was to renew the attempt, which had already been fruitlessly made, to withdraw him from the cause he had espoused, and engage him on the side of the king.

The most liberal promises were made, both of rank and emolument, including the most desirable provision for his sons, in case of his compliance. But they were all spurned with contempt, and with the assurance, that nothing could win him back to his old allegiance, or induce him to lay down his arms, but an utter and eternal abandonment, on the part of Great Britain, of those unrighteous principles of administration, which had given rise to the present contest, and to the maintenance of which every true American had pledged his fortune and his life. The nature and result of this conference were communicated to Washington, at whose suggestion the whole affair was kept secret, and remained so for many years.

Intrenchments were already thrown up on Winter and Prospect Hills—about a mile westward from that division of the enemy which lay on the Peninsula of Charlestown, and in full view of it. Eastwardly of the works on Winter Hill, towards Mystic River, redoubts were thrown up, to prevent the enemy from passing up that river, or effecting a landing opposite the fort on the hill. At Ploughed Hill, much in advance of Prospect Hill, and within half a mile, on a direct line, of the British intrenchments on Bunker Hill, a formidable breast-work was thrown up, in the face of an incessant cannonade from the enemy's works. Putnam was exceedingly active and energetic in forwarding the completion of these defences; not only directing others in their toils, but putting his own hands to the work, like one who felt that there was dignity in labor, when consecrated to a holy cause. "On one occasion," says the Rev. Mr. Harvey, "he came along near where I was at work, and, seeing a quantity of sods which had just been brought up, he addressed himself to one of the men, directing him to place them on the wall; remarking at the same time, 'You are a soldier, I suppose?' The order

17

not being executed on the instant, the General added, 'Oh! I see you are an officer,' and immediately took hold, and placed the sods himself. Meanwhile, the balls were continually pouring in from the British forts; sometimes killing our men, and sometimes tearing our works; but they went forward, nevertheless, and were soon in a condition to return the compliment."*

About the 20th of July, the declaration of the Continental Congress, setting forth the grievances of the country, and the reasons which rendered necessary a resort to arms, was read before the several divisions of the army. The paper concluded with the following noble sentiments: " In our own native land, in defence of the freedom that is our birthright, and which we ever enjoyed until the late violation of it; for the protection of our property, acquired solely by the honest industry of our forefathers and ourselves; against violence actually offered, we have taken up arms. We shall lay them down when hostilities shall cease on the part of the aggressors, and all danger of their being renewed shall be removed, and not before.

" With an humble confidence in the mercies of the Supreme and impartial Judge and Ruler of the Universe, we most devoutly implore his divine goodness, to conduct us happily through this great conflict, to dispose our adversaries to reconciliation on reasonable terms, and thereby to relieve the empire from the calamities of civil war."

* Rev. Mr. Harvey, of Herkimer, N. Y., an aged veteran of the Revolution, who, on the 11th of July, 1846, completed his 111th year. He is hale and hearty, and in perfect possession of his faculties. All that is here referred to him as authority, was taken down from his own lips by the compiler, during his visit to New York, in May. When requested to state, in a few words, his own estimate of the character of Putnam, and of his standing in the regards of his countrymen, he replied, with the solemn emphasis of an aged prophet, " He was a man animated for the good of his country."

Agreeably to orders previously issued by General Putnam, the troops under his immediate command were assembled in full parade on Prospect Hill, on this occasion. When the last words of the declaration were pronounced, the whole division, at a signal from the general, shouted in unison their loud and thrice repeated *Amen* to its solemn appeal to heaven. At the same instant, a gun was fired from the fort, and the new standard, just received from Connecticut, was run up, and, unfolding itself to the air, displayed on one side, the motto, in letters of gold, " An Appeal to Heaven ;" and on the other, the armorial bearings of Connecticut—consisting of three vines, without supporters or crest, with the motto " *Qui transtulit, sustinet ;*"* a beautiful allusion to the confidence our pilgrim fathers placed in the protecting care of providence, and to the three allegorical scions, Knowledge, Liberty, and Religion, which they had transplanted to America.

An animated, pathetic, and highly patriotic address to the army, was then made by the Rev. Mr. Leonard, Chaplain to General Putnam's division, followed by prayer. " The whole," says an eye-witness, " was conducted with the utmost decency, good order and regularity, and to the universal acceptance of all present. And the Philistines on Bunker's Hill heard the shout of the *Israelites*, and being very fearful, paraded themselves in battle array."†

As evidence of the cheerful spirit and good humor, which prevailed at this time among the defenders of liberty, and a specimen of the manner in which Putnam encouraged his men, by endeavoring to make their toil a recreation, the following anecdote, related by the venerable Captain Foster, of Danvers, is given. Captain Foster belonged to Colonel Mansfield's regiment, which was sta-

* He who transplanted will support them.
† Am. Archives, 4th Series, vol. ii., page 1687.

tioned on Prospect Hill, within the command of General Putnam. By orders from the General, all the Captains were desired to meet. It was then stated to them that a secret and hazardous expedition was planned, and it was desired that one of their number should volunteer to take the command.

After waiting a short time for his seniors to have an opportunity to offer, Captain Foster stepped forward with a proffer of his services. Six or eight men were drafted from each company They were ordered to arm and equip themselves completely, and repair to General Putnam's quarters. On presenting themselves before his tent, the bluff old general came out, and reviewed them in due form ; when, having commended their spirit and good appearance, he ordered them to lay aside their arms and equipments, provide themselves with axes, and go into a neighboring swamp and cut a quantity of fascines, which they were to bring in upon their shoulders. The men expected to gain honor by their cheerful exposure to unknown dangers and hardships ; but their greatest danger was from the attacks of the musquitoes, and their greatest exposure was to the mirth of their fellow-soldiers.

With a view to acting upon Boston, a large number of boats were prepared, and kept in readiness in Charles River. It was a part of Putnam's duty, as commanding officer at this station, to exercise his men in the proper management and discipline of these boats. On one occasion, about the middle of July, it happened, that, in executing a certain manœuvre, one of the smaller boats, either from mistaking the order, or from want of skill in following it, ran athwart the track of the larger one, of which Putnam had the command. With his usual impetuosity, without checking his course in the least, or deviating from his track, he ran the disorderly shallop down, staving in her side, and tumbling her whole crew into the water. Having completed the movement he had ordered, the delinquents were all carefully picked up, and cautioned to be, for the future, more attentive to the word of command.

In November, General Putnam was ordered to erect another fortification on Cobble Hill. This was the spot where the Asylum for the Insane now stands. It was about the same distance from the British works on Charlestown heights, as Ploughed Hill, but nearer to those in Boston. As soon as the Americans were perceived to be engaged in this work, the British ships of war in Charles River, as well as the forts on Bunker's Hill, opened a severe fire upon them, which was kept up without respite during their entire progress. Captain Putnam, a son of the General, held a command at this post. As some of his men were one day reclining upon the greensward, taking some refreshments, the General coming along, cried out—" Up in a moment, or you are all dead men." They started up at the word, and hastened to their work. No sooner had they cleared the way, than a ball from the enemy ploughed the ground where they had been lying, and buried itself deep in the earth. It was thus necessary to keep a watchful eye to the side of the enemy, and to labor in the constant expectation of an iron mandate to abandon the work. It went forward, however, with the same rapidity and energy as all the others had done. The fort was soon completed and mounted—affording another proof of the indomitable spirit and ready skill of the defenders of the soil. This fort was known, at the time, as " Putnam's impregnable fortress ;" while that at Prospect Hill, where Putnam held his quarters, is designated, in the correspondence of the day, as " our main fortress." This post was occupied by about one thousand men of the Connecticut Line—the remainder being at Roxbury under

17*

General Ward.   As soon as these works were completed, they opened their batteries upon the floating batteries of the British in Charles River, with such effect, as soon to drive them from their moorings.

Not long after the works on Cobble Hill were completed, General Putnam, wishing to give his men some active employment, of a more stirring character than digging trenches, or raising walls of earth and stone, sent out a small party, under Major Knowlton, who, passing across the mill-dam into Charlestown, attacked the advanced guard of the British, near the western base of Bunker Hill. They made several prisoners, set fire to the guard-house, and retired without receiving any injury to life or limb.

This was on the 8th of January, 1776.   The detachment marched between eight and nine o'clock in the evening.   While engaged in executing its work, it was saluted by a brisk fire from the British garrison on the hill above. Those only, who are acquainted with the situation of Bunker Hill, and the places adjacent, at the time of this expedition, can fully appreciate the danger and delicacy of the task, so handsomely executed by Knowlton, and his brave associates.   They passed from the main-land in Charlestown, over the mill-dam (the Neck being protected by the garrison), round the base of the hill, and directly under the garrison, which crowned its summit.   They set fire to eight out of fourteen scattering houses, which were standing in full view of the garrison, secured six prisoners, and effected an orderly retreat, under the very guns of the enemy's batteries which poured upon them an unremitted but ineffectual fire.

On the evening, when this brilliant sortie was accomplished, the farce of " *The Blockade of Boston*," of which General Burgoyne was the reputed author, was performed for the amusement of the British army.   The person, designed to burlesque General Washington, was dressed in the most uncouth style, with a large wig and a long rusty sword, and attended by an orderly sergeant, in a coarse country dress, having on his shoulder an old rusty gun, seven or eight feet long. At the moment when this figure appeared on the stage, one of the regular sergeants came running in, quite out of breath, with alarm depicted in his countenance, and, throwing down his bayonet, exclaimed, " *The Yankees are attacking our works on Bunker Hill.*" Those of the audience, who were not familiar with the plot of the piece, supposed that this was only a part of the farce. But when General Howe, rising suddenly in his place, called out, in tones of earnest command, " *Officers, to your alarm posts* "—the play was instantly changed to a stern reality, having more resemblance to the fast gathering plot of some terrible tragedy, than to the laughter-provoking incidents of a broad farce. The theatre was all confusion and dismay—officers and soldiers rushing this way and that, ladies shrieking and fainting, children screaming with terror, and all ranks and classes, in boxes, pit and stage, mingling frantically together, as if the theatre itself had been attacked, and delivered up to the tender mercies of war.

The utmost industry, tact, and skill of the American commander, and his Generals, were now required, to increase, organize and discipline the army, and procure the necessary supply of arms, ammunition, and the various paraphernalia of war. Assembled, at a moment's warning, from various quarters, enlisted for various terms, unaccustomed to subordination and restraint, they neither felt the inclination, nor realized the importance, of a rigid subjection to military rules. Never, perhaps, in the history of the world, was an army assembled in the presence of an enemy, with so little preparation to sustain a regular campaign. Had that enemy been fully informed of the destitution of powder, of bayonets, and of other essential equipments in the camp, it is altogether improbable he would have remained quiet so long in his narrow quarters in Boston. It was a period of comparative inactivity to both armies, though by no means one of rest or indolence to the American officers. Besides his immediate duties in the camp, each one exerted all the influence he possessed with his own colony, to procure the necessary supplies for the troops under his command. It is interesting to read the voluminous correspondence of the time. There are frequent letters from General Putnam to the Governor and Council of Connecticut, requesting supplies of powder, &c., and corresponding votes to meet the demand. One of the latter, which, for its considerate humanity, is worthy of particular mention, is a vote, passed on the 19th of July, ordering a sufficient number of tents to supply General Putnam's regiment, and directing that they should be made " *by some of the poor tent-makers escaped from Boston.*"

CHAPTER XV.

BOSTON EVACUATED BY THE BRITISH.

General Lee ordered to New York—Volunteers raised in Connecticut—Washington's desire for an attack on Boston—General Thomas takes possession of the Heights of Dorchester—Lord Percy attempts to dislodge him—A severe storm interrupts his movements—Intended attack on Boston by General Putnam—The council of war—Nook's Hill fortified—General Gage suddenly evacuates Boston—Putnam takes possession—Wooden sentries on Bunker Hill.

EARLY in January, 1776, General Washington received unquestionable information, that an armament was equipping at Boston, to sail, under General Clinton, on a secret expedition. Many considerations induced him to believe, that the design of this movement was to take possession of New York, and establish the British Head Quarters there ; not only as a more commanding post, but as a more central theatre of operations against the now united colonies. He, therefore, ordered General Lee to repair immediately to that place, with such volunteers as he could assemble on his march, and to make the best arrangements for its defence that circumstances would permit. He was also instructed to disarm all disaffected persons, of whom there were known to be many in New York—and especially on Long Island—and to collect the arms and ammunition in their possession, for the use of the continental army.

General Lee found no difficulty in raising volunteers

among the zealous patriots of Connecticut. At the head of twelve hundred men, he marched into New York, and commenced his works of defence in that city, on Long Island, and in the Highlands. It soon appeared, however, that General Clinton's expedition was destined farther south; and Lee was ordered by Congress to take command of the Southern department of the army.

Meanwhile, the army and the people were growing restive under this long season of fruitless inactivity. They were anxious to come to another open conflict with the enemy, and to make a serious effort to dislodge him from his position in Boston, before he should be rendered impregnable by the large reinforcements which were expected early in the spring. Washington was as desirous of an engagement as any one, and was deterred from making the attempt, only by the want of ammunition and arms, suitable to contend with an army so well provided as the British. Congress had earnestly suggested the propriety of an attack, and Washington had digested a plan of operations; but, on laying it before a council of war, it was deemed altogether too hazardous to attempt, in the then condition of the army.

Late in February, various appearances among the British troops indicated an intention to evacuate Boston; but, as these appearances might be deceptive, and as the ice now well formed in Charles River, and a small supply of powder recently received, favored his designs, General Washington determined to prosecute vigorously the plan he had formed—to force General Howe either to come to an action, or to abandon his post. The regular continental force now amounted to somewhat more than fourteen thousand men. In addition to these troops, the commander-in-chief called to his aid about six thousand of the militia of Massachusetts. Thus reinforced, he determined to take immediate possession of the Heights of Dorchester —now known as South Boston—and construct fortifications there, from which he could greatly annoy the ships in the harbor, and the soldiers in the town. He was persuaded that, by this means, a general action would be brought on, as the enemy must inevitably attempt to drive him from a position so dangerously near to their own camp. But in case he should fail in bringing on an engagement in this manner, he determined to make the fortification of the heights of Dorchester merely preparatory to seizing and fortifying Nook's Hill,* and the other points opposite the southern end of Boston. These eminences commanded entirely the harbor, a large part of the town, and the beach from which the enemy must embark, in the event of a retreat.

To facilitate the execution of this plan, a heavy bombardment of the town, and the lines of the enemy, was commenced from the forts, on the night of the second of March, and was repeated the two succeeding nights. On the evening of the fourth, soon after the firing had begun, a large detachment, under the command of General Thomas, passed unperceived from Roxbury, and took possession of the heights without any opposition. Although the ground was frozen to a great depth, yet such was their activity and industry through the night, that a considerable breast-work was thrown up by morning, so as to nearly protect them from the shot of the enemy. When the dawning light revealed the position and works of the Americans, which were magnified to the view by a hazy atmosphere, the beleaguered British were no less embarrassed than astonished at the sight. They immediately commenced an ineffectual fire, which was returned

* That point where South Boston is connected with the peninsula by a bridge, called the South Boston Bridge.

by those in possession of the heights, while they still continued, with unremitting labor, to strengthen their position.

This bold and successful movement of the American army left but two alternatives to the choice of the British commander. He was compelled either to dislodge the enemy from their new position, or to abandon his own ; and General Gage, as had been foreseen and desired by Washington, determined on the former alternative. Lord Percy, with about three thousand chosen men, consisting of parts of five regiments, and the grenadiers and light infantry, was ordered on this service. The next day, the troops were embarked and fell down to the castle, in order to proceed up the river to the scene of action ; but a furious storm coming up, they were scattered, and prevented from prosecuting their enterprise at this time. Before they could be again in readiness for the attack, the works had been rendered so strong, that it was thought unadvisable to attempt to force them. The evacuation of Boston followed as a matter of necessity.

In the expectation that the flower of the British troops would be employed against the Heights of Dorchester, General Washington had concerted a plan for availing himself of that occasion to attack the town of Boston—little doubting that he should be able, with so favorable a disposition of his forces, to obtain complete possession of the enemy's quarters, if not to achieve an absolute conquest of their army. Four thousand chosen men were held in readiness to embark, at the mouth of Charles River in Cambridge, on a signal to be given, if the enemy should come out in such force, as to justify an opinion that an attack on them might be made with a good prospect of success. They were to embark in two divisions ; the first to be led by Brigadier-General Sullivan, the second by Brigadier-General Greene ; and the whole to be under the command of Major-General Putnam. The boats were to be preceded by three floating batteries, which were to keep up a heavy fire on that part of the town where the troops were to land. It was proposed that the first division should land at the powder-house, and gain possession of Beacon Hill; the second at Barton's Point, or a little south of it, and after securing that post, to join the other division, and force the enemy's works at the Neck, so as to give admission to the troops from Roxbury.

If this plan had succeeded, the whole British army in Boston must have been destroyed, or taken prisoners. General Washington entertained the most sanguine hopes of its success, and greatly regretted the storm, which prevented the intended attack on the Heights of Dorchester, and, consequently, the residue of his plan, the execution of which was entirely dependent on that attack.

At the council of war, in which this plan of an assault upon the enemy was under discussion, General Putnam, who was always restless, and more disposed to action than to deliberation, was continually going to the door and the windows, to see what was passing without. At length, General Washington said to him, with some earnestness, " Sit down, General Putnam, we must have your advice and counsel in this matter, where the responsibility of its execution is devolved upon you." " Oh, my dear General," he replied, "you may plan the battle to suit yourself, and I will fight it."

On the morning of the 17th of March, the British discovered a new breast-work, that had been thrown up during the night on Nook's Hill, which perfectly commanded the Neck, and all the south part of Boston, and rendered their position there wholly untenable. There was no longer safety in delay. By sunrise in the morning, the king's troops, with those of the Americans who were

18

attached to the royal cause, began to embark; and before ten, they were all under sail, leaving behind them, in the haste of their forced departure, a considerable quantity of valuable stores.

As soon as it was reported in Cambridge that the enemy were making preparations to evacuate Boston, several regiments, under the command of General Putnam, were embarked in boats, and dropped down the river, to watch and take advantage of their movements. On landing at the mouth of the river, it was ascertained that the fleet had actually sailed; and a detachment was ordered to take possession of the town, which they did by landing on its western shore, near Sewall's Point, which formed the southern limit of the Mill Pond. Another detachment marched in, at the same time, over the Neck from Roxbury. The whole was under the command of General Putnam; who, amid the cheering welcomes and hearty congratulations of the citizens, proceeded to take formal possession, in the name of the Continental Congress, of all the fortified posts, as well as of the military stores, and other property, which had been abandoned by the retreating foe.

One historian of the day relates, that when the British retreated from Bunker's Hill, they left sentries standing in effigy, with muskets shouldered, and having the usual appearance of being on duty. If this were so, it was a harmless joke, and gave no alarm to the Americans; who deigned not to waste their powder upon wooden images, though clothed in the king's livery. Two men only were sent from the camp to reconnoitre the post, who entered unchallenged, and made signals for their friends to follow, and take full possession.

CHAPTER XVI.

MAJOR-GENERAL LEE, during the brief period of his com
mand at New York, had planned and laid out some works
of defence, which, in his hasty departure for South Caro-
lina, were left to be prosecuted by his successor.   Believing that this place would be the next point at which the
enemy would aim, and deeming its preservation to be of
the last importance to the American cause, General Washington, immediately after his triumphal entry into Boston,
sent thither a portion of his troops, assigning the command
to Major-General Putnam—with instructions to carry forward as rapidly as possible the plan of defence, which had
been projected by General Lee.

The following " Orders and Instructions " were issued
on this occasion.

" As there are the best reasons to believe that the
enemy's fleet and army, which left Nantasket Road last

Wednesday evening, are bound to New York, to endeavor to possess that important post, and if possible to secure the communication by the Hudson River to Canada, it must be our care to prevent them from accomplishing their designs. To that end I have detached Brigadier-General Heath, with the whole body of riflemen, and five battalions of the Continental army, by the way of Norwich in Connecticut, to New York. Six more battalions, under General Sullivan, march this morning by the same route, and will, I hope, arrive there in eight or ten days at farthest. The rest of the army will immediately follow in divisions, leaving only a convenient space between each division to prevent confusion, and want of accommodation on their march. You will, no doubt, make the best despatch in getting to New York. Upon your arrival there, you will assume the command, and immediately proceed in continuing to execute the *plan* proposed by Major-General Lee, for fortifying that city, and securing the passes of the East and North Rivers. If, upon consultation with the Brigadiers-General and Engineers, any alteration in that *plan* is thought necessary, you are at liberty to make it; cautiously avoiding to break in too much upon his main design, unless where it may be apparently necessary so to do, and that by the general voice and opinion of the gentlemen above-mentioned.

"You will meet the Quarter-Master General, Colonel Mifflin, and Commissary-General,* at New York. As these are both men of excellent talents in their different departments, you will do well to give them all the authority and assistance they require ; and should a council of war be necessary, it is my direction they assist at it.

"*Your long service and experience will, better than my particular directions at this distance, point out to you the*

* Colonel Joseph Trumbuil.

*works most proper to be first raised; and your perseverance,
activity and zeal will lead you, without my recommending it,
to exert every nerve to disappoint the enemy's designs.*

" Devoutly praying that the POWER which has hitherto
sustained the American arms, may continue to bless them
with the divine protection, I bid you FAREWELL.

" Given at Head-Quarters, in Cambridge, this twenty-
ninth of March, 1776.

" G. WASHINGTON."

Entrusted with these responsibilities, General Putnam
hastened to New York, where he was, for some time, the
chief in command, in the absence of Washington, and the
executive commander, during the entire occupancy of the
city. His head-quarters were at the house, now occupied
by Mr. Prime, No. 1 Broadway, facing the Bowling
Green. Here he established himself, with his family about
him, receiving and entertaining his friends, both in the
army and in the city, with great hospitality, when the
arduous duties of his station allowed him time for such
indulgence. During a part of this time, Major Burr
served him as aide-de-camp, and resided in his family.
His son, Major Putnam, and Major David Humphreys,
who afterwards became his biographer, were also attached
to his staff.

As has been already observed, there was some diversity
of opinion among the Americans, in respect to the contest
which was now going on. Some opposed the war through
fear of the consequences, believing it impossible, for a few
weak, half-united colonies, to resist the omnipotence of
Great Britain. Many were loyally devoted to the king
and the mother-country, and felt a kind of holy horror at
the thought of open resistance to authority. There were
persons of this description in all the colonies. There had

18*

been some in New England.   A considerable number had abandoned their homes in Boston, and followed the British army in its retreat.   But they were much more numerous in and about New York, on Long Island, Staten Island, and in New Jersey.   This made the position of the American army, and the duty of its commanders, much more difficult than it would otherwise have been.   They could not rely upon the support of all those, for whose liberties they were contending.   Some of them were secret enemies, and spies in the service of the British; and not a few were associated in a scheme to get possession of the person of the commander-in-chief, and deliver him up to the enemy.   General Putnam, and other principal officers, were at different times the objects of similar plots.   This will account for the frequent orders respecting the seizure of disaffected persons, disarming the suspicious, &c., which occur in the correspondence of Washington ; and the frequent allusions to other perplexities, than those which were occasioned by the direct action of the British generals, and their forces.

The city being, of necessity, under martial law, General Putnam's first object, on assuming the command, was to regulate its police, and put in operation such precautionary measures, as would prevent disturbance or surprise in the night, and enable him to keep a stricter watch upon the movements of spies, and disaffected citizens.   For this end, after posting the necessary guards, he issued the following

" General Orders.

" *Head Quarters, New York, April* 5, 1776.

" The soldiers are strictly enjoined to retire to their barracks and quarters at tattoo beating, and to remain there till the *reveille* is beaten.

" Necessity obliges the General to desire the inhabitants of the city to observe the same rule, as no person
will be permitted to pass any sentry, after this night, without the countersign.   The inhabitants, whose business
requires it, may know the countersign, by applying to any
of the Brigade Majors."

Although the war had raged, in some other parts of the
country, with a severity that cut off all voluntary intercourse between the British and Americans, there had, as
yet, been no outbreaking of hostilities at New York, beyond
the firing of a few guns from one armed vessel upon the
city ; which, however, was attended with no material
damage.   Consequently, the intercourse between the British vessels and the shore was not wholly interrupted.
Through the favor of the loyalists, or the connivance of
those whose avarice was stronger than their patriotism,
the commanders had hitherto found means to secure ample
supplies of fresh water and provisions.   General Putnam
resolved to put an effectual stop to all such commerce at
once, and, accordingly, issued a prohibition in the following very pointed terms.

" Prohibition.

" *Head Quarters, New York, April* 8, 1776.

" The General informs the inhabitants, that it is become
absolutely necessary that all communication between the
ministerial fleet and the shore should be immediately stopped ; for that purpose he has given positive orders that
the ships should no longer be furnished with provisions.
Any inhabitants, or others, who shall be taken, that have
been on board (after the publishing this order), or near
any of the ships, or going on board, will be considered as
enemies, and treated accordingly

" All boats are to sail from Beekman slip. Captain James Alner is appointed inspector, and will give permits to oystermen. It is ordered and expected that none attempt going without a pass.

" ISRAEL PUTNAM,

" Major-General in the Continental Army, and Commander-in-chief of the Forces in New York."

In the expectation of the arrival of the British fleet, and with a view to protect the harbor and city, and prevent the passage of vessels up the North River, a detachment of one thousand continentals was sent to occupy Governor's Island, and put it in a state of defence. A regiment was also detached to fortify Red Hook, so as to command the entrance by Buttermilk Channel. Several companies were advantageously posted on the Jersey shore, and fortifications were commenced, and carried forward with great activity, at every available point. The most active measures were taken to break up all attempts, on the part of the enemy, to hold any kind of intercourse with the shore. The Americans had nothing that could be called a navy, at this time, nor any vessels capable of maintaining a conflict with the British armed cruisers. They could, therefore, with perfect impunity, remain on the coast, and hover about the harbors, as they pleased. Two of them, lying at the Narrows, sent their boats to the watering-place on Staten Island to procure a fresh supply. By the vigilance and activity of General Putnam, one was driven off with the loss of two or three men, and the other, with her crew, amounting to thirteen, was captured. Soon after this, finding that no good purpose could be accomplished by remaining at a post that was so vigilantly guarded at all points, and not being sufficiently strong to attempt offensive operations, the ships withdrew from the harbor, and put to sea, awaiting the arrival of the fleet, with reinforcements for the army, then in repose at Halifax.

Besides the correspondence which he maintained with the Commander-in-chief at this time, General Putnam held free communication, by letter and personally, with the New York Committee of Safety, on all the questions of public interest requiring their attention. At one time, we find him calling urgently for the levies, which were needed for the construction and defence of his works (Am. Arch., vol. vi., page 1164), and at another making provision for guarding the City Records, and other public property (page 1432). Nothing that could in any way subserve the public good, was too minute for his vigilance, nothing too difficult for his industry and zeal.

In his correspondence with Congress, he shows the enlarged views he entertained of the measures to be adopted, and the boldness and confidence with which he entered upon the execution of his important trust; while the replies of the President of that body indicate an entire reliance on the patriotism, skill, judgment, and integrity of the General. Large sums of money are demanded on the one part, and remitted on the other, with the same tone of lofty courtesy, and mutual esteem and confidence, that characterized the correspondence with the Commander-in-chief. The following extract from the first letter to Congress, written the third day after his arrival at New York, furnishes some of the details of the capture of the boat's crew on Staten Island.

"*Head Quarters, New York, April* 7, 1776.

" Sir :—

" I arrived here on Wednesday evening last, having his Excellency General Washington's orders to take com-

mand of the forces in this city, and to erect such works as
I should think necessary for its defence ; in which we are
busily employed.

" After getting the works in such forwardness, as will
be prudent to leave, I propose immediately to take possession of Governor's Island, which I think a very important post. Should the enemy arrive here, and get post
there, it will not be possible to save the city, nor can we
dislodge them without great loss. * * *

" On Friday, arrived at the Narrows a small ship of
eighteen or twenty guns*—sent her boat immediately on
board the *Duchess of Gordon* ; soon after which the Governor in the ' Duchess ' sailed—where bound we know
not.

" This morning the ship sent a boat to the watering
place for water. The day before, I had detached three
companies of the Rifle Battalion to Staten Island, with
orders to scour the shores. A midshipman and twelve
sailors were in the boat. She was fired upon, and lost
two men. The Riflemen took the rest prisoners, and
hauled up the boat. The ship immediately began a
heavy fire, and slightly wounded one man. She has since
fallen down below the Narrows.

" I am, &c ,
" ISRAEL PUTNAM.
" *To the Honorable John Hancock, President of Congress.*"

On the arrival of General Washington at New York,
which took place on the 13th of April, the same measures

* The ship here mentioned was the *Savage.* The account of the
attack upon her boat, and the taking of the prisoners, may be found
in a very spirited letter from Captain Stephenson to General Putnam, dated April 8th, in which he also speaks of making sundry
arrests of persons, concerned in sending provisions, or giving information, to the enemy. Am. Archives, vol. iv., page 820.

were vigorously pursued for strengthening his position there, and endeavoring to render the passes of the Hudson and the East River inaccessible to the enemy's ships. Other measures were also concerted, for the same end, and put in execution with the utmost spirit and despatch. Hulks were sunk in the channel, to obstruct the navigation of the river. The most advantageous positions, not already occupied, on both sides of the North River, and of the narrow passages between the islands, were taken and fortified, as far as the limited means at the command of Washington rendered possible. Of all these works, General Putnam had still the chief superintendence and direction. The defences were well placed, and constructed with a skill and science that was highly honorable to the officers and engineers who planned and superintended them. But they were too feebly mounted, and too scantily supplied with munitions of war, as the sequel proved, to answer the principal purpose for which they were designed. In all the early operations of the continental army, the want of heavy cannon was most sensibly felt.

The Commander-in-chief, having inspected the works in progress, and carefully examined the condition and discipline of the army, availed himself of the first public orders, issued in his own name, to compliment the officers who had successively commanded New York, for their capacity and diligence ; and to return his thanks to them, as well as to the officers and soldiers under their command, for the many works of defence which had been so expeditiously erected, and for others so well and courageously begun. At the same time, he expressed his confidence, that the same zeal and spirit would continue to animate them in their future conduct.

On the 21st of May, at the urgent request of Congress, General Washington proceeded to Philadelphia, to confer

with that body—remaining absent until the seventh of
June. During this interval, General Putnam was again
invested with the supreme command at New York, with
directions to open all letters addressed to General Washington on public business, and regulate his conduct by
their contents ; to carry on with spirit the works of defence ; to establish signals for communicating an alarm, on
the appearance of the enemy ; and to make arrangements
to put the posts in the Highlands into a proper condition
of defence. The following letter, taken in connection
with the statements given above, of the arduous duties
required of him, will serve to show that the life of a vigilant officer, in active service, is not a life of idleness

"To MAJOR-GENERAL PUTNAM.

"*Instructions.*

"SIR :—I have reason to believe, that the Provincial
Congress of this colony, have in contemplation a scheme
for seizing the principal tories, and disaffected persons on
Long Island, in this city, and the country round about ;
and that, to carry the scheme into operation, they will
have recourse to the military power for assistance. If
this should be the case, you are hereby required, during
my absence, to afford every aid, which the said Congress,
or their committee, shall apply for. I need not recommend secresy to you, as the success, you must be assured,
will depend absolutely upon precaution, and the despatch
with which the measure, when once adopted, shall be
executed.

"General Greene will, though not in person perhaps,
have a principal share in ordering the detachments from
his brigade on Long Island ; of course he will be a proper
person to be let into the whole plan. I would, therefore,
when application is made by Congress, have you and him

concert measures with such gentlemen as that body shall please to appoint, and order the execution with as much secresy and despatch as possible, and at the same time, with the utmost decency and good order.

"Given under my hand, at Head-Quarters, in the city of New York, this 21st day of May, 1776."

The machinations of disaffected persons, or *Tories*, as they began to be universally called, in the lower counties of New York, had, for some time, excited serious apprehensions as to their effect on the army, and particularly when the British fleet should arrive on the coast. Governor Tryon was at their head. His influence in the colony was great, and justly feared. The Mayor of the city was deeply involved, being the principal agent of communication between Tryon and the main body of Tories. The disaffection had even been communicated to the army, and a part of Washington's Guard had engaged in it. The Provincial Congress, in the measures which were concerted between their committee and General Washington, laid themselves under an oath of secresy. It was then reported to them that a scheme of junction was forming, between the Tories in Connecticut and those on Long Island, in order to join the ministerial army, and oppress the friends of liberty in the colonies. The result of their action, under the spirited co-operation of the Commander, was, that a considerable number of disaffected persons were seized, and put in confinement; and one, named Thomas Hicks, a member of Washington's Guard, who had enlisted himself, and induced others to do the same, was tried by a court-martial, and executed, on the 28th of June, for mutiny, sedition, and treachery.

The following letter from General Washington, dated Philadelphia, June 3, 1776, will serve to introduce ano-

19

ther department of duty, to which General Putnam's attention was urgently directed, and to which he devoted a
great deal of thought and care.

" DEAR SIR :—I received your favor by yesterday evening's express, with the several letters and intelligence from
General Schuyler, and am much concerned for the further
misfortunes that have attended our arms in Canada.   I
have laid the whole before Congress, who had before
resolved to send a considerable augmentation to our army
there ; and I doubt not that General Schuyler may receive
assistance from the militia most convenient to him, for
securing the different passes and communications, till they
can be relieved.   As to sending a reinforcement from New
York, neither policy nor prudence will justify it, as we
have the strongest reasons to believe the day not far distant, when a large armament will arrive, and vigorously
attempt an impression there ; to oppose which, the forces
we have, will not be more than equal, if sufficient.

" Congress have determined on sundry gondolas, and fire-
rafts, to prevent the men-of-war, and enemy's ships, from
coming into New York or the Narrows.   I must, therefore, request, that you will make inquiries after carpenters,
and procure all you can, with materials necessary for
building them, that they may go on with all possible expedition, as soon as the person arrives from hence, whom I
have employed to superintend the work.   He will be there
in a day or two.

" I am, dear Sir, &c.,

" GEO. WASHINGTON."

On evacuating Boston, General Howe had retired to
Halifax.   His purpose seems to have been to wait there
for the large reinforcements expected from England, and

not to approach his adversary, till he possessed a force sufficiently large to act on the offensive, and with such success as would make a very serious impression.   The situation of his army was very uncomfortable, however, and the delay of the arrival of the troops from England so great, that he determined to proceed at once to New York, with such forces as were under his command—knowing that he could take a station of perfect security in one of the islands on its seaboard, and there wait, until he should be strong enough to commence his intended plan of operations.

In the latter part of June, he arrived off Sandy Hook, in the Greyhound, and on the twenty-ninth of the same month, the first division of the fleet from Halifax reached the same place.   The rear division arrived soon after, and landed the troops on Staten Island, where there was no military force, with the exception of a small number of men sent to drive off such cattle as might supply the enemy with fresh provisions.

The people of this island, as well as those of Long Island, and the neighboring parts of New Jersey, expressed a favorable disposition towards the royal cause.   General Howe, therefore, chose Staten Island as his station, until the arrival of the expected troops.   General Washington, foreseeing the distress which would be occasioned by cutting off the supply of fresh provisions, had urged the removal of the stock and grain in the small islands near the coast ; but this, owing to the large extent of the coast, and the necessity of keeping every effective hand at work upon the fortifications, had been only partially attended to, and Howe was in a measure supplied with what he wanted.

The opposition which the British troops had encountered in New England, had given rather a serious complexion to the war, and proved to the British Ministry the necessity of employing a much larger force, than had at first been thought sufficient, for the suppression of the rebellion. In addition, therefore, to the national troops, they employed about thirteen thousand Hessians and Waldeckers.

As had been foreseen by General Washington, the great effort was now to be made on the Hudson. A variety of considerations suggested the policy of transferring the seat of war to this part of the continent. The country on the sea-board being divided into islands, is assailable in every direction by a maritime force, and, accordingly, requires for defence against a conjoint attack by land and water, not only complete fortifications, but also a very large and powerful army. The very same causes, which render this part of the United States so vulnerable to an invading enemy commanding the sea, secure that enemy in the possession of it, after it has been acquired. A naval superiority will, consequently, be nearly always necessary, to drive even an inferior enemy from this post.

From this position, he could either carry the war eastwardly into New England, northwardly into the State of New York, or westwardly into the Jerseys and Pennsylvania ; or, if too weak to do either, he could retire into a place of security, and harass the enemy in his neighborhood, or carry on expeditions against distant parts of the continent. In fact, it left him at entire liberty to choose the scene of action, and the kind of operations by which to annoy his enemy. If he should get possession of the Hudson, he would also be enabled to open a direct communication with Canada, and have it in his power to interrupt the intercourse between the eastern and southern states. In addition to all this, he would cover his friends, who in turn would supply him with all those necessaries he had so much wanted in his old station.

The command of the fleet was given to Lord Howe, brother of General Howe ; and they were both constituted commissioners for restoring peace to the colonies and granting pardons. Lord Howe arrived at Halifax a short time after his brother's departure, and reached Staten Island about the 12th of July.

In the meantime, the great decisive measure, which fixed the character of this conflict, and elevated a rebellion into a Revolution, had been adopted, and made public, by the Congress of the United States. The Declaration of Independence, the Magna Charta of American liberty, had received the signatures of the immortal fifty-six. It was immediately transmitted, by President Hancock, to the Commander-in-chief, with a request to have it suitably proclaimed at the head of the army. The following order was accordingly issued :

" The Continental Congress, impelled by the dictates of duty, policy, and necessity, have been pleased to dissolve the connection which subsisted between this country and Great Britain, and to declare the United Colonies of North America *Free and Independent States.* The several brigades are to be drawn up this evening on their respective parades, at six o'clock, when the Declaration of Congress, showing the grounds and reasons of this measure, is to be read with an audible voice. The General hopes, that this important event will serve as a fresh incentive to every officer and soldier, to act with fidelity and courage, as knowing that now the peace and safety of his country depend, under God, solely on the success of our arms ; and that he is now in the service of a state possessed of sufficient power to reward his merit, and advance him to the highest honors of a free country."

19*

This Declaration was received by the army with the highest satisfaction and enthusiasm ; the expressions and behavior, both of officers and men, testifying their warmest approbation of the measure, and their determination to sustain and defend it, to the last drop of their blood.

CHAPTER XVII.

THE BRITISH FLEET AND ARMY AT STATEN ISLAND.
PUTNAM'S CONTRIVANCES TO ANNOY THEM.

Comparative force of the English and Americans—Two frigates pass
up the North River—Confined to Tappan Sea—Conflict with the
American galleys—*Chevaux-de-frise*—Described by General Putnam—Its ill success—The fire-ships alike unsuccessful—Bushnell's
American Turtle—The expedition of Abijah Shipman.

THE arrival of Admiral Howe with his fleet at New York,
and the return of General Clinton from the south, which
took place about the same time, placed at the command
of General Howe, an army of twenty-four thousand men,
composed of the best troops of Europe, and officered by
men of tried courage and experience. A further reinforcement of eleven thousand was instantly expected,
which would swell their numbers to thirty-five thousand.
It was the design of the British to seize New York, with
a force sufficient to keep possession of the Hudson River
—open a communication with Canada—separate the Eastern States, where the rebellion began, from the Middle
and Southern, where there was still a strong leaven of
loyalty to work upon—and overrun the adjacent country
at pleasure.

To oppose this large, highly disciplined, and well-appointed force, the Americans had, in this vicinity, an army
of seventeen thousand troops, of whom little over ten
thousand were deemed effective, and fit for duty—poorly

provided with arms—without treasure, and almost without ammunition. Ten thousand more were expected, who reached the camp about the first of August. The result, defying all human calculations, is one of those remarkable events, in which the working of an Almighty providence is manifest to every eye, causing justice and truth to prevail, in the unequal contest with power.

Immediately on the arrival of the British fleet, an attempt was made to force the passage of the North River, and try the force of the American batteries. Availing themselves of the combined aid of the flood tide, and a brisk south wind, the Phœnix of forty guns, and the Rose of twenty, accompanied by three tenders, ran boldly up, and passed the batteries, without sustaining any material damage from the heavy and incessant cannonade, which saluted them from both sides as they passed. Their decks were guarded with ramparts of sand-bags, which served to protect the men from the small shot, and their motion was so rapid, that they remained but a short time within the range of the heavy guns. They ascended to the broad part of the river, called Tappan Sea, about forty miles from New York, where they could cast anchor so far from the shore on either side, as to be out of danger from the American guns. Their object was, to obstruct the supplies which came down the river to New York, and to cut off the communication between Washington and the army on the Lakes. They frequently attempted to land with their boats, but were driven back by the militia of the neighborhood, on both sides of the river ; who watched their motions so narrowly, that for several weeks they were unable to hold any *direct* intercourse with the fleet, though, by means of their Tory friends on shore, they had contrived to make known to the Admiral their safe arrival at their point of destination. It was probably a part of their design to supply the Tories with arms, and otherwise encourage and assist them in their disaffection. But in this they were completely foiled, by the vigilance and activity of the New York patriots, who, with General George Clinton at their head, guarded every point with so watchful an eye, that they could make no signal for the shore that was not intercepted.

Several methods were adopted to drive the enemy from this position, and to annoy and weaken his naval force, as well as to prevent further advances of the same kind. A considerable number of galleys, hastily provided in New York, and placed under the command of Colonel Tupper, came to an engagement with the Phœnix and the Rose, in the North River. General Washington, referring to it, in his despatch to Congress, under date of the 5th of August, says : " What injury was done to the ships, I cannot ascertain. All accounts agree, that our officers and men, during the whole affair, behaved with great spirit and bravery. The damage done to the galleys, shows, beyond question, that they had a warm time of it. The ships still remain up the river, and, before anything further can be attempted against them, the galleys must be repaired."

He then refers to another plan which was in progress of execution, to prevent the other ships from proceeding up the river. " The hulks, and three *chevaux-de-frise*, that have been preparing to obstruct the channel, have got up to the place they are intended for, and will be sunk as soon as possible." The mode of constructing the *chevaux-de-frise*, was a contrivance of General Putnam's. It is thus described, in a letter from him to General Gates, dated July 26th.

" The enemy's fleet now lies in the bay very safe, close under Staten Island. Their troops possess no land here but the island. Is it not strange, that those invincible troops, who were to destroy and lay waste all this country with their fleets and army, are so fond of islands and peninsulas, and dare not put their feet on the main ? But I hope, by the blessing of God and good friends, we shall pay them a visit on their island. For that end, we are preparing fourteen fire-ships to go into their fleet, some of which are ready charged and fitted to sail, and I hope soon to have them all fixed. We are preparing *chevaux-de-frise*, at which we make great despatch by the help of ships, which are to be sunk—a scheme of mine, which, you may be assured, is very simple ; a plan of which I send you. The two ships' sterns lie towards each other, about seventy feet apart. Three large logs, which reach from ship to ship, are fastened to them. The two ships and logs stop the river two hundred and eighty feet. The ships are to be sunk, and, when hauled down on one side, the pricks will be raised to a proper height, and they must inevitably stop the river, if the enemy will let us sink them."

This *chevaux-de-frise* was sunk just above the entrance of the Palisades, stretching from Jeffery's Hook, at Fort Washington, to the northernmost redoubt at Fort Lee. But, though much relied on, it proved insufficient for the purpose for which it was designed. The rapid current, changing with every turn of the tide, and continually wrenching the work, so weakened it, that it gave way before the weight and momentum of the heavy armed ships, and left them a free course as before.

The fire-ships, before referred to, were scarcely more successful. Two of them were sent up, on the 16th of August, to operate against the Phœnix and Rose, in Tappan Sea. One of them boarded the Phœnix, and was grappled with her for some minutes, but she succeeded in clearing herself. The only damage the enemy sustained, was the destruction of one of the tenders. The men engaged in this affair, behaved with great resolution and intrepidity. Though the enterprise did not succeed according to the wishes of those who directed it, it so alarmed the enemy, as to compel him to abandon his position. The second day after this attempt, both ships, with their remaining tenders, took advantage of a favorable gale and tide, to run down the river, and rejoin the fleet at the Narrows. They were handsomely saluted by the batteries, as they passed, and not without effect, though they did not suffer any material loss or damage.

Among the Connecticut troops, was an officer, named Bushnell; a man of education, of somewhat eccentric habits, but of a strong mechanical turn of mind. While at college, he had prepared a model of a submarine explosive machine, or torpedo, of a very ingenious construction. He gave it the name of "The American Turtle." The report of this contrivance coming to the ears of General Putnam, he sent Major Burr, his *aide-de-camp*, to invite Bushnell to come and see him. After a little conversation, the model was sent for, examined, explained, and highly approved ; and Bushnell was immediately furnished with the necessary funds to construct a full machine, and put it in operation.

In the course of ten days it was completed. Outwardly it bore some resemblance to a large sea-turtle. Hence, the origin of its name. In the head there was an opening, sufficiently large to admit a man. This apartment was air-tight, and was designed to be supplied with air sufficient to support life for half an hour. At the bottom, opposite this entrance, was a deposit of lead for ballast. The operator sat upright, holding an oar for rowing forward or backward, and having command of a rudder to direct his course in any direction. An aperture at the bottom, with its valve, admitted water, for the purpose of descending, while two brass forcing-pumps served to eject the water, when necessary to rise to the surface.

Behind this vessel, and above the rudder, was a place for carrying a large powder-magazine. This was made of two pieces of oak timber, large enough when hollowed out, to contain one hundred and fifty pounds of powder, with the apparatus used for firing it; and was secured in any place, where it was designed to act, by means of a screw turned by the operator. Within the magazine, was a piece of clock-work, capable of running twelve hours, and so arranged as to be set to any moment, at the will of the manager. When it had run out its time, it unpinioned a strong lock, resembling a gun-lock, by means of which the explosion was produced.

Unfortunately for the contriver and his patron, this well-managed scheme failed, not, it appears, for any want of skill in the construction of the machine, but for another reason, which will appear in the sequel.

A brother of Captain Bushnell was appointed to go down with the machine, but falling sick the day before the experiment was to have been made, it was necessary to find a substitute. A sergeant in the regiment from New London, volunteered for this service. His name was Abijah Shipman, better known among his comrades as "Long Bige." He was an amphibious kind of a fellow—had been in early life a sailor, engaged in carrying " stock " to the West Indies ; and was a genuine specimen of what would be called a " queer fish," or " a live Yankee." He stood six feet two or three inches, was remarkably lean and bony, and full of dry wit and humor. Fear formed no part of his composition, his chief faults were rather too strong a liking for St. Croix and tobacco.

Before daylight, on a morning in July, Abijah was put

on board the torpedo on the North River side, preparatory
to being pulled off into the stream, from whence he was
to drop down with the tide, and get under the bottom of
the Eagle, which was the flag-ship of Admiral Howe.
Putnam, Bushnell, Heath, Knowlton, Burr, and many
other officers, accompanied him to the shore. The undertaking was regarded as extremely hazardous, and no little
skill and coolness were required for the successful management of the machine. If he could once strike the ship,
and attach the magazine to any portion of the bottom, her
destruction was inevitable. But to do this, great care and
judgment were needed, and there were many circumstances that might interfere with its successful operation.

Every thing being ready, Abijah went on board the Turtle, and was about to screw himself into the air-tight
chamber, when, suddenly thrusting his head out again, he
exclaimed—

"Thunder and marlinspikes! who's got a cud of tobacco? This old cud won't last, any how!"' at the same
time pulling out an ounce or more of the weed, and throwing it away.

The officers, not being addicted to this peculiar indulgence, or having left their boxes at home, the sergeant's
odd appeal excited only a laugh. Not even a bit of pig-
tail could be found, and Abijah was absolutely obliged to do
without it—for daylight was near at hand, and it was necessary he should move, without a moment's delay.

"Ah! my brave boy!" said Putnam, "you see how it
is—we continental officers are too poor to raise even a
tobacco plug. Push off, my fine fellow, and to-morrow,
when yonder Eagle has taken his last flight, some of the
southern officers shall give you an order for a keg of old
Virginia."

"Too bad!" answered Abijah, despondingly; "but

20

mind, Gen'ral, if the old Turtle doesn't do her duty, it's all because I go to sea without tobacco."

The machine was towed into the stream, and cast off, and Abijah, in his narrow chamber in the Turtle's head, disappeared under water. For the space of an hour or more, Putnam and his friends waited upon the Battery, expecting every moment to see the Eagle ascend into the air. When the morning broke, suspense gave way to fear. Nothing was to be seen of the torpedo, and the officers began to mourn for Abijah, as one to be reported among the " missing," at the next call of his regimental muster-roll.

Putnam had been intently examining the vicinity of the Eagle with his glass, when he suddenly exclaimed, " There he is." The top of the machine was just emerging from the water, in a little bay, to the left of the Eagle. It did not escape the observation of the watchful sentinels on board the ship. A volley of musketry was fired into it, and down popped the Turtle in a twinkling, Abijah not relishing this kind of salutation. Boats were immediately sent from the shore to his assistance, and the Eagle was observed to be getting under weigh in great haste. The sergeant was taken up near Governor's Island. The magazine had been cast off, and being set to run an hour, exploded, at the expiration of that time, with tremendous force, throwing up the water in every direction. The alarm on board the men-of-war was very great. There was an instant heaving at the anchors of the Eagle, the Asia, the Chatham, and all the rest. The harbor was evacuated without the ceremony of a salute; and, from that time, till the morning of the battle of Long Island, not an English vessel moved from Staten Island up the bay.

On landing, the eccentric sergeant gave the following account of his perilous submarine expedition—

"Just as I said, Gen'ral! it all failed for want of that cud of tobacoo.‑ You see I am *narvous* without tobacco. I got under the Eagle's bottom, but somehow the screw struck the iron bar, that passes from the rudder pintle, and wouldn't hold on, any how I could fix it. Just then I let go the oar to feel for a *cud*, to steady my *narves*, and I hadn't any. The tide swept me under her counter, and away I slipped top o' water. I couldn't manage to get back, so I pulled the lock, and let the thunder-box slide. I say, can't you raise a cud among you, *now* ?"*

The immense advantage, which the British commander possessed over his antagonist, in the well-appointed fleet, under the command of his brother, Admiral Howe, constituted one of the many inequalities in this contest, which the Americans found it most difficult to overcome. They had neither navy, nor seamen, nor the means of raising and equipping them ; while the enemy, being amply provided with both, had every facility for moving in any direction, transporting forces and provisions from place to place, and protecting their movements, and flanking their batteries, by the heavy guns of their ships, as well as cutting off the communication of their adversary with his different posts. It was, therefore, of the highest importance, that some efficient means should be devised, to resist, and, if possible, destroy this powerful engine of offence ; or, at least to protect from its approaches some of the most vulnerable and important points in the line of their defences. The best mode of doing this became a subject of intense interest, and deep study, with all those who were actively engaged in the good cause. From the Commander-in-chief to the humblest artisan in his service, every inge‑

* Noah's Weekly Messenger.

nious mind was bent upon devising schemes of annoyance, which should, in some degree, supply the deficiency of a naval force. Necessity, as in all similar cases, became the mother of invention. A variety of experiments were made, and a very considerable expense incurred, in the prosecution of these inventions. Putnam, who was apt and ingenious in such contrivances, devoted a great deal of attention to them, and was encouraged in doing so, by the approval of Washington, and of Congress. From this source sprung not only torpedos and turtles, but *chevaux-de-frise*, both in the Hudson and Delaware, with booms, chains, and sunken hulks, row-galleys, fire-rafts, and other devices. It is true, they were not, in many instances, successful. They answered but little purpose, in checking the movements of the enemy, and only in a few cases, disabled any of their vessels. The ships passed over the *chevaux-de-frise* without damage. The row-galleys were too feeble to compete with their heavy guns. The fire-ships failed for want of skill in their management ; and the torpedo was lost by an unfortunate sweep of the tide, or, if we may credit the story of Abijah Shipman, for lack of a quid of tobacco. This torpedo was the most promising of all the inventions of the day, and would, if successful in one instance, have done more than any or all the rest, to intimidate the enemy, and take away the strength from this right arm of his power. Not knowing when or where to expect it, he would always have approached the shore with fear and trembling, and Putnam and Bushnell would have been regarded as the ablest and most favored of the defenders of thier country. Whether it was owing to want of confidence in the scheme, or the feeble state of Bushnell's health, does not appear ; but the experiment was never tried again.

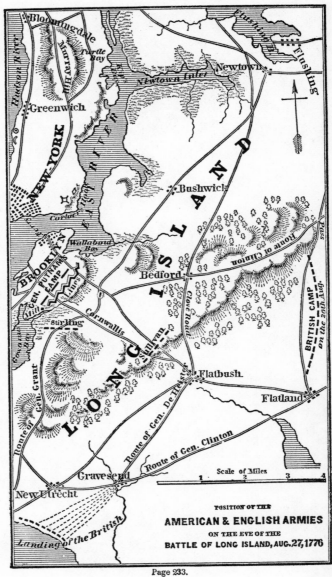

POSITION OF THE

AMERICAN & ENGLISH ARMIES

ON THE EVE OF THE

BATTLE OF LONG ISLAND, AUG. 27, 1776

CHAPTER XVIII.

THE BATTLE OF BROOKLYN, AND RETREAT FROM LONG ISLAND.

Fortifications on Long Island—General Sullivan in command, in consequence of the illness of General Greene—Landing of the British at the Narrows—Sullivan reinforced—Putnam sent to take the command—His orders—Relative position of the armies—General Clinton seizes one of the passes through the hills—General Grant makes a feint in the opposite direction—General Stirling detached to meet him—De Heister advances towards Bedford—Clinton gains the rear of Sullivan, while De Heister attacks him in front—Sullivan, in an attempt to retreat, is taken prisoner—Stirling, attempting to regain the lines, is met by Cornwallis—Engages him, to cover the retreat of his division—Is made prisoner—The greater part of his division escapes—Loss of the Americans—Washington in the camp, a witness of the battle—The difficulty of his position—Comments upon the Battle—Masterly retreat.

A PORTION of the American army was stationed at Brooklyn, on Long Island, under the command of Major-General Greene. It was an important position, and its defence was deemed absolutely necessary, to secure the possession of the city of New York. It was strongly fortified against an attack from within the island, by a line of defences, extending along the high grounds, from Wallabout to Gowanus Bay, at a distance of about a mile and a half from "The Heights." The remains of its northern redoubt, called Fort Greene, are still to be seen, between Myrtle and Fulton Avenues, above Navy Street. A portion of the line of intrenchments from that point towards Red

20*

Hook, may also be easily traced, on the south side of Fulton Street, just below its junction with the Avenue. These will soon disappear before the rapid advances of a populous and thriving city, but Fort Greene is to be preserved, in perpetuo, and ornamented as a public park.

These fortifications commanded, from the various points of their extended line, all the approaches from the interior, and from the northern and southern shores of the Island. The rear was covered and defended against an attack from the ships, by strong batteries on Red Hook and Governor's Island, which, in a great measure, commanded that part of the bay, and by other batteries on the East River, which kept open the communication with the main army in the city of New York. In front of these defences, was a range of hills covered with thick woods, extending eastwardly nearly the whole length of the Island. They were everywhere passable by infantry, and were traversed, at three different points, by roads leading to the Brooklyn Ferry. These were the only points, or passes, through which artillery or cavalry could approach.

On the eve of an expected attack from the enemy, General Greene was seized with a raging fever, and the command of this important post devolved upon General Sullivan. On the 22d of August, a large body of the British, under the command of General Clinton, landed near the Ferry at the Narrows, and marched through Utrecht and Gravesend, across the low grounds at Flatbush, approaching within three or four miles of the American lines. Their principal encampment was near the village of Flatland, under Clinton, Earl Percy and Lord Cornwallis. The centre, at Flatbush, was composed of Hessians, under the command of General De Heister. The left wing, under General Grant, extended to the place of landing, on the coast. The landing was effected without opposition, under cover of the ships that lined the coast—Colonel Donop's corps of chasseurs and Hessian grenadiers, with forty pieces of cannon, being in the van. A party of Pennsylvania troops, under Colonel Hand, whose duty it was to guard the coast at this place, retired before them, and took a position on the high grounds, commanding the pass from Flatbush to Brooklyn. Lord Cornwallis was detached to seize this pass, if not in the hands of the Americans ; but was commanded not to engage with them, if they were there in any force. Finding the pass guarded, he moved on, and took post with the British right wing at Flatland.

Immediately on the landing of this force, Washington detached six battalions from the army in New York, to reinforce General Sullivan, and ordered five battalions more to be in readiness to join them, at a moment's warning.

On Sunday, the 25th, Major General Putnam was directed to take command at Brooklyn, carrying with him these additional reinforcements—General Sullivan still holding the immediate command of all the troops not within the lines. In his orders from the Commander-in-chief, Putnam was urgently enjoined to put everything in readiness for a resolute defence ; and, in particular, to guard well the passes between his lines and the enemy's camp. "The wood next to Red Hook should be well attended to. Put some of the most disorderly riflemen into it. The militia are the most indifferent troops, those I mean who are least tutored, and have seen the least service, and will do for the interior works ; whilst your best men should, at all hazards, prevent the enemy's passing the woods, and approaching your works. The woods should be secured by *abattis* when necessary, to make the enemy's approach as difficult as possible. Traps and ambuscades should be laid for their parties, if you find they are sent out after cattle."

On Tuesday, the 27th, two days after General Putnam took the command, the attack was made. Agreeably to the leading suggestion in his orders, as well as to the natural facilities of the place, he expected the first and principal offensive demonstration to be made, by way of the passes near the western shore. To these, therefore, he directed his first attention.

In order to a perfect understanding of the details of the battle which ensued, it will be necessary to obtain a clear view of the relative position of the two armies, previous to the engagement. The range of hills before-mentioned lay between them. The British centre, at Flatbush, was scarcely four miles distant from the American lines at Fort Greene—a road leading directly across from one to the other. Another road, diverging a little northwardly from this, led through another pass, by way of Bedford village. The right and left wings of the British army, the former near Flatland, the latter near Utrecht and Gravesend, at the Narrows, were each between five and six miles from the American works. From the position occupied by the right wing, there was another and somewhat circuitous route, through a pass on the north, leading into the main road from Jamaica to Bedford. All these several roads met in the plain, between Bedford and Brooklyn, within less than half a mile from the American lines.

The road first mentioned, leading direct from Flatbush to Brooklyn, was defended by a strong redoubt, under the immediate command of General Sullivan. To this point Colonel Hand had retired with his detachment, on the landing of the British, burning, as he passed along, several parcels of wheat, and such other valuables as he supposed would fall into the enemy's hands. The pass on the other road from Flatbush, leading to Bedford, was occupied by Colonel Williams on the north, and a regiment of Pennsylvania riflemen, under Colonel Miles, on the south. The road from Jamaica, on the north side of the hills, guarded by light parties of volunteers, was less ably protected than either of the others—partly because less danger was apprehended from that quarter, and partly because the change of command, consequent upon the illness of General Greene, who superintended the erection of the works, and was thoroughly acquainted with the lay of the land, left the whole affair to the direction of those, who did not fully understand the ground, and who had not sufficient time, before the action, to acquire a thorough knowledge of their position.

About nine o'clock on the evening of the 26th, General Clinton, having ascertained the weakness of the party at the pass on the north of his position, silently drew off the van of his army in that direction. Arriving at the pass, unperceived, before day-break, he surprised and secured the whole party stationed there—thus cutting off from his enemy all knowledge of his approach. On the appearance of day, his whole column passed the heights, and advanced into the level country, between them and Brooklyn.

Before Clinton had secured this movement, on which the fate of the day turned, General Grant, being ordered to make a diversion in the opposite direction, advanced along the coast, at the head of the left wing, with ten pieces of cannon. His main object being to draw the attention of the American commander from his left, now exposed, without knowing it, to the whole force of the British right, he moved slowly, skirmishing, as he advanced, with the light parties stationed along the road.

This movement of General Grant was communicated to

General Putnam about three o'clock in the morning, who immediately detached Brigadier-General Lord Stirling, with strong reinforcements, to meet and resist it. He reached the summit of the hill a little before sunrise, and was there joined by the troops which had been already engaged, and were now slowly retiring before the enemy. Their retreat being arrested by this timely reinforcement, the enemy soon appeared in sight. A brisk cannonade was immediately commenced on both sides, which con--tinued for several hours ; while some spirited, but not very effective skirmishing took place between the infantry. Lord Stirling, being ordered to act only on the defensive, was anxious only to keep possession of the pass. He could not, therefore, descend in force from the heights, to bring on a general engagement ; and General Grant had no desire to drive· him back, until that part of the plan, which was under the direction of Sir Henry Clinton, should be executed.

Soon after daylight, General De Heister commenced a distant cannonade upon the American redoubt above Flat-bush, where General Sullivan was stationed. He did not, however, advance from his position at Flatbush, until he had notice that the British right had turned the left, and gained the rear of the American lines. In the meantime, the more effectually to divert attention from the actual point of attack, the fleet was put in motion, and a heavy cannonade commenced upon the battery at Red Hook.

About half-past eight, the British van having reached Bedford, and thrown forward a detachment to the rear of General Sullivan, General De Heister ordered Colonel Donop's corps to advance upon the redoubt on the hill, himself following with the whole of his division. At the moment that this movement was attempted, General Sullivan was made aware of the presence of the main division of the British at Bedford, and an effort was immediately made to regain the camp at Brooklyn. While retiring from the woods, by regiments, with this view, they encountered the British front. At the same instant, De Heister came up from Flatbush, to attack them on that side. Such was the confusion and consternation, occasioned by this sudden discovery of an unknown and unexpected danger, that, though General Sullivan commanded the post in person, and exerted all his accustomed energy and skill, with the most determined bravery, he found it difficult to keep his troops together long enough to meet the first onset. The brisk firing from the Bedford quarter had disclosed to his whole detachment the alarming fact, that their left flank was already turned, and their rear completely exposed to the enemy. Apprehending, at once, the full danger of their position, and the utter futility of any attempt to defend themselves in it, they thought only of escaping from the snare, by an instant retreat upon their own camp.

The sudden rout of this party enabled De Heister to detach a part of his force upon the upper road to Bedford, to fall upon the rear of Colonels Williams and Miles. The American lines, in that quarter, had already been broken, and driven back into the woods; while the British van, led by General Clinton, was moving forward, to intercept and engage those who were endeavoring to secure their retreat along the direct road from Flatbush. Thus attacked both in front and rear, and alternately driven by the British on the Hessians, and by the Hessians back again on the British, they were drawn into a succession of skirmishes, in the course of which, some considerable parties forced their way through the columns of the enemy, and, fighting all the way, as they retreated, regained the lines at Brooklyn. Some individuals also saved themselves under cover of the woods, and ultimately effected their escape. But a large proportion of the whole detachment were either killed or taken prisoners. General Sullivan was among the latter. Surrounded and hemmed in as he was, and with greatly inferior numbers, he made a most gallant resistance, and maintained it, with such force as he had, more than two hours ; bravely illustrating the difference between a retreat and a flight.

So silently had Clinton's first grand movement been accomplished, and so rapidly had all the subsequent steps been taken, that the American right received no notice of these events, until the firing in the vicinity of Brooklyn announced that the enemy had gained their rear. Lord Stirling was sensible of his danger, and perceived that the only safety for his division was in an instant retreat. This he hoped to effect by crossing Mill Creek, below the swamp. To this point Lord Cornwallis had advanced, with a view to cut off the retreat of the American right. He took his station under cover of a house near the Upper Mills. To cover the intended movement of his detachment, by occupying Lord Cornwallis till it should be achieved, Lord Stirling determined to attack him in person. For this purpose, six companies of Smallwood's regiment of Maryland riflemen were drawn out, and the attack was made with great spirit. Several times, successively, they charged the enemy with great bravery, and with such admirable effect, that they were on the point of dislodging Lord Cornwallis from his post, when, some considerable reinforcements arriving to his aid, at the same time that General Grant, with his division, advanced upon their rear, they were compelled to give way, and follow their comrades in the retreat. They were all, with their General, made prisoners of war. But they had accomplished the main object of their brave attack, by diverting the attention of the enemy from the remainder of their detachment—who, while *they* were engaged, succeeded, with the loss of one man, in crossing the creek, and gaining the American lines.

The loss sustained by the Americans, in this battle, has been variously estimated. It was probably not far from eleven hundred, of whom by far the greater part were taken prisoners. The number, who took part in the action, was about five thousand. About two-thirds of these were with Lord Stirling's division, on the right, most of whom, as is seen above, effected their retreat across the creek. Of Colonel Hand's regiment, and those of Williams and Miles, in the hills between Bedford and Flatbush, a considerable number made good their retreat. But the larger proportion of the prisoners taken, were from this division, and their number was afterwards swelled, by the capture, at Jamaica, of two hundred of the Long Island militia, under General Woodhull, whose movements were wholly independent of the army. As General Howe, in his report of the battle, stated the number of prisoners, including General Woodhull and his corps, at one thousand and ninety-seven, the number of killed must have been very small. His own loss, killed, wounded and taken, was set down at three hundred and sixty-seven.

In the heat of the action, General Washington passed over to the camp at Brooklyn, where he witnessed, with feelings, which can better be imagined than described, the utter rout of his choicest troops, without the power of relieving them, or of doing anything to change the fate of the day. General Putnam had already detached from his camp every man that could be spared, consistently with the defence of his own position, on which that of New York, and the army there, depended. It was more than probable that the British commander would follow up the successes of the day, by combining all his forces for an attack upon the American camp. The main body of his army was posted a short distance in front of the lines, and it was supposed he intended to force them by regular approaches, while the ships of war, coming round into the East River, and cutting off all communication with New York, should equally prevent General Putnam from effecting a retreat, or receiving reinforcements. In this state of things, the numbers of the enemy being greatly superior, and elated with recent success, it would have been madness to offer him further battle. The entire hope of the Americans was in continuing to act on the defensive. This was the judgment of Washington, and his council, as well before the battle as after it. The relative numbers and character of the two armies, and their position during the engagement, fully vindicates the soundness of that judgment. The subsequent retreat, and the events connected with, and following it, disclosing the ulterior designs of the enemy, confirm and establish, beyond a cavil, the wisdom of that decision, and show clearly that the fate of the whole American army, and with it the American cause, was, at that moment, suspended upon the prudent generalship of a great commander.

The unfortunate issue of this battle of Long Island, has made it the subject of many and severe comments, by that class of critics, who estimate actions only by the measure of success which attends them. Some have censured freely the Commander-in-chief, while others have laid the onus of blame upon General Putnam, charging him with unpardonable neglect, in not posting a sufficient force on the Jamaica road, to protect the pass. To every charge of this kind, it ought to be a sufficient answer, that he was unexpectedly assigned to that command on Sunday, the 25th, and that the pass was taken by General Clinton before break of day, on Tuesday, the 27th. Without any previous knowledge of the posts which had been fortified beyond the lines, or the passes by which the enemy could make their approach, and with scarcely *two days** to make himself acquainted with his extended lines, the condition of his forces, and the nature of the grounds without, through a circuit of more than twenty miles—there is certainly no show of reason, in attributing the disastrous issue of the day, to any lack of watchfulness or activity on *his* part.

The first duty of the good officer is to execute the orders of his superior. It is manifest from the orders of Washington, that he regarded the pass on the south as the most important, and first to be attended to. To that Putnam, accordingly, devoted his first care, and provided it with an ample defence. It was stoutly defended, as it was, and would have been maintained against all the force of the British left, if it had not been attacked in the rear. At the same time, the other passes were not overlooked. That, by which Clinton came down upon the plain, was provided with a patrolling party, whose duty it was to report to the commanding officer, any and every movement of the enemy in that quarter. The misfortune was, that this

---

* General Sullivan, in his letter to the President of Congress, says, "General Putnam had taken the command from me *four* days before the action." Colonel Humphreys says it was *two days;* and General Washington, writing to the President of Congress, on the 23d, four days before the battle, says, "I have been obliged to appoint Major-General Sullivan to the command on the Island, owing to General Greene's indisposition." The only "orders" given to General Putnam, bearing upon this command, are dated of the 25th, to which date Marshall assigns the beginning of Putnam's command. Dr. Sparks, in a note attached to the above-mentioned order of the 25th, says, "Putnam had just been sent over to take the general command on Long Island."

party suffered a surprise. They were all taken prisoners, and therefore were not able to give the desired notice of the enemy's approach.

Both Marshall and Sparks fully vindicate General Putnam from any charge of neglect, or oversight, in this matter. The latter* says, " He (Putnam) had not time to acquire this knowledge (of the various posts, passes, &c.) before the action. The consequence was, that, although he was commander on the day of the battle, he never went beyond the lines at Brooklyn, and could give no other orders, than for sending out troops, to meet the enemy at different points."

Judge Marshall says,† " *His* (Putnam's) *numbers were not sufficient to furnish detachments for all the defiles through the mountains; and, if a corps, capable of making an effectual resistance, had been posted on this road, and a feint had been made upon it, while the principal attack was by the direct road from Flatbush, or by that along the coast, the events of the day would probably have been not less disastrous.* The columns, marching directly from Flatbush, must, on every reasonable calculation, have been in possession of the plains, in the rear of the detachment posted on the road from Jamaica, so as to intercept its retreat to the camp. So great is the advantage of those who attack, in being able to choose the point against which to direct their grand effort.

" The most advisable plan, then, appears to have been, to watch the motions of the enemy, so as to be master of his designs ; to oppose, with a competent force, every attempt to seize the heights ; and to guard all the passes in such a manner, as to receive notice of his approach

* Writings of Washington, vol. iv., page 513.

† Life of Washington. Second Edition. Philadelphia, 1832. Vol. i., page 93.

through any of them, in sufficient time, to recall the troops maintaining the others.

"*This plan was adopted—and the heavy disasters of the day, are attributable, principally, to the failure of those charged with the execution of that very important part of it, which related to the Jamaica road.* The letter of General Howe states, that an American patrolling party was taken on this road ; and General Washington, in a private and confidential communication to a friend, says, ' This misfortune happened, in a great measure, by two detachments of our people, who were posted in two roads leading through a wood, to intercept the enemy in their march, (one of them) suffering a surprise, and (the other) making a precipitate retreat.'

"The events of this day, too, exhibited a practical demonstration of a radical defect in the structure of the army. *It did not contain a single corps of cavalry.* Had the General been provided with a few troops of light horse, to serve merely as vedettes, it is probable that the movement, so decisive of the fate of the day, could not have been made unnoticed."

A more complete and triumphant vindication of General Putnam, from the charge of neglect, inefficiency, or a lack of judgment, decision, or any other martial virtue, in the conduct of this affair, could not be desired. If anything is wanting to relieve him from all responsibility in relation to it, it is found in the fact, that General Washington passed the whole of the 26th, the day previous to the battle, at Brooklyn, and assisted in all the arrangements for the expected action. He was in the camp with Putnam, almost up to the very hour when Clinton began his stealthy advance from Flatland, to surprise the fatal pass. With equal clearness of perception, and force of argument, is the generalship, foresight and skill of the Commander-in-chief,

21*

defended from all reproach, by the same masterly hand, than whom, for his commanding genius, his fearless impartiality, and his personal acquaintance with the principal actors in these scenes, there can be no better or more satisfactory authority.

The truth is, that the greatest error, committed on this occasion, was committed by General Howe, in not following up his victory by an immediate attack on the American lines. With his superior numbers, and flushed with success, he would undoubtedly have carried them, and either killed, or made prisoners of the flower of the American army, at the same time laying open to immediate attack, on its most vulnerable side, the main body of the reserve in New York. Had he not been greatly deceived in his estimate of General Putnam's real strength, he would certainly have attempted this move, in which case, the great cause of American liberty would have been staked upon one cast of the die, and that, under circumstances, in which all the advantage was on the side of the enemy.

It may be questioned, indeed, if the defeat of this day should not be regarded, rather as a kind, providential interposition, to save the cause of freedom from a sudden and hopeless overthrow, than as a disaster. It was deemed important and possible, by Congress, by Washington, and by a majority of his advisers, to retain possession of New York. It was certainly desirable that they should have been convinced, by the indirect attack upon the outpost on Long Island, that their main position was not tenable, rather than to have held it undisturbed, as they would have done if the success of this battle had been on their side, till the enemy had driven his ships up the North and East Rivers—which he had shown himself able, by favor of wind and tide, to do—and landed on the main, above

Haerlem River, a sufficient force to confine his antagonist to the Island.* Let any one look at the ground, remembering that the Americans had no ships, and but few heavy cannon, while the British were amply supplied with both, and he will be forced to the conclusion, that, if Washington made a mistake, in attempting to occupy and defend Long Island, in the hope of thereby retaining New York as his main position, Howe committed a capital error, in making his first attack upon that quarter; and another, of scarcely less importance, in not following up his victory, by a bold assault upon Putnam's defences.

In front of those defences, he immediately fixed his camp, and commenced his arrangements to force them, by a series of regular approaches. But his prudent enemy did not leave him opportunity to finish them. On the night of the day succeeding the battle, Clinton broke ground for the erection of a battery, within six hundred yards of a redoubt on the left. On the same night, the entire American force was withdrawn to New York, with such silence, order, and despatch, that all the troops and military stores, with the greater part of the provisions, and all the artillery, except a few heavy pieces, were carried over in safety, before the movement was revealed to the enemy. At break of day, the British outposts discovered the rear-guard crossing the East River, and out of the reach of their guns.

This retreat, in its plan, execution and success, was one of those masterly manœuvres, which distinguish the man of commanding genius, consummate skill, and inexhaustible resources, from the mere military chieftain. To convey, in boats, during the brief hours of a summer's night, across an arm of the sea, half a mile in width, an army of

* See Washington's Letters of this period, particularly those of the 8th and 14th of September, to the President of Congress.

nine thousand men,* with all the arms, ammunition, provisions, camp equipage and military stores of every description, required for lines as extensive as those at Brooklyn—to accomplish all this in the near vicinity of a watchful and victorious foe, and that without the loss of a single man, is an achievement, worthy of the ablest general, that ever guided the destinies of war—worthy of a Hannibal or a Cæsar, a Turenne or a Napoleon, a Marlborough or a Wellington—worthy of a WASHINGTON.

Governor's Island was abandoned two days after, so that the entire force, then under the immediate command of Washington, with the exception of a few detachments in the garrisons along the Jersey shore, was concentrated on the island of New York. In all these laborious and fatiguing operations, during which there was no rest, for mind or body, to the commander or any of his principal officers, the activity, energy, and unwearied industry of General Putnam, were everywhere seen and felt. And, although as commander of the abandoned post, he was retiring from a lost field, it is certain that he had lost nothing of the confidence or respect of his superior, who had been present during a part of the engagement, and witnessed the difficulties of his position, and the judgment with which he had conducted his arrangements for defence. In the subsequent dispositions of the army, as will be seen, he was still assigned to the post of difficulty and danger, which is always the post of honor.

* This was the number that joined in the retreat, five battalions having gone over from New York, on the 27th, after the engagement. The whole number on the island, at the time of the battle, was seven thousand seven hundred—the British being considerably more than twice as many.

CHAPTER XIX.

THE British General took immediate possession of all the
fortified posts on Long Island, extended the line northwardly to Hell Gate, and put the whole in a condition to
render him effective service. The two armies were separated only by the East River, on both sides of which were
batteries, which now kept up a continual cannonade upon
each other; the exposed lines extending nearly to the
Heights of Haerlem, a distance of about nine miles.

Dispositions were immediately made to attack New
York on every side. A part of the fleet sailed round
Long Island, and made their appearance in the Sound.
Two frigates passed up the East river, receiving but little
injury from the batteries, and anchored behind a small
island, which protected them from the American guns.

At the same time, the main body of the fleet lay at anchor, close in with Governor's Island—now in the hands of the British—ready to pass up either the North or the East River, or both, and act against any part of the American lines.

These movements, indicating a purpose, rather to effect a landing above, and gain his rear, and thus cut off his communication with the country, than to attack him in his post, General Washington began at once to remove such stores as were not immediately necessary, and to prepare for an instant evacuation of the city. In the latter movement, he was overruled by the decision of a council of general officers, which was summoned on the seventh of September, to advise him in the present exigency. His own opinion, in which Generals Putnam, Greene, and a further respectable minority coincided, was in favor of an immediate removal. The majority, however, while they regarded the post as ultimately untenable, advised that a middle course should be taken between abandoning the city entirely, and concentrating their whole strength for its defence. It was, consequently, concluded to arrange the army under three divisions; five thousand to remain for the defence of the city, and nine thousand at King's Bridge and its dependencies; the remainder to occupy the intermediate space, and be in readiness to support either of the other divisions, in case of an attack.

The rear division, occupying the city, was under the command of Major-General Putnam. Generals Greene and Spencer were assigned to the centre; but the whole command of that division devolved upon Spencer, Greene not having recovered sufficiently to appear at his post. General Heath commanded the advance.

In this position they remained five days—days of watching, weariness, and incessant exertion—during which the movements of the enemy were such, as to compel the officers to change their opinion. Everything indicated an immediate attack upon some quarter, though it was impossible to decide what point they would choose for the assault. It was resolved in council on the 12th, to abandon the city altogether. From this opinion, Generals Spencer, George Clinton, and Heath still dissented. In the meantime, the utmost diligence had been used to remove the stores to a place of safety—a work which was attended with the greatest difficulty, the British ships having taken so many positions in the two rivers, as to render the communication by water of no avail.

Meanwhile, active preparations were made for the retreat. On Sunday, the fifteenth, those preparations were suddenly precipitated, by a decided demonstration on the part of the enemy. Under cover of a heavy fire from the ships lying in the East River, Sir Henry Clinton, with four thousand men, passed over from the head of Newtown Inlet, and effected a landing in Kip's bay, about three miles above the city. The works at this place were of sufficient strength to have withstood the advance of the enemy for a considerable time, if the force stationed there had been disposed to offer resistance. But they abandoned them at once, without waiting for an attack. Two brigades from General Putnam's division, commanded by Parsons and Fellows, being ordered to their support, infected with the same panic, broke in the utmost disorder on the approach of the enemy, and fled. Their commanders made every effort to rally them, but in vain. Washington himself, who flew to the spot, was equally unsuccessful in his endeavors to arrest their flight, and bring them back to their duty. He was so incensed with their dastardly conduct, that he drew his sword, and threatened them with death, if they did not turn and face the enemy.

But they heeded neither menaces nor entreaties, flying with such indecent haste, as to leave their General in a most exposed and perilous situation, from which he was only extricated by some of his immediate attendants seizing his bridle, and turning his horse's head from the enemy.

Orders were now given to occupy the heights of Haerlem, where it was resolved to concentrate the whole force of the army, and make a desperate stand against the advance of the enemy. To that place the Head-Quarters of the Commander-in-chief were removed, his own residence being at the house of Colonel Morris, about a mile and a half below Fort Washington, and nearly midway between the Haerlem River and the Hudson.

About the same time that the landing was effected at Kip's Bay, three ships of war moved up the North River to Bloomingdale, and commenced offensive operations there. In the meantime, General Putnam, with the remnant of his division, which was strengthened rather than weakened by the absence of the two brigades that had so shamefully deserted their commander at Kip's Bay, was at his post in the city. It was every hour growing more and more perilous, as the forces of the enemy, taking one position after another, were closing around it. The retreat was ordered at the last critical moment, in which it was possible to have effected it. The enemy, by the advantage so basely given them at Kip's Bay, already had possession of the main road, on the east side of the island, which made it necessary to take the route by Bloomingdale. That route, also, as we have seen, was now exposed, in one point at least, to a raking fire from the ships in the North River.

Calling in his pickets and guards, Putnam set his brigades in motion. The day was oppressively hot, and the

Washington in imminent Danger at Kip's Bay. PAGE 252.

men suffered so severely from fatigue and thirst, that they could scarcely have made a very resolute defence, if the enemy had attempted to cut off their retreat. Some fainted by the way, and some died at the brooks, where they halted to drink, by indulging in that luxury to excess. Col. Humphreys, who was at this time in Putnam's division, and acting Adjutant to the last regiment that left the city, writes thus of the conduct of his general, on that occasion : " I had frequent opportunities, that day, of beholding him, for the purpose of issuing orders, and encouraging his troops, flying on his horse, covered with foam, wherever his presence was necessary. Without his extraordinary exertions, the guards must inevitably have been lost ; and it is probable the entire corps would have been cut in pieces. When we were not far from Bloomingdale, an aide-de-camp came from him at full speed, to inform us that a column of British infantry was descending upon our right. Our rear was soon fired upon, and the colonel of our regiment, whose order was just communicated for the front to file off to the left, was killed on the spot."

The force under Putnam's command at this time was about three thousand. They were encumbered with wives, children, and all kinds of hangers-on ; with a great variety of baggage, tools, camp utensils, and all the numberless and nameless *et cetera*, which the ancient Romans embraced under the appropriate and comprehensive term, *impediments*. These, together with the extreme heat of the weather, the narrowness of their routes, and the perils which surrounded them, rendered the retreat an arduous and difficult achievement.

Sir Henry Clinton, having met with nothing to hinder his landing, or employ his troops at Kip's bay, immediately put them in motion, to cut off the retreat of Putnam —whose men he supposed were of the same class of soldiers, with those he had just encountered, and, therefore, little to be feared, whatever might be their numbers, or by whomsoever they might be led. In attempting to effect this object, he was obliged to pass under the eastern side of Murray Hill, where was the residence of a well known and worthy old Quaker lady—a true-hearted American woman, and the mother of Lindley Murray, the celebrated grammarian. Feeling that, with his enemy several miles in advance, he could not hope to escape him, without the aid of some well managed diversion, Putnam sent one of his Aids to Mrs. Murray, requesting her, if possible, to detain General Clinton, by offering to him and his staff the hospitalities of her house, and entertaining his officers, till the Americans should have gained the point of the hill.

Mrs. Murray was well known to many of the British officers, and her polite invitation to halt at her door, and take a friendly glass of wine, was very courteously accepted. The quality of the wine was excellent. The society and conversation of the ladies was an agreeable episode to the stirring scenes of war, and the hour flew by, before they were aware that it had begun to wane. At length a faithful negro servant, whom she had stationed at the look-out on the top of the house, entered the parlor, made a sign to his ·mistress, and instantly retired. Upon this, Mrs. Murray, rising with the true dignity of an American matron, requested Sir Henry Clinton to follow her, as she had something interesting to show him. Ascending to the look-out, she pointed out to him the banner of Freedom, proudly waving amid the columns of the retiring army; which had now gained the northern side of the hill, and was moving in close array, into the open plains of Bloomingdale. Without waiting for the ordinary etiquette of leave-taking, the disconcerted General rushed down, sprang upon his horse, and gave orders for instant pursuit.

It was a beautiful piece of strategy, delicately managed, and ably executed, and proved the turning point in the fate of Putnam's division. Says Humphreys : " Before our brigades came in, we were given up for lost by all our friends. So critical, indeed, was our situation, and so narrow the gap by which we escaped, that the instant we had passed, the enemy closed it by extending their line from river to river." But for the delay at Murray Hill, the extension of this line would inevitably have cut off the rear, and perhaps brought on a general engagement. The British were now landing in force at all the deserted posts. Their numbers, already greatly superior to their foes, were constantly increasing ; and any attempt to accept their offer of battle, would have shown an utter destitution of " the better part of valor." But, though there was no regular fighting, there was necessarily, as an accompaniment to a difficult retreat, and a close pursuit, considerable skirmishing, sharp-shooting, and other mutual annoyances. General Putnam's loss was not inconsiderable, having fifteen killed, and three hundred taken prisoners. Nearly all the heavy cannon, and a considerable quantity of baggage, stores and provisions, were also left behind, and fell into the hands of the enemy. Most of this might have been saved, had General Clinton been detained at Kip's bay, by a tolerable defence of that post.

General Howe now took formal possession of New York, posting a small force in the city, for the preservation of order, and the defence of his rear, and planting the main body of his army at the upper end of the island, near the American lines. His right was at Horen's Hook, on the East River, his left extending to the Hudson, near Bloomingdale—making a continuous encampment from river to river, two miles in extent—both flanks being covered by the ships.

The Americans were strongly posted at King's Bridge, the natural position of the place being favorable for works of defence. There was also a strong force at Morris's Heights; and another at Haerlem and McGowan's Pass, within about a mile and a half of the British lines. Each of these posts was so fortified, as to be supposed capable of being defended against superior numbers. The distance between Haerlem and King's Bridge is between five and six miles—Morris's Heights being nearly half way between. Of the advanced posts, General Putnam commanded the right at McGowan's Pass, and General Spencer the left, at Haerlem.

It was Washington's desire, to embrace every opportunity to give his men some active service, without bringing on a general engagement. By thus habituating them, in a series of skirmishes, to meet the enemy in the field, he hoped to show them what they were capable of doing, and encourage them to entertain confidence in themselves An opportunity was soon offered to gratify this desire.

The day after the retreat from New York, several parties of the enemy appeared in the plains between the two camps. On receiving intelligence of this movement, General Washington rode quickly to the out-posts, to order the necessary dispositions to meet it. Soon after his arrival, Lieutenant-Colonel Knowlton, of the Continental division, and one of Putnam's bravest officers, who, with a fine corps of Yankee Rangers, had been skirmishing with one of the advanced parties of the enemy, came in and reported their numbers at about three hundred. Some of them were concealed in a wood, in the rear of a small eminence. The General ordered Knowlton, with his rangers, assisted by Major Leitch, with three companies from Weedon's regiment of Virginians, to make an effort to gain their rear, and cut them off, or bring them in as prisoners ; while, to divert them from this movement, another party should attack them in front.

As soon as this attack was attempted, the British retreated with some precipitation, in order to secure a more advantageous position, under cover of some fences and bushes, which skirted the hill. A brisk but distant and ineffectual fire immediately commenced. In the meantime, Colonel Knowlton, who had not been informed of this new position of the enemy, having made his circuit, came upon them with great bravery, but, unfortunately, rather in flank than in rear. A warm action ensued. Major Leitch was soon brought from the field, severely wounded in three places. The gallant Knowlton fell, mortally wounded, soon after. Their men, notwithstanding the loss of their commanders, stood their ground, and maintained the conflict with the greatest resolution, under the lead of their brave and experienced captains. Being reinforced from the camp, they charged the enemy with such intrepidity, as to compel him to leave his covert ; and would have driven him from the field altogether, had not General Howe sent a battalion of Hessian grenadiers and a company of *chasseurs* to his aid. Not wishing to bring on a general action, or expose himself to unnecessary loss, Washington ordered a retreat.

In this affair, the loss of the British was ascertained to be about a hundred. That of the Americans was not half that number ; but the difference was more than balanced by the fall of the two brave leaders, Knowlton and Leitch. The former was a special favorite with General Putnam. He was trained up under his own eye, having entered the army, under his command, at the early age of sixteen, and served with him in most of those brilliant

22*

affairs, which distinguished his name in the Seven Years'
War. He was with him in the forest of Wood Creek,
where he was taken prisoner. He was with him in the
expedition to Montreal, under General Amherst; and in
the closing scene of that protracted conflict, the expedition
to Havana;—having been promoted through all the
grades, from a private to a lieutenancy, before he was
twenty-one years of age. He was one of the foremost,
under his old commander, to rush to the rescue, on the
breaking out of hostilities at Lexington; and was the
General's right hand man in the skirmish at Noddle Island,
and in the battle of Bunker Hill. He was also in the heat
of the action on Long Island, and effected his escape with
great difficulty. He entered the Revolutionary service as
a captain, and, in less than a year, had risen to a lieuten-
ant-colonelcy. Colonel Burr, who was intimately acquainted with him, and sometimes associated with him in
service, remarked that " it was impossible to promote
such an officer too rapidly." He lived an hour after his
fall, and had the satisfaction of receiving from the lips of
Washington, an unqualified commendation of his conduct
on all occasions; and from Putnam the assurance that to
him, and his division, his loss was irreparable. He died
at the age of thirty-six, lamented by the army and the
country, but by no one more than the General, who had
trained him to war, and knew how well he could rely
upon him in the most trying exigencies of the service.

This little skirmish, though attended with so serious a
loss, had an important effect upon the American army.
It encouraged them to face the enemy boldly, and to believe themselves capable of victory, under all the inequalities of their condition. They had wiped away the stain
of the previous day, and they resolved that no such dastardly act should again tarnish the name of the defenders

of liberty. To encourage this sentiment, as well as to do justice to his able and faithful soldiers, Washington publicly commended their conduct in the following

"ORDERS.

"*Head Quarters, Haerlem Heights, Sept.* 17, 1776.

"Parole, *Leitch ;* countersign, *Virginia.*

"The General most heartily thanks the troops, commanded yesterday by Major Leitch, who first advanced upon the enemy, and the others who so resolutely supported them. The behavior yesterday was such a contrast to that of some of the troops the day before, as must show what may be done, where officers and soldiers will exert themselves. Once more, therefore, the General calls upon officers and men, to act up to the noble cause in which they are engaged, and to support the *honor* and *liberties* of their country.

"The gallant and brave Colonel Knowlton, who would have been an honor to any country, having fallen yesterday, while gloriously fighting, Captain Brown is to take command of the party, lately led by Colonel Knowlton. Officers and men are to obey him accordingly."

If the army of the Revolution had been composed, in chief, of such men as these, the contest would have been of shorter duration, and the toils and anxieties of the general officers infinitely less severe. But, unfortunately, they were mostly of a different class, while the circumstances and terms, under which they engaged in the war, rendered them far less serviceable and trustworthy, than the same men might have been under a different system. An extract from one of Washington's letters of this period, addressed to the President of Congress, will show the matter at a glance : "To place any dependence upon militia is assuredly resting upon a broken staff. Men, just dragged from the tender scenes of domestic life, unaccustomed to the din of arms, totally unacquainted with every kind of military skill (which is followed by a want of confidence in themselves, when opposed to troops regularly trained, disciplined, and appointed, superior in knowledge, and superior in arms), are timid, and ready to fly from their own shadows. Besides, the sudden change in their manner of living brings on an unconquerable desire to return to their homes, and produces the most shameful and scandalous desertions. Again, men accustomed to unbounded freedom, cannot brook the restraint, which is indispensably necessary to the good order and government of an army, without which, licentiousness and every kind of disorder triumphantly reign."

Such were the unpromising materials, out of which these able officers were compelled to fashion an army, to resist the best troops of the most powerful nation on the globe. It must be admitted that none but the most able and competent officers, with a righteous cause to sustain, could have accomplished the herculean task.

CHAPTER XX.

THE British commander, aware of the advantages which his enemy would derive from a series of partisan skirmishes, under cover of his intrenchments, was as desirous to bring on a general engagement, as Washington was to avoid it. The latter, sensible of his great inferiority in numbers, discipline, experience, and equipment, was, at the same time, confident in the strength of his defences, and his ability to repel, with advantage, any assault that might be made upon them. He, therefore, prudently contented himself with annoying and weakening his adversary, whenever opportunity offered, rather than by bolder and more brilliant movements, hazarding his whole cause upon one cast of the die. In constant readiness for an attack, which, if made anywhere, was to be expected at the advanced post, at McGowan's Pass, where General Putnam was stationed, he gave orders to General Spencer, who commanded at Haerlem, to be prepared to reinforce that Pass, at a moment's warning. But the enemy prudently refrained from any attempt upon the defences.

Among the multitude of cares which bore upon the mind of General Washington, at this period, was the protection of the property of American citizens—especially that of persons known, or supposed, to be attached to the royal cause. The army was composed, in great part, of men who made no scruple of plundering whatever they could lay their hands upon, and burning, or otherwise destroying, what they could not carry away. Every effort was made, on the part of the General, to punish and suppress this spirit of rapacity, but the means within his power were hardly adequate to the end. On the 24th of September, he addressed a strong representation to Congress on the subject. " Of late," says he, " a practice prevails of the most alarming nature, and which will, if it cannot be checked, prove fatal both to the country and the army—I mean the infamous practice of plundering. For, under the idea of Tory property, or property that may fall into the hands of the enemy, no man is secure in his effects, and scarcely in his person. In order to get at them, we have several instances of people being frightened out of their houses, under pretence of those houses being ordered to be burnt ; and this is done with a view of seizing the goods. Nay, in order that the villainy may be more effectually concealed, some houses have actually been burned to cover the theft. I have, with some others, used my utmost endeavors to stop this horrid practice." In these endeavors, he was constantly and zealously aided by General Putnam, who abhorred every species of robbery and injustice ; and who, in the discharge of the com-

mon duties of equity and humanity, recognized no difference between patriot and tory, or friend and foe. His
good offices, in this respect, secured for him the confidence
and respect of many among the enemies of his cause;
while some of his own countrymen, whose party prejudices
obscured their sense of private right, did not hesitate to
condemn a virtue, to which they did not pretend to aspire.

General Howe, finding that he could neither force the
American defences, nor decoy them into an action where
all the advantage would be on his side, resolved to make
another effort to gain their rear, cut them off from all supplies, and so compel them to an unconditional surrender.
With this view, leaving a sufficient force below for the
protection of New York, he sent several frigates up the
North River, which came to an anchor at some distance
above Fort Washington—having passed the batteries at
that place and Fort Lee, without material damage. A
few days after, on the 12th of October, he embarked a
great part of his army in flat bottomed boats, and, passing
through Hell Gate into the Sound, landed at Frog's
Point, near the town of Westchester, about nine miles
above the camp on the Heights of Haerlem.

Frog's Neck is covered with water, at full tide; and
the Point, on which the British had landed, was connected with the main by bridges. These bridges the Americans took good care to destroy; at the same time,
throwing up some slight works, to obstruct the enemy in
his march. The road from this place to King's Bridge,
led through a difficult country, intersected everywhere by
stone walls; rendering the passage of artillery, or even of
infantry in compact order, almost impracticable.

On the 18th, General Howe, being strongly reinforced,
moved forward, with all his force, to New Rochelle.
Some skirmishing took place on the march, in which the

Americans fought with great bravery, and gained some advantages. At New Rochelle, the British army was still further strengthened, and soon commenced a movement towards White Plains. The main body of the American troops formed a long line of intrenched camps, extending from twelve to thirteen miles, on the different heights from Valentine's Hill, near King's Bridge, to White Plains, fronting the British line of march, and the River Bronx, which divided the two armies.

It was while the two armies were watching each other in this position, that Colonel Haslet succeeded in surprising Colonel Rogers,* "the late worthless Major," as he calls him, at Mamaroneck, taking thirty-six prisoners, a pair of colors, sixty stand of arms, and other valuable booty. About the same time, Colonel Hand, with a regiment of Pennsylvanian riflemen, engaged an equal number of Hessian *chasseurs*, with considerable advantage.

General Washington was encamped on high broken ground, his right flank resting on the Bronx, which, by a bold curve at this place, covered also the front of his right wing, extending along the road towards New Rochelle, as far as the brow of the hill on which his centre was posted. His left, forming almost a right angle with his centre, and nearly parallel to his right, extended along the hills northward, so as to keep possession of the commanding ground, and secure a retreat, should it be necessary, to a still stronger position in his rear. General McDougall, with a detachment of sixteen hundred men, principally militia, occupied Chatterton's Hill, on the west side of the Bronx, about a mile from the camp. The river being fordable at that place, his communication with the main army was open.

General Howe having advanced in force, on the 28th,

* Appendix, No. 1.

to attack General Washington in his camp, determined, as a measure preliminary to a general assault, to dislodge General McDougall from this post. He, therefore, directed Colonel Rahl, with a brigade of Hessians, to make a circuit so as to gain his rear, while Brigadier-General Leslie, with a strong corps of British and Hessian troops, should attack him in front. This being done with great vigor, the militia in the front rank immediately gave way; but Colonel Haslet's Delaware regiment, Colonel Smallwood's Maryland battalion, and Colonel Reitzimer's New York corps, advanced boldly, and in good order, to meet the foe, and gallantly defended their post, till they were overpowered by numbers; when they reluctantly retired, keeping up, in their retreat, an irregular, but not ineffectual fire, from behind the stone walls that lined the way General Putnam, receiving orders to support General McDougall, hastened to the scene of action, with a considerable detachment. But the post was already abandoned to the enemy, and its late defenders were met in full retreat towards the camp. Notwithstanding this reinforcement, it was deemed unadvisable to attempt to regain the hill, and all moved on, in order, to rejoin the main army.

The loss in this action has been variously stated by historians. The most probable report makes that of the Americans not much over two hundred, with nearly double that number to the British.

A general assault was now momentarily expected, and every arrangement was made for it in the British camp, the whole army reposing on their arms, in order of battle, during the night. But, perceiving in the morning that Washington had improved the night, in adding to the strength of his works, and disposing his forces to better advantage to meet the expected attack, Howe concluded

23

to postpone further offensive operations, till the arrival of six battalions, which had been ordered up, under command of Lord Percy. A violent rain, which fell immediately on the accession of this reinforcement, occasioned a further delay. General Washington, having, in the meantime, removed his provisions and heavy baggage to a stronger position at North Castle, about five miles distant, availed himself of the darkness of the night, on the first of November, to withdraw his whole army to that place Deeming this post too strong to be attempted with prudence, General Howe changed his plans, and directed his attention to Forts Washington and Lee, which, being still ably garrisoned by the Americans, proved a check upon the contemplated movements of the British commander, by leaving a well-posted enemy in his rear. His first effort was against Fort Independence, at King's Bridge, upon which a descent was made by General Knyphausen. The garrison abandoned it on his approach, and retreated to Fort Washington, followed by Knyphausen, who pitched his camp between the two forts. In the meantime, General Howe, with his whole force, retired slowly down the North River, towards New York.

Apprehending, from these new movements, that an invasion into New Jersey was intended, Washington detached all the troops belonging to the States west of the Hudson, five thousand in number, under command of General Putnam, to provide against such a design. They crossed the river on the 8th of November, and took post at Hackensack, which they reached after a circuitous route of sixty miles, to avoid the parties of the enemy. General Greene was in command at Fort Lee, on that side of the river, and was now invested with discretionary powers, in relation to the defence of Fort Washington, on the New York side, towards which the British were concentrating their movements. It had been intended and resolved, by the strong recommendations of Congress, to maintain these two posts to the last extremity. The Commander-in-chief believed that this last extremity had already come, and that it was vain to attempt to hold them, in the present position of affairs. General Greene entertained a different opinion, in which he appears to have been sustained by General Putnam, and consequently availed himself of the discretion allowed him, to reinforce Colonel McGaw, with directions to defend the post at every hazard.

General Howe, in retiring southward, encamped near King's Bridge on the 13th. On the 15th, he summoned the garrison to surrender, on pain of being put to the sword. Colonel McGaw replied, with becoming manliness, that he should defend the place to the last extremity; and immediately communicated the summons, with his answer, to General Greene, who transmitted them to the Commander-in-chief, then just arrived at Hackensack. Washington proceeded at once to Fort Lee, and, though late in the night, was hastening over to Fort Washington, whither Generals Putnam and Greene had already gone. In crossing the river, however, he met those officers on their return. They reported the garrison in high spirits, ready and able to make a good defence, and General Washington returned with them to Fort Lee. The next day the fort was carried by storm, with a loss of nearly three thousand men, by far the most severe that had yet befallen the American army. The loss of the British was about eight hundred.

The evacuation of Fort Lee was a necessary consequence upon the loss of Fort Washington, and immediate preparations were made for the removal of the stores. Before this could be completed, however, Lord Cornwallis had crossed the North River, with a strong detachment of six thousand men, and made an attempt to enclose the garrison, upon the narrow neck of land, between the North and Hackensack Rivers. By a rapid and well-conducted movement, they were so fortunate as to escape, with all their ammunition and small arms ; their heavy cannon, with several hundred tents, a large quantity of baggage and valuable stores, being unavoidably left behind.

The retreat across the Hackensack, left the American army in a position but little better than that which they had just left. The Passaic runs nearly parallel with that river for many miles. They were consequently in the same danger, as before, of being enclosed between two barriers, which it would be difficult to pass. There was, therefore, no alternative but to retreat still further across the Passaic. Their forces were daily diminishing, by the withdrawal of great numbers of the militia, who, dispirited by their late reverses, returned to their homes as fast as their terms of enlistment expired, so that, by the last of November, Washington had scarcely three thousand men under his immediate command. These were exposed in an open country, among a part of the people by no means cordially favorable to the cause of Independence, without intrenching tools, without stores, without tents to shelter them from the growing inclemency of the season.

A division of three thousand five hundred men, under General Heath, had been stationed among the Highlands, for the defence of the Hudson, and the mountain passes. Another division of four thousand, many of whom were militia, whose term of service was soon to expire, was left in the camp at White Plains, commanded by General Lee, with discretionary instructions, to continue on that side of the Hudson, or to follow the Commander-in-chief into New Jersey, according to the movements of the enemy

Newark, New Brunswick, Princeton, and Trenton, successively fell into the hands of the enemy, as they were successively abandoned ·by the retreating " phantom of an army ;" and, finally, on the eighth of December, Washington crossed the Delaware, then the only barrier which prevented the British from taking possession of Philadelphia. So rapidly had the pursuit been urged, that the rear of one army was often within sight and shot of the van of the other ; and before one party had completed the destruction of the bridges, by which they fled, the other had commenced repairing them for the pursuit.

It was the darkest period in the history of the Revolution. The campaign, now so darkly closed, had been a continued series of disasters and retreats. The enemy was now in possession of Rhode Island, Long Island, the City of New York, Staten Island, and almost the whole State of New Jersey, and was apparently on the point of extending his conquests into Pennsylvania. The commander of the victorious army, in conjunction with his brother, the Admiral, had issued a proclamation, which was widely scattered on every side, offering a full pardon, in the name of his Majesty, to all who should take the oath of allegiance, and come under his protection, within sixty days. Great numbers, and among them men of fortune and respectability, had accepted the terms, and gone over to the enemy. Others, especially in New Jersey, took the oath, but did not leave their usual places of abode. In short, so great was the panic, and so dark the prospect, that a general despondency pervaded the continent. Many of the strongest spirits quailed before the accumulating difficulties that encompassed the cause of freedom. Washington stood firm and unmoved as a rock. " Undismayed by the dangers which surrounded him, he did not for an instant relax his exertions, or omit anything which could

23*

obstruct the progress of the enemy, or improve his own
condition.   He did not, for a moment, appear to despair
of the public safety, but struggled against adverse fortune,
with the hope of yet vanquishing the difficulties which
encompassed him ; and constantly showed himself to his
harassed and enfeebled army with a serene, unembarrassed
countenance, betraying no fears in himself, and invigorat-
ing and inspiring with confidence the bosoms of others."
Among his principal officers, none was more hopeful,
more courageous, more determined than General Putnam.
Through all this season of peril, disaster and discourage-
ment, he was ever at his Commander's side, and was
among the last of the fugitive band, that crossed the Delaware, and drew up   its   diminished lines on the other
side, not to give over the fight in despair, but, like a hunt-
ed wolf at bay, to turn upon its   pursuers with redoubled
fierceness, and drive them back from the field they had so
lately won.

CHAPTER XXI.

GENERAL HOWE, having now, as he supposed, broken the spirits, as well as scattered the forces, of the rebel army, promised himself a certain and easy victory. His next immediate object was the possession of Philadelphia; through which so large a portion of the American supplies were obtained, that, in the earnest language of Washington, " upon the salvation of that place, their cause almost depended." With this view of its importance, and with a determination to leave no effort untried to secure it against the approach of the enemy, General Putnam was sent forward to take the command, and to superintend the works to be erected for its defence

In a letter from General Washington to the President of Congress, under date of the 9th of December, after remarking " that the security of Philadelphia should be our next object," he suggests, that " a communication of lines and redoubts might be formed from the Delaware to the Schuylkill, on the north entrance of the city—to begin on the Schuylkill side, and run eastward to the Delaware, upon the most advantageous and commanding grounds. We have ever found," he continues, " that lines, however slight, are very formidable to the enemy ; they would at least give a check, till the people could recover from the fright and consternation, that naturally attend the first appearance of an enemy.

" In the meantime, every step should be taken to collect a force, not only from Pennsylvania, but from the neighboring States. If we can keep the enemy from entering Philadelphia, and keep the communication by water open for supplies, we may yet make a stand, if the country will come to our assistance till the new levies be collected. * * *

" P. S. General Mifflin is this moment come up, and tells me, that all the military stores yet remain in Philadelphia. This makes the immediate fortifying of the city so necessary, that I have desired General Mifflin to return and take charge of the stores ; and have ordered Major-General Putnam immediately down, to superintend the works, and give the necessary directions."

The difficulties to be encountered in this new sphere of action, were many and severe. But the hardy old veteran proved himself equal to them all. Here, as well as in New York, there were many persons strongly disaffected towards the American cause—men, who, from attachment to royalty, or from fear of losing their property, shrunk from the unequal contest, or lent their aid, secretly, to further the designs of the enemy. Many of them were so decided in their hostility, that it was at one time thought unsafe to withdraw the forces from the city, though their aid was much needed to strengthen the army in the field, lest, in their absence, the whole city should declare for the enemy. It was this, as will be seen hereafter, that deprived General Putnam of a share in one of the most brilliant and successful enterprises of the army of the Revolution.

The danger apprehended from the steady approaches of General Howe was imminent, and the works of defence were required to be constructed with the greatest despatch. The labor was severe and unintermitting, and General Putnam never spared himself, when there was work to be done, any more than when danger was to be braved. " His personal industry," says Humphreys, who was with him at this time, " was unparalleled, and his health was, for a while, impaired by his unrelaxed exertions." The city was placed under martial law, and his authority, during his command in it, was paramount and supreme. But he made no unnecessary display of his power, scrupulously avoiding everything that would needlessly disturb the usual order, or restrain the usual freedom of intercourse among the citizens. He made a diligent use both of authority and example, to conciliate, as far as possible, the contending factions,—to win over the disaffected to the cause of freedom,—and to excite all the citizens to use their utmost diligence in preparing to repel the expected approach of the enemy. He took good care, as he had done in New York, to regulate and sustain the police of the city, by bringing his own military authority to bear upon it, and by encouraging a cheerful obedience to the laws. The following order will illustrate his care and prudence in this respect :

" GENERAL ORDERS.

" *Head Quarters, Philadelphia, Dec.* 14, 1776

" Colonel Griffin is appointed Adjutant-General to the troops in and about this city. All orders from the General through him, either written or verbal, are to be strictly attended to, and punctually obeyed.

" In case of an alarm by fire, the city guards and patroles are to suffer the inhabitants to pass, unmolested, at any hour of the night; and the good people of Philadelphia are earnestly requested and desired to give every assistance in their power, with engines and buckets, to extinguish the fire. And, as the Congress have ordered the city to be defended to the last extremity, the General hopes that no person will refuse to give every assistance possible, to complete the fortifications that are to be erected in and about the city.

" ISRAEL PUTNAM."

Soon after his arrival in Philadelphia, General Putnam was called, with General Mifflin, to a special conference with Congress upon the expediency of adjourning their meeting to some place less exposed to interruption from the enemy. By their advice, and urgent counsels, and directly in the face of a vote taken only the day before, the resolution to adjourn was adopted on the 12th of December, to assemble in Baltimore on the 20th.

The labor of constructing fortifications was regular and monotonous, and but few incidents of sufficient interest to be recorded, marked the toilsome residence of the General in this capital. Everything was proceeding well and prosperously under his direction, when he was suddenly called off from this position, to take part in other and more important movements of the army.

Contrary to all expectation, and to all human proba-

bility, General Washington, with the poor remnant of an
army that had escaped with him over the Delaware, had
suddenly recrossed that river, in the dead of winter, and
struck a blow upon the victorious and too confident enemy
at Trenton, that astonished alike both friend and foe—
reviving and inspiriting the one, as much as it discomfited
and chagrined the other. Before the enemy had quite
recovered from the panic occasioned by this masterly
movement, the American general had crossed the Delaware the second time, and, prudently avoiding the prof-
ferred encounter with Lord Cornwallis, had struck another
blow upon Princeton, killing and capturing almost an
entire regiment.

It was a part of his original design, in planning these
bold movements, to unite the troops employed in fortifying Philadelphia, with those of Brigadier-General Cadwallader at Bristol, and to place the whole under the
command of General Putnam, with a view to carrying the
post at Mount Holly, about ten miles back of Burlington,
where the advanced guard of the British army was posted.
But so alarming were the indications, at that time, of an
insurrection in the city, in favor of the royal cause, that
the execution of this part of the plan was entrusted to
General Cadwallader alone ; and General Putnam remained at his post, to prosecute the works of defence which
were to guard against an invading enemy from without,
and to quell the incipient organization of a more dangerous
enemy within. He was, therefore, denied the opportunity—which to his active and enterprising spirit would
have seemed one of the *privileges* of the service—of sharing
in two of the most brilliant achievements which distinguished the Revolutionary War. Had the original plan
been carried out, and the river been found passable, at the
place appointed for crossing, there is no doubt that it

would have been completely successful, and greatly enhanced the advantages of that glorious day. It was ascertained, by persons despatched to reconnoitre the post at Mount Holly, that the soldiers were in a state of comparative helplessness from intoxication—having indulged freely in spirituous liquors the preceding day, which was Christmas-day. There was no apprehension of danger, and no precaution to guard against it.

On the eve of the execution of the first of these enterprises, the Commander-in-chief addressed a letter to General Putnam, expressing his great satisfaction in learning the improved state of his health—which had been impaired by his excessive labors and exposures—and informing him that the design of the enemy to gain early possession of Philadelphia, was fully confirmed, by an intercepted letter from a gentleman of Philadelphia, who had joined the enemy, to his partner in that city, which declared that their plans were laid to enter it within twenty days, or as soon as the ice in the river should be sufficiently strong to enable them to transport their artillery across it. He added, that, if the citizens of Philadelphia had any regard for the town, not a moment's time was to be lost, until it should be put in the best possible posture of defence. Fearing that, through their indifference, or the want of time to accomplish it, this would not be done, he directed all the public stores, except such as were necessary for immediate use, to be removed at once to places of greater security.

Ten days after, on the 5th of January, 1777, Washington wrote to Putnam, from Pluckemin, giving an account of his second successful stroke, and expressing the hope—as the enemy appeared to be quite panic-struck—that he should be able to drive them out of the Jerseys. The new aspect which their late brilliant successes had put upon the American cause, so completely changed the current of popular opinion, that the defection of Philadelphia was no longer feared, and Putnam could now be spared from that post. He was, accordingly, ordered to take the field, and assist in pushing the advantages so unexpectedly gained. " It is thought advisable for you," continues the letter, " to march the troops under your command to Crosswicks, and keep a strict watch upon the enemy in that quarter. If the enemy continues at Brunswick, you must act with great circumspection, lest you meet with a surprise. As we have made two successful attacks upon them by surprise, if there is any possibility of retaliating, they will attempt it. You will give out your strength to be twice as great as it is.* Forward on all the baggage and scattered troops belonging to this division of the army as soon as may be.

" You will keep as many spies out as you shall see proper. A number of horsemen, in the dress of the country, must be constantly kept going backwards and forwards for this purpose, and if you discover any motion of the enemy, which you can depend upon, and which you think of consequence, let me be informed thereof as soon as possible, by express.

" I am, dear General, yours, &c."

In obedience to these orders, General Putnam took the field at once, leaving suitable directions for the prosecution of the works of defence in the city. The design of the Americans was to hold the advantages already gained, and to harass the enemy, by all the means in their power—for

---

* So successfully was this species of deception practised upon the enemy, that letters from officers in the army to their friends in England, represented the Americans, at this very time, as forty thousand strong. See Almon's Remembrancer.

they had neither men nor ammunition to attempt a battle. They had succeeded in driving them from all their newly acquired posts in the Jerseys, except Brunswick and Amboy, and had thus opened to themselves a large field for supplies, and given encouragement to multitudes of those, who, while they were at heart friendly to the American cause, had begun to despair of ever bringing it to a successful issue.

Putnam's first movement was to Crosswicks, a few miles southeast of Trenton, on one of the routes by which the enemy might attempt to regain his lost position at Mount Holly. As no attempt was made to do this, and Howe's forces seemed to be concentrating for winter quarters, Putnam was ordered to advance to Princeton. At this post he continued, during the remainder of the winter, within fifteen miles from the enemy's stronghold at Brunswick. His force was exceedingly small, never more than a few hundred. At one period, from a sudden diminution, occasioned by the withdrawal of those whose terms of enlistment had expired, and who peremptorily refused to remain till their places could be supplied by new recruits, he had fewer men on duty than he had miles of frontier to guard. There was no time, during the winter, when he could have sustained, for a single hour, the attack of a respectable body of regulars. Yet, so good a front did he maintain, and so successfully did he blind the eyes of his adversary to his real position and strength, that no effort was made to dislodge him.

Among the British who were left on the field at the battle of Princeton, was Captain M'Pherson, of the 17th regiment, a very worthy Scotchman, who was desperately wounded through the lungs. He had been left for dead, and on General Putnam's arrival on the ground, he found him languishing in extreme distress, without a surgeon, without a single accommodation, and without a friend to solace the troubled spirit in the hour of death. He visited him, and immediately caused every possible comfort to be administered to him. Captain M'Pherson, who, contrary to all appearances, recovered, after having demonstrated to General Putnam the dignified sense of obligations which a generous mind wishes not to conceal, one day, in familiar conversation, demanded—" Pray, Sir, what countryman are you?" "An American," answered the latter. " Not a Yankee?" said the other. " A full blooded one," replied the General. " I am sorry for that," rejoined M'Pherson, " I did not think there could be so much goodness and generosity in an American, or, indeed, in anybody but a Scotchman."

While the recovery of Captain M'Pherson was doubt ful, he desired that General Putnam would allow a friend in the British army at Brunswick, to come and assist him in making out his will. Putnam had then only fifty men in his command—the remainder being out, in detachments, to cover and protect the country. He was, consequently, very much embarrassed by this proposition. He was not content that a British officer should have an opportunity to spy out his weakness, nor was it in his nature to refuse complying v th a dictate of humanity. He luckily thought of an expedient, which he hastened to put into practice. A flag of truce was despatched with Captain M'Pherson's request, but under an injunction not to return until after dark. In the evening, lights were placed in all the rooms of the College, and in every apartment of the vacant houses throughout the town. During the whole night, the fifty men, sometimes all together, and sometimes in small detachments, were marched from different quarters, by the house in which M'Pherson lay. It was afterwards known, that M'Pherson's friend, on his return, reported that General Putnam's army, upon the most moderate calculation, could not consist of less than four or five thousand men.

The harshness and cruelty of the invaders, and particularly the German mercenaries, during the period of their temporary occupancy of New Jersey, reacted with a most salutary effect upon the American cause, alienating from the British interest the affections of those who had been hitherto loyal, confirming in their opposition those who had before espoused the cause of liberty, and rousing to instant and spirited revolt such as had been compelled to take sides with the conquerors, or at least to render a seeming submission. The humane and generous treatment they everywhere experienced at the hands of Washington, and his compeers, settled for ever the question of their allegiance ; and, from the time when General Howe evacuated his short-lived possessions on and about the Delaware, there were no truer or more devoted supporters of the cause of independence in the States, than those of New Jersey.

While affording every possible protection to the persons and property of American citizens, the principal officers, in their various stations, seemed constantly to vie with each other, in giving proofs of vigilance, enterprise, and valor, against the common foe. The numbers under the command of each were necessarily very small. But they were always on the alert for opportunities to annoy the enemy, incessantly hovering, in small scouting parties, about their quarters, interrupting their communications, cutting off their supplies, surprising their foraging parties and pickets, and, in every other way, showing them that, though broken, they were not subdued. They maintained a constant communication with each other, and, by mutual counsel and assistance, and a perfect harmony of operation, contrived, in a great measure, to remedy the evil of scanty numbers, and scattered posts.

Lord Cornwallis was in command of the British forces at New Brunswick. General Dickinson, of New Jersey, was stationed on the west side of Millstone river, not far from Somerset Court-House, and about ten miles from New Brunswick. On the opposite side of the river was a mill, in which was deposited a large quantity of flour. Tempted by such a booty, of which he was in no small need, Lord Cornwallis sent out a party, about the 25th of January, with wagons and horses, to seize the flour, and collect such forage as fell in their way. While engaged in this enterprise, General Dickinson fell upon them in a most spirited manner, and drove them back, with some loss, taking from them forty wagons, and upwards of a hundred valuable horses, with a considerable number of sheep and cattle, which they had collected on their march. The two parties were nearly equal in number. The bridge over the Millstone was in possession of the British, and defended by their field-pieces; so that General Dickinson, to accomplish his purpose, was compelled to break the ice, and cross the river in three feet of water.

General Putnam was still more successful in several expeditions, undertaken by his orders, during this trying winter. In the course of January, Colonel Gurney and Major Davis were detached from his command, with such parties of militia as could be spared from the garrisons, to protect the citizens of Monmouth county from the predatory incursions of the royalists, to which they were much exposed. Several severe skirmishes took place, in which the British invariably were the sufferers, losing large numbers of men, as well as horses and wagons. So well, indeed, did they cover the country, for a season, as to induce many of the most respectable inhabitants to declare, that

24*

for the security of their persons, as well as the salvation of their property, they were wholly indebted to the spirited exertions, and well-conducted manœuvres, of these two detachments. Nor was this the only service rendered by such parties. While they rescued the country from the tyranny and depredations of the tories, they encouraged the militia to come boldly out, and embody themselves for their own defence.

On the expiration of their term of service, which happened soon after, Putnam was compelled to part even with such valuable and efficient coadjutors as these. How reluctantly he parted with them, in the then reduced state of his forces, may be gathered from the following letter, dated

" *Princeton, February* 5, 1777.

" To Major John Davis, of the Third Battalion of Cumberland County Militia.

" Sir—I am much obliged to you for your activity, vigor and diligence, since you have been under my command. You will now march your men to Philadelphia, and there discharge them, returning into the store all the ammunitions, arms and accoutrements you received at that place.

" I am, sir, your humble servant,
" ISRAEL PUTNAM."

Two weeks after this, having received information that a considerable party of refugees, in the pay of the British commander, had taken post at Lawrence's Neck, and were proceeding to erect some works of defence there, General Putnam despatched Colonel Nelson, of Brunswick, with one hundred and fifty men, with orders to surprise and take them prisoners. That able officer conducted the affair with so much secresy and decision, that the entire party was secured, with their arms, and considerable booty. They were about sixty in number, and were commanded by Major Stockton, having been detached, on this service, from the brigade of the celebrated General Cortlandt Skinner, a New Jersey royalist, who, with his corps of kindred spirits, had taken advantage of General Howe's gracious Proclamation of pardon, and given in their adhesion to the King.

In a letter to the Council of Safety for Pennsylvania, dated at Princeton, February 18, 1777, General Putnam thus speaks of Nelson's success, and commends the good conduct of the party:

" Yesterday evening, Colonel Nelson, with a hundred and fifty men, at Lawrence's Neck, attacked sixty men of Cortlandt Skinner's Brigade, commanded by the enemy's RENOWNED LAND-PIRATE, *Major Richard Stockton*, routed them, and took the whole prisoners. Among them the Major, a captain, and three subalterns, with seventy stands of arms. *Fifty of the Bedford, Pennsylvania, Riflemen behaved like veterans.*"

As has been already remarked, General Putnam was proverbially lenient to his prisoners, so much so as sometimes to incur the censure of those who had not learned to make the proper distinction between an armed and an unarmed foe. In the case of Major Stockton, he exercised an unusual severity, sending him to Philadelphia in irons, and ordering him to be placed in strict confinement there. The particular reason for this severe treatment does not appear in any of the official documents of the day, so far as I have had opportunity to examine them. General Washington, writing, on the 10th of March, to General Gates, then in command at Philadelphia, says, " I am informed that General Putnam sent to Philadelphia in irons, Major Stockton, taken upon the Raritan, and that he continues in strict confinement. I think we ought to avoid putting in practice, what we have so loudly complained of, the cruel treatment of prisoners. I therefore desire, that, if there is a necessity for confinement, it may be made as easy and comfortable as possible to Major Stockton and his officers. This man, I believe, has been very active and mischievous, but we took him in arms, as an officer of the enemy, and by the rules of war, we are obliged to treat him as such, and not as a felon."

General Cortlandt Skinner, and his corps, were so notorious for their cruel depredations upon the property of American citizens, that his name became a familiar appellative for that class of land-pirates, from whom the country suffered, if possible, more severely than from their British enemies, or even their mercenary German allies. The Yagers, the Cow-Boys, and the Skinners, were but different names for the three grades of lawless banditti, that prowled about the precincts of the two armies, in quest only of plunder, and reckless of the means of obtaining it. The Yagers and the Cowboys plundered both parties alike, indifferent to whom the booty belonged, so that they could secure it for their own use. The Skinners, though Americans, plundered only their own countrymen, and served the British as the dastardly jackal serves the lion. They were mere patricides, who, for British gold, sold themselves to rob the houses and fields, and cut the throats, of their more patriotic neighbors and relatives. It was this that made them so peculiarly obnoxious to our people. And it was, probably, either on account of some peculiar acts of violence and outrage that he had committed, or from some special danger to be apprehended from suffering him to go at large on his parole, that the humane General Putnam distinguished him from ordinary prisoners by a close confinement. When General Lee was made a prisoner by the British, General Howe refused to receive his parole, on the ground that he was a deserter from the British service, and should be treated rather as a traitor to his king, than as an ordinary American prisoner. If there was even a show of justice or reason in this case, it was surely no great stretch of the same general principle, to accord to any of the Skinners, and especially to Major Stockton, the distinction of irons, and a guarded cell.

Shortly after the capture of Stockton and his detachment, General Putnam received, from his scouts, intelligence of another party of foragers, sent out by Lord Cornwallis towards Bound Brook. Immediately detaching Major Smith, with a few riflemen, to hang on the rear of the party, and annoy them, till he should come up, he made his dispositions to follow, with all the little force at his command. Before he reached the ground, however, the gallant Major, eager to secure for himself the honors of the day, had laid an ambush, sprung upon and surprised the enemy, killed several of his horses, and driven him back, with the loss of several prisoners and sixteen baggage-wagons—his own little band sustaining no injury in life or limb.

A large accession of strength to the British army in Brunswick, which took place towards the latter end of February, induced General Washington to believe, that another movement towards the Delaware would soon be made, with a view to gaining possession of Philadelphia. He accordingly wrote to General Putnam, advising him of this reinforcement of the enemy, and directing him to be ever on the alert, and prepared for any movement that might take place. In case it should appear that Philadelphia was to be their object, Putnam was to cross the river at once, with such force as might be then at his disposal, assume the command of the militia, who might assemble, secure all the boats on the west side of the Delaware, and adopt every other measure that he might deem necessary, to facilitate the passage of the rest of the army, if circumstances should require them again to retire from the Jerseys ; the possession of which he, at the same time, resolved to contest, inch by inch.

But Lord Cornwallis, notwithstanding his vastly superior advantages, was in no haste to advance. The two armies retained their relative position some two months longer, undisturbed by any event of greater importance than an occasional skirmish between their foraging and scouting parties.

General Putnam continued at his post in Princeton, until near the middle of May, when a more important service was assigned him, in the northern department. During his command in New Jersey, a period of four winter months, he had, by his several parties, taken from the enemy nearly a thousand prisoners, and more than a hundred and twenty baggage wagons, besides a large amount of other valuable booty. At one time, about the first of February, in an enterprise, the details of which are not given, he took ninety-six wagons, laden with provisions, on their way to the British army.* At another, as above described, sixteen. In services of this kind, he was not excelled by any other officer in the American army. During all this period, Major Aaron Burr was attached to his staff, and lived with him as a member of his family. This singularly gifted man, though not more deficient in ambition than in gallantry and intrigue, wrote to a friend, on the 7th of March, from Princeton, remarking, that, as for promotion, he did not expect it, and hardly desired it ; and adding, as the only apparent reason for his contentment, " I am at present quite happy in the esteem and entire confidence of my good old General."

* Almon's Remembrancer. It was probably one of the expeditions under the direction of Major Davis.

CHAPTER XXII.

PUTNAM'S COMMAND IN THE HIGHLANDS.

Importance of the Highlands—Destruction of American stores at Peekskill and Danbury—Good conduct of McDougall, Arnold and Wooster—Generals Greene and Knox examine the posts in the Highlands, and advise a mode of defence—General Putnam put in command at Peekskill, with directions to carry out that plan—Obstructions in the river—Arduous labors and exposures of Putnam—Washington's opinion of his character—Desires him to surprise the enemy's post at King's Bridge—Abandons the project, and removes his camp to Middlebrook—Putnam's force greatly reduced to reinforce the main army—Reduced still further, to support General Schuyler, on the north—Doubtful movements of the enemy—Marches and countermarches of the Americans—First anniversary of the Declaration of Independence—Evacuation of Ticonderoga, and advance of Burgoyne—American force concentrated in the Highlands—Howe's clumsy attempt to deceive Washington—The latter withdraws his force again into New Jersey—Orders and countermands—Edmund Palmer, the spy, in Putnam's camp.

THE British having just organized a considerable army in the north, for which it was important to open a free communication with their centre of operations in New York, the possession of the North River, and of the passes of the Highlands, became a matter of deep interest to both parties. Washington had always foreseen the necessity of holding these passes—not only for commanding supplies from the interior of New York, and guarding the western frontier of New England, but for cutting off the communication of the enemy with their loyal supporters in

Canada. On retiring into New Jersey, near the close of the previous year, he had stationed a considerable force at Peekskill, under the command of General Heath. It was only in an extreme exigency, when it became necessary to concentrate all his force upon the one object of driving the enemy from the Jerseys, that he withdrew a considerable portion of that force, for a brief season.

The recent successful attempts of the enemy to destroy the stores collected at Peekskill, and at Danbury in Connecticut, indicated not only a watchfulness in that direction, but a purpose to force a passage that way for more extensive and important operations. In the former of these affairs, General McDougall, under the most unfavorable circumstances, had gained for himself the praise of prudent generalship. In the latter, Arnold had shown the coolness, intrepidity, and energy, for which he was conspicuous ; and the veteran Wooster, in the seventieth year of his age, had exhibited a spirit, zeal, and bravery, worthy of the best days of his youth, in attacking the retiring foe, with a few raw, undisciplined troops, hastily collected from the highways and hedges, and gallantly maintaining the conflict with vastly superior numbers, till he fell mortally wounded.

About the middle of May, Generals Greene and Knox were directed to proceed to the Highlands, and examine the river and passes, in company with Generals McDougall, George Clinton, and Wayne. They were instructed to look to the state and condition of the forts in the Highlands—especially Fort Montgomery—and to view them, both with reference to the probability of an attack by water, and the practicability of approaching them by land, and then to give such directions, as should appear to them necessary, for their greater security. Their attention was particularly directed to the pass through the Highlands, on the west side of the North River, lest the enemy should possess themselves of it by a *coup de main,* before a sufficient force could be assembled to oppose them.

Having faithfully discharged the duty assigned them, these officers made report to General Washington, recommending that the obstruction across the river at Fort Montgomery, which had already been proposed, should be completed. This was to be done by a boom, or chain, from bank to bank, in front of which should be one or two cables, to break the force of a vessel, before she should strike the chain. Two ships, and two row-galleys, were to be manned, and stationed just above this boom, in such a position as to fire advantageously upon the enemy's ships when they approached. This force, with the land batteries on the margins of the river, they supposed amply sufficient to defeat any efforts of the enemy to ascend by water. And on this they deemed it safe to rely, for the entire defence of this important pass ; remarking with confidence, that, " if the obstructions of the river could be rendered effective, the enemy would not attempt to operate by land—the passes through the Highlands being so exceedingly difficult." The result proved that this confidence was not well grounded, as fort Montgomery was afterwards assaulted and taken by a party, which penetrated the defiles of the Highlands on the west side of the river.

Arnold, who had been strangely, and, in the view of Washington, unjustly overlooked, in the recent promotions by Congress, had just received his commission as Major-General. But its date, being subsequent to those of five others who had been his juniors in rank, still left him subordinate to those whom he had once commanded. To make amends as far as he could, for this singular treatment, Washington offered him the command on the North

25

River ; which, at that juncture, was as honorable a post as any officer in the army could hold. But his private affairs calling him to Philadelphia, the place was assigned to General Putnam. He was instructed to use every means in his power for expediting and effecting the works and obstructions mentioned in the report above referred to. His attention was particularly directed to fixing the boom. This work, which was completed only with great labor and difficulty, was well suited to the ingenuity and industry of Putnam ; and no man in the service could have been better chosen to superintend and direct such a plan. To support the weight of the chain, it was necessary to place under it large rafts of timber, at small distances from each other. These, together with the chain itself, presented such obstructions to the descending current, as to raise the water several feet, by which its force was so much increased, that the chain was broken. It was soon replaced, and the recurrence of a similar accident prevented, by several of the largest sized cables being passed round the lower side of the rafts, and made fast on either shore. Some idea may be formed of the extent and difficulty of this undertaking, when it is stated, that the width of the river, at this place, is five hundred and forty yards, and that, being laid diagonally, the better to resist the current, the cables required for the service were not less than four hundred and fifty fathoms in length.*

These works were well and faithfully executed under the able guidance of General Putnam ; and it is not improbable, that the arduous labor performed here, connected with the constant exposure of his person, in and about

---

* A letter from an officer in the royal army, that removed the chain, dated Oct. 7, 1777, and published in the Pennsylvania Ledger of that year, describes the chain as near a mile in length, each link weighing sixty pounds.

the water, may have been the principal means of undermining his health, and subjecting his iron constitution to the peculiar infirmity, by which, in a little more than two years after, he was compelled, in the vigor of an otherwise green old age, to retire from the field.

On his appointment to this station, the Commander-in-chief addressed a letter to Brigadier-General McDougall, who had previously held the command there, in which he states, in a few words, some of the prominent traits in his character, as a man, and shows how truly that character was appreciated by one who had had the best possible means of proving it, under some of the most trying circumstances to which it could have been exposed. " I have ordered General Putnam to Peekskill. You are well acquainted with the old gentleman's temper ; he is active, disinterested, and open to conviction, and I, therefore, hope that, by affording him the advice and assistance which your knowledge of the post enables you to do, you will be very happy in your command under him."

To Brigadier-General Parsons he wrote, about the same time, as follows : " As I consider the defence of the fortifications and passes through the Highlands an object of the last importance, and possessing them most probably to form the chief end of the enemy's councils and immediate operations, I wish you to come to Peekskill, and there continue with the troops, till some further disposition shall become necessary." And again, on the 29th : " The passes and fortifications in the Highlands are of the last importance, and every means in our power must be employed to secure them." The troops at this post were chiefly those from New England and New York.

But it was not in raising fortifications alone, or in planning and completing obstructions to the navigation of the river, that the talents of this tried soldier and able com mander were expected to be employed. The following letter shows that he was still relied upon, as an accom-plished general, to order and execute important and deli-cate movements against the enemy.

" To Major-General Putnam.

" <i>Morristown</i>, 25 <i>May</i>, 1777.

" Dear Sir :—

" Would it be practicable, do you think, under the present circumstances and situation of the troops at Peeks-kill, to surprise the enemy at King's Bridge ? It must be effected by surprise, or not at all ; and must be undertaken by water—which would also prove abortive, if the enemy have vessels of any kind above Fort Washington. The undigested ideas which I have entertained of the matter are these : to embark a number of troops, supposed ade-quate to the enterprise, in boats, under pretence of trans-porting them and their baggage to Tappan, as a more easy and expeditious method of joining the army under my immediate command. To cover this the better, a number of wagons might be ordered to assemble at the landing on this side, in order to receive your baggage. Or, if it should be thought that moving a body of men so near the enemy would put them too much on their guard, could not the troops be embarked at Peekskill, under pretence of reinforcing the garrison on the river, in order to expe-dite the works, and actually set off as if bound thither; but, under cover of darkness, turn and push down the river ? But here, possibly, a difficulty will arise on account of the impracticability of getting down in the night, and the difficulty of being concealed in any creek or inlet on the western shore in the day. These are all mat-ters worthy of consideration, and I have nothing more in view than to lead you into a train of thinking upon the subject. Let the matter be communicated to Generals McDougall and George Clinton for their sentiments, but under strong injunctions of secresy ; for it always happens, that, where more than two or three are apprized of an undertaking of this kind, the knowledge of it gets abroad, which must immediately defeat any measure that depends upon secresy.

" The place at which I should propose your landing would be in the hollow between Fort Washington and Spiten Devil. It is a good landing place, and affords a good passage into the road leading from Fort Washington to the Bridge. It is very obscure, and would enable you to fall in upon the back of the troops at Fort Independence, by which the surprise would be greater, and their retreat cut off. Thence your troops might, or might not, march up by land, and sweep the country before them of the enemy and provisions, as circumstances would justify. After consulting the gentlemen before mentioned on the propriety of this measure, let me know the result, by a careful person, and when the plan could be conveniently carried into execution.

" I am, dear Sir,

" Your most affectionate, &c.,

" GEO. WASHINGTON."

Three days after the date of this letter, General Washington removed his camp from Morristown to Middlebrook, and the subsequent movements of General Howe requiring his utmost watchfulness and activity, the plan of surprising his outposts was, for the time, abandoned. There was no officer in the army, who would have performed a service of this kind with more alacrity or effect than General Putnam. His successes in the previous campaign in New Jersey fully demonstrated that he had lost none of the

25*

energy, promptness and skill, which had distinguished his partizan adventures in the Seven Years' War.

It was not until the 10th of June that the British army, under the immediate command of Sir William Howe, left its quarters at Brunswick. For a considerable time, the movements of that commander were so uncertain and inexplicable, as greatly to puzzle and perplex his sagacious antagonist; for, while it was necessary for him to watch every point, it was still more so, that he should be at hand to meet the blow whenever it should be struck. The preservation of Philadelphia and the Highlands were objects of equal importance and interest. The former appearing to be the first aim of the British commander, General Washington prepared to gather all his scattered forces about him, to contest the passage through the Jerseys. To this end, General Putnam was ordered on the 12th of June, to send forward Generals Parsons, McDougall, and Glover, with all the Continental troops, at Peekskill, except one thousand effective men; which number, in connection with the militia and convalescent at that post, was deemed equal to the number of the enemy then on the east side of the Hudson. The above detachments were ordered to march in three divisions, each to follow one day's march behind the other, and each of the first two divisions to be attended by two pieces of artillery.

A few days after this, while these orders were in the course of execution, intelligence was received, through a Canadian spy, of the probable advance of General Burgoyne from that quarter. To provide against this event, General Putnam was ordered still further to reduce his effective force, by holding four regiments of Massachusetts militia in readiness to go up the river at a moment's warning. He was also directed to order a sufficient number of sloops from Albany, to serve as transports for the troops.

Ever on the watch for any intelligence, which might indicate the real designs of the enemy, General Putnam was enabled, on the 30th of June, to transmit to his Commander papers of great importance, in consequence of which a new disposition was made of the American forces, and Putnam, anticipating the wishes of Washington, put a portion of his own command in readiness to meet the exigency. In reply to this communication, Washington wrote, under date of July 1st, "The intelligence, contained in the copies of the letters you transmitted, is truly important. It appears almost certain to me, that General Howe and General Burgoyne design, if possible, to unite their attack, and form a junction of their two armies. I approve much of your conduct, in ordering Nixon's brigade to be in readiness, and I desire that it may be embarked immediately, with baggage, to go for Albany, as soon as General Varnum's and General Parsons' brigades are so near Peekskill, that they can arrive to supply their place, before any troops can come up the river, and effect a landing, or as soon as a number of militia, equal to them, can be got in. It seems absolutely necessary for you to pursue the most speedy and effectual measures, to obtain a respectable reinforcement of the neighboring militia. No time is to be lost. Much may be at stake; and I am persuaded, if General Howe is going up the river, he will make a rapid and vigorous push to gain the Highland passes. You will not think of sending Glover's brigade to White Plains in the present situation of affairs."

Thus it continued during a considerable part of this perplexing season. Time was consumed, and strength and patience were tried, in marches and countermarches, which resulted in nothing but weariness. Before one order was fully executed, it was countermanded by another of an opposite character. Before the last of the three divisions ordered from Peekskill was ready to leave that post, the demand for its removal was recalled, and one of the others was on its return, in company with a fresh brigade, to reinforce the garrison, now regarded as the post of peculiar danger. General Clinton was, at the same time, urgently requested, without loss of time, to call out a considerable body of the New York militia, from the neighboring counties of Orange and Ulster, to support General Putnam, while the latter called upon those of Connecticut, to swell the reinforcement.

To meet these rapidly shifting movements, and execute skilfully these continually conflicting orders, in connection with the other arduous duties of his station, demanded a degree of activity, industry and talent, scarcely inferior to that of the Commander-in-chief, and a spirit and energy not always to be found in men of three score years.

But though the labors of the season were exceedingly arduous, and the perils of war imminent and incessant, there was occasional opportunity even with the soldier, for pastime. And Putnam, with his wonted good humor, seized every opening that would justify a little recreation for himself and his men. A fine opportunity was offered on the first anniversary of the Declaration of Independence, and liberal arrangements were made to improve it. It was celebrated with feast and song, and *feu de joie*— with eloquent speeches and patriotic toasts, in which success to the blessed cause of liberty, and confusion to all its enemies, were pledged as heartily and truly as they have ever been by their successors. The concluding scene of that day's sport was peculiar and emphatic. On the top of one of the rugged eminences that overhang the Hudson, in the vicinity of his post, Putnam had discovered an immense rock, of several hundred tons weight, so perfectly

First Celebration of the 4th of July in the Highlands.   PAGE 297.

poised in its rest, that a comparatively small power, well applied, would destroy its balance, and send it thundering down into the dark ravine below.

Having made his preparations, he drew up a handsome detachment of his force upon the height, accompanied by his principal officers, in full uniform, when, after an animated and amusing address, he gave orders for the lever to be manned. The mighty mass trembled and quivered, and fell with a tremendous crash, accompanied by a simultaneous discharge from the whole corps, and immediately followed by the thunder of the artillery and heavy guns in forts, whose echoes bellowed and reverberated a long time from the heights and cliffs around. As the huge rock toppled from its old resting place, one party of the officers on one side of it, shouted in admirable unison—" So may the thrones of tyrants fall !"   And when it settled into its new bed below, the other responded—" So may the enemies of freedom sink to rise no more !"

The danger from the north becoming more imminent, by the evacuation of Ticonderoga and its dependencies, and the consequent advance of Burgoyne to the vicinity of the Hudson, Putnam was ordered to furnish General Schuyler with still further aid, including ten pieces of artillery, with the proper officers to direct in their use, and a considerable quantity of powder and ball.

The following order to his aide-de-camp, Major Burr, appears under date of the 14th July:

" Pursuant to orders from his Excellency, General Washington, you are forthwith to repair to Norwalk, Fairfield, and other places, adjacent on the Sound, and to transmit to me intelligence of the movements of the enemy.   On your return you will pass through Litchfield, and leave orders for all detachments of any regiments of Nixon's brigade, to take the most direct route to Albany.

"ISRAEL PUTNAM."

In the meantime, General Washington, with the army under his command, was gradually moving up towards the Highlands, on the western side of the Hudson, and, by the middle of July, had advanced, by way of Pompton Plains, as far as the Clove, a narrow passage leading through the mountains, about eighteen miles from the river—near the entrance of which he fixed his camp. From this place, General Sullivan and Lord Stirling, with their divisions, were successively sent across the river, to swell the already formidable force of General Putnam, the main body being held in reserve, to operate on either shore, as the movements of the enemy should require.

Having, on the 20th, in consequence of information, which proved to be premature, advanced eleven miles within the Clove, General Washington addressed an earnest letter to Putnam, requesting the most accurate and detailed account of the movements and designs of the enemy, both by sea and by land, his present position being in the highest degree embarrassing and perilous. Putnam had, in the meantime, despatched General Sullivan, and other trusty and intelligent persons, to various points of the river, and the coast, to obtain such intelligence as could be safely relied on. Having by this means ascertained, beyond a doubt, that the British fleet, with a large number of troops on board, had passed the Hook, and put out to sea, the army returned into New Jersey, and prepared to oppose, with all its force, the meditated movement upon Philadelphia. General Sullivan, and Lord Stirling, with their divisions, were immediately detached by General Putnam, in the same direction, accompanied by all the

field-pieces at Peekskill, except two pieces for each brigade that remained for the defence of that post.

The next day, he received orders to " keep as many of
his remaining troops, as could possibly be spared from the
defence of the forts and passes of the Highlands, in the
most perfect readiness to move, either to the southward or
to the eastward, as occasion should require.   I do not pretend," continued the letter, " to fix upon the number
which may be necessary for those defences.   You and
your officers must determine this point, proportioning your
defence to the troops left by General Howe on York Island.
If you have not already done it, let the eastern States be
immediately advised of the fleet's sailing from the Hook,
that they may be in a posture of defence, as no person can
with certainty say where the blow will be struck."

At this critical juncture, an attempt was made to blind
the eyes of Washington as to the real movements of the
enemy.   A young American, who had been a prisoner in
New York, was employed to convey a letter from General
Howe to General Burgoyne, with the apparent design of
notifying the latter of the intended movements of the former.   The messenger—whether in obedience to his instructions, or not, does not appear, but certainly in accordance
with the wishes of the writer—immediately hastened to
Peekskill, and delivered up the letter to General Putnam,
by whom, after perusal, it was communicated to the Commander-in-chief.   It was in the handwriting of General
Howe, and read as follows :

                    " *New York*, 20 *July*, 1777.

" Dear Sir,
        " I have received your letter of the 14th of May from
Quebec, and shall fully observe its contents.   The expedition to B——n [Boston] will take the place of that up

the North River. If, according to my expectations, we may succeed rapidly in the possession of B., the enemy having no force of consequence there, I shall, without loss of time, proceed to coöperate with you in the defeat of the rebel army opposed to you. Clinton is sufficiently strong to amuse Washington and Putnam. I am now making demonstrations to the southward, which I think will have the full effect in carrying our plan into execution. Success attend you.

" W. HOWE."

It was a clumsy plan, and clumsily executed; and produced no other impression on the mind either of Washington or Putnam, than to establish, beyond a doubt, the design upon Philadelphia, and hasten the march of the forces in that direction.

Notwithstanding this decisive movement, and the concentrated interest which it created towards the capital of Pennsylvania, the posts in the Highlands were still deemed so important, and the necessity of the possession of them by the British, in order to a junction of their two armies, seemed so manifest and urgent, that Washington, to use his own expression, " could not help casting his eyes continually behind him." That they might not be left too much exposed, General Sullivan's division was ordered to halt at Morristown, and be in readiness to return, at a moment's warning, if necessary.

On the arrival of the enemy's fleet at the Cape of Delaware, General Putnam was directed to send forward two other brigades, which he had already, in anticipation of the demand, transported across the river, and put in readiness for instant departure. The deficiency thus created in his own garrison, now reduced to two thousand Continental troops, he was requested, if possible, to supply by immediate requisitions upon the militia of Connecticut and New York.

The very next day, August 1st, in consequence of a new *ruse* on the part of the enemy's fleet, all these orders were countermanded, and General Sullivan's division, with the two brigades on the western bank of the Hudson, were directed immediately to return and recross the river, while the main body of the army prepared to follow with all possible expedition. Says Washington, in his letter to General Putnam, on this occasion, "The importance of preventing General Howe's getting possession of the Highlands by a *coup-de-main*, is infinite to America ; and, in the present situation of things, every effort that can be thought of, must be used."

By this continual marching and countermarching, in the hottest season of the year, the American troops were more harassed, than by all the fatigues and duties of the campaign, and many of them became so discouraged and disgusted with the service, as to embrace every opportunity to desert.

On the third of August, Sir Henry Clinton, who had recently returned from England, and now commanded the British forces in the City of New York, sent up a flag of truce to General Putnam, at Peekskill. Edmund Palmer, a lieutenant in a regiment of American Tories, had been detected in the American camp, in disguise as a spy, and the object of the flag was to claim him as an officer in the British service. The message, accompanying it, expatiated upon the heinous crime of bringing to an ignominious death, by execution, a man bearing his Majesty's commission, and threatened signal vengeance, in case of such a violation of his person. The flag was taken up the river to Verplank's Point, by Captain Montagu, in the ship Mercury, and thence forwarded to the camp. General

Putnam instantly returned the following characteristic reply :

" Head Quarters, 7 August, 1777.

" Edmund Palmer, an officer in the enemy's service, was taken as a spy, lurking within our lines ; he has been tried as a spy, condemned as a spy, and shall be executed as a spy, and the flag is ordered to depart immediately.

" ISRAEL PUTNAM.

" P. S. He has accordingly been executed."

In the meantime, Burgoyne was advancing on the north, and the army in that quarter stood greatly in need of reinforcements. General Putnam's post at Peekskill was the only one from which such aid could be immediately sent Washington, addressing him on the subject, on the 7th of August, remarks, " I would not wish to weaken you, as the enemy seem to bend their course again towards ·you. I desire that you, and the general officers, would consider the matter fully, and, if you think that you can spare Cortlandt's and Livingston's regiments, they may be put in readiness to move." He also recommended highly the plan, in which Putnam was engaged, of fortifying, by various works of defence, the entrance to the passes in the vicinity of his post.

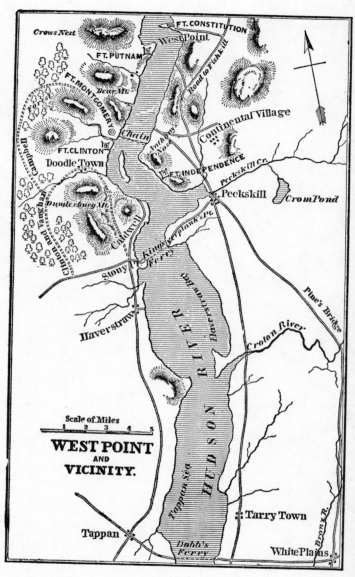

Crows Nest

FT. CONSTITUTION

West Point

FT. PUTNAM

Road to Fishkill

Bear Mt.

FT. MONTGOMERY

Forts

Continental Village

Chain

Anthony's Nose

FT. CLINTON

FT. INDEPENDENCE

Doodle Town

Peekskill Cr.

Campbell

Peekskill

Crom Pond

Dunderburg Mt.

Clinton and Vaughan

Caldwell

Stony Pt.

Kings Ferry

Verplank's Pt.

Pine's Bridge

Haverstraw

Haverstraw Bay

Croton River

HUDSON RIVER

Scale of Miles
1 2 3 4 5

WEST POINT
AND
VICINITY.

Tappan Sea

:. Tarry Town

Bronx R.

Tappan

Dobb's Ferry

White Plains.

Page 303.

CHAPTER XXIII.

Extent of Putnam's command—Relative position of the forts—Plans
an attempt on the posts of the enemy—His force greatly reduced—
Sir Henry Clinton in New Jersey—Detachments for the main
army delayed—Peremptory order to hasten their march—Militia
of little service—Sir Henry Clinton in Haverstraw Bay—Favored
by circumstances—Lands at Tarrytown—at Verplank's Point—at
Stony Point—covered by a dense fog—Diverts General Putnam
from his main object—Gains the rear of Forts Montgomery and
Clinton—His advance resisted—Severe action—Gallant assault—
Putnam orders a reinforcement—Works carried—Escape of part
of the garrison—Putnam retires to Fishkill—Frigates burnt—
British advance, burning villages and houses—Hearing of the
surrender of Burgoyne, they return again to New York—Death of
Mrs. Putnam—Peekskill retaken—Comments upon the late dis-
asters.

SIR HENRY CLINTON'S object in sending the unfortunate
Lieutenant Palmer into Putnam's camp, was to obtain
accurate knowledge of the condition of that post, and the
force stationed there, with a view to turning his arms
against it. This General Washington fully expected, and,
accordingly, wrote to General Putnam, on the 11th of
August, as follows: "If General Clinton is left upon York
Island, with the number of men you mention, it is probably
to attack you below, while Burgoyne comes down upon
you. It is a matter of great consequence to ascertain that
fact. I beg you will use every method to come at the

knowledge of his force." This duty Putnam faithfully fulfilled, and obtained, by means of his spies, accurate information respecting the strength of the garrison in New York; which he intended, if Providence should favor his plans, soon to turn to good account.

General Putnam's command embraced the fortified posts in the Highlands, on both sides of the river. His head-quarters were at Peekskill, on the eastern side. Forts Montgomery and Clinton were situated on the western side—the former in the township of Cornwall, the latter in Monroe—being separated from each other by Poplopen Kill, a narrow stream, which runs down from the mountains in their rear. These forts were placed on very high ground, so that they could not be safely stormed in front; and, being deemed—as was stated in the report of Generals Knox and Greene—inaccessible in the rear, were considered, in the ordinary acceptation of the term, impregnable.* They were garrisoned chiefly by the militia of New York, who, to the number of about six hundred, were then under the immediate command of General George Clinton, Governor of the State; of whom General Washington remarked, in reference to his command at this post: "There cannot be a more proper man upon every account."

Fort Independence was just under Anthony's Nose, about three miles below forts Montgomery and Clinton, and on the opposite side of the river. It was situated on a high point of land, in the town of Cortland, Westchester County. Fort Constitution was rather more than six miles

---

* The mountains which commence five or six miles below these forts, are so high and rugged, the defiles, through which the roads leading to them pass, so narrow, and so commanded by the heights on both sides, that the approaches to them are exceedingly difficult and dangerous.--MARSHALL.

above them, on an island, near the eastern shore. Peeks-kill Village, the general Head-Quarters of the officer commanding at the station, was about two miles below Fort Independence, with a considerable creek, or inlet, between them, into which two respectable streams flowed from the north and east. The latter, being Peeks' Kill, gives its name to the village, which is included in the town of Cortland. Continental Village, where most of the stores were deposited, was situated on high ground, in the rear of Fort Independence, and about two miles north of Peeks-kill, on the road to Fort Constitution. It was a military settlement only—its population being made up of those artizans, mechanics, and other laborers, who were employed about the various works connected with the army.

Having a very respectable force under his command, and being encouraged by Governor Trumbull to expect large reinforcements of militia from Connecticut, for that purpose, General Putnam formed a plan for a very important blow upon the enemy's posts. He had informed himself accurately of their force, and the condition of their defences at Staten Island, Paulus Hook (Jersey City), York Island, and Long Island, and was making his arrangements for a simultaneous assault upon all these posts. Extensive preparations were making for carrying this plan into execution. In the view of his counsellors, who were able and judicious men, the position of the enemy justified the attempt. Success, which was probable, would be attended with the happiest consequences, by wrenching from the enemy all that he had hitherto gained, and getting possession of an immense amount of valuable stores of every description. This plan, which was formed early in September, was in very promising progress, when the demands for reinforcements to the main army became so urgent, that it was necessary to abandon it for a season

26*

About a month later, a similar attempt, upon a smaller scale, was suggested to Putnam, by the Commander-in-chief, and a movement in that direction was made, the details of which will be given in its appropriate place.

General Sullivan's division was held *in medio*, at Morristown, till the British fleet returned into the Chesapeake. They were then ordered to join the main army on the Delaware. General McDougall was also immediately ordered down from Peekskill, as well as General Dickinson from New Jersey.

The State of New Jersey becoming defenceless by the withdrawal of the main army to Pennsylvania, Sir Henry Clinton seized that opportunity for effecting an incursion into the country. His troops landed, in four divisions—at Elizabethtown Point, Schuyler's Landing on the Hackensack River, Fort Lee, and Tappan—approaching, at this last point, the vicinity of General Putnam. The object was to drive off the cattle, and to attack any small party of the enemy that might be met with ; as it was known that, in the divided state of the American army, no force of much magnitude could at this time be in Jersey. The number of troops engaged in the enterprise amounted to more than two thousand.

Colonel Malcom's regiment, then stationed at Ramapo, just below the entrance of the Clove, watched their motions, but was not in force to offer much resistance. A party of that regiment, under command of Lieutenant-Colonel Burr, who had just been promoted to that rank, and who was eager to be engaged in some active enterprise, was sent down to collect intelligence, and to prevent the ravages of the enemy's small detachments. There was also some skirmishing with the militia of the several places through which they passed. The enemy lost, in this way, eight killed, and eighteen wounded ; and, according to the account of their own commander, seventeen were taken prisoners.

As soon as General Putnam received intelligence of this movement, he ordered General McDougall to cross the river, with fifteen hundred men, and advance to meet them. The order was obeyed, but not in time to overtake the enemy, who were already retiring with their booty.

This incursion caused great alarm in New Jersey, and rendered it necessary for General Dickinson to leave behind him one thousand of the militia, who were intended to reinforce the army of Washington ; while it occasioned some delay, on the part of Putnam, in forwarding the detachments ordered from Peekskill—the necessity of meeting and resisting the hostile movements of the enemy in his own immediate vicinity, being supposed paramount to any order from his superior, issued in ignorance of those movements.

The situation of the main army on the Delaware being critical in the extreme, a further order upon General Putnam was issued, on the 23d of September, requiring from him a further detachment of sixteen hundred men, under General Varnum. This was to include the regiment of Colonel Malcom, which had been posted in the Clove, to guard the passes to the forts on the west bank of the river. In consequence of the previous delay in forwarding the expected reinforcements, Washington concludes his letter thus : " That you may not hesitate about complying with this order, you are to consider it peremptory, and not to be dispensed with." Putnam was, at the same time, required, for the protection of his own post, and the passes in the Highlands, to call in all his outposts, and, if threatened with an attack, to get what aid he could from the militia.

These orders being obeyed, General Putnam's force

was reduced to fifteen hundred—three hundred of whom were militia, on whom no dependence could be placed. Many of those who had been sent in to reinforce this post, had deserted, and others became so restive and uneasy that the General, who well knew of how little value they would be to the service, if compelled to remain against their will, suffered them to depart. The three hundred who remained, were but little better than men of straw. They would answer to count, when it was necessary to make a fair show of numbers ; but could not *be counted upon,* in the hour of danger.

Knowing what heavy drafts had been made upon the Highland fortresses, and having himself received considerable reinforcements from Europe, Sir Henry Clinton resolved to avail himself of the opportunity to attack them with the flower of his force, and thus, if possible, break a way through to the assistance of Burgoyne. He had an eye also, in this expedition, to the extensive and valuable military stores collected in the Highlands. Accordingly, with a force of between three and four thousand men, he sailed up the North River, and made his appearance on the 5th of October, in Tarrytown Bay.

Everything combined to favor the movement of the British in this case. The forces of the Americans, which were not more than half those of the enemy, were necessarily divided between four points—two on each side of the river, and separated miles from each other. All of these must be guarded alike—the most important, as well as the most exposed, being those on the east side, which covered the military stores and provisions for the army. While, therefore, it was incumbent on Putnam to have his eye upon all these points at once, with a view to adapt his defence to the attack, Clinton fixed his attention upon one only, and concentrated his whole force upon that—

only making such demonstrations towards the opposite side, as to mask his real designs. This is ever the advantage of him who takes the offensive attitude ; that, by a well managed feint, he can withdraw the strength of his enemy from the post where he intends to strike his decisive blow. By this means, General Clinton succeeded, on this occasion—being remarkably favored in the operation by a heavy fog, which hung over the river, and concealed the greater part of his movements from the view of his adversary.

After some manœuvring in the bay, he landed his whole force at Tarrytown, whence he marched about five miles up the country, with no other object but to mislead and divert his enemy, and then returned at night to the landing. Embarking again the next morning, he proceeded up the river to King's Ferry, and made another landing at Verplanck's Point, about three miles below Peekskill ; upon which General Putnam retired to the fortified heights in his rear, covering the Continental Village. In the evening of the same day, a part of these troops re-embarked, and the fleet moved up to Peekskill Neck, in order to mask their movements at King's Ferry, which was below them. The next morning, at break of day, large detachments of more than two thousand men, destined for an enterprise against the fortifications on the western side, landed at Stony Point, just opposite to Verplanck's Point, and commenced their march through the mountains, into the rear of Forts Clinton and Montgomery. This disembarkation was observed on the other side, but the state of the atmosphere was such that no estimate could be formed of its numbers. A large fire which was soon afterwards perceived at the landing place, led to the belief that it was only a small party, detached for the purpose of destroying the store-houses on that side. The manœuvres of the vessels confirmed this suspicion; and the troops remaining at Verplanck's Point, whose numbers, though they could not be correctly ascertained, were nearly if not quite equal to his own, fully satisfied General Putnam that the meditated attack was to be directed against Fort Independence. His whole attention was, accordingly, turned that way, and every preparation was immediately made for a resolute defence.

The enemy remaining quiet at Verplanck's Point, and Putnam not being able to gain from his pickets and scouts any satisfactory report of their numbers or apparent designs, he went down, in company with Brigadier-General Parsons, and Adjutant-General Root, to reconnoitre their position in person.

In the meantime, the detachments which had landed at Stony Point in the morning, were pursuing their march towards the rear of the mountain fortresses. Long before the fog had cleared away from the bank, they were lost to the view of those who were eagerly watching for them on the other side, and who now supposed they had returned to the ships, having accomplished their object of burning the storehouses. Avoiding the Clove, which they supposed too well defended to be forced, they filed off to the west, and passing to the rear of Dunderberg, began to climb the rugged and difficult passes toward Fort Clinton. Leaving a battalion at the pass of Dunderberg, to protect his rear, and keep open the communication with the river, Sir Henry Clinton formed his army into two divisions. One, consisting of nine hundred men, commanded by Lieutenant-Colonel Campbell, made a circuit by the forest of Deane, in the rear of Bear's Hill, in order to fall on the back of Fort Montgomery. The other, consisting of twelve hundred men, commanded by General Vaughan, and accompanied by Sir Henry Clinton in person, advanced slowly towards Fort Clinton, intending so to time their movements, as to make their attacks simultaneously upon both fortresses.

General George Clinton, apprehending from the movements below, that an attack on his position was intended, had despatched Major Logan, on the evening of Sunday, the 5th, to gain intelligence. He returned·on Monday morning, and reported the landing of a considerable body of troops at the Point, but so dense was the fog, that he was not able to form any judgment of their numbers. Lieutenant Jackson was immediately despatched with a small party, on the Haverstraw road, to watch their motions. He had not proceeded more than two miles, when he was attacked by a party in ambuscade, at a place called Doodletown. Returning their fire with spirit, he fell back toward the fort. As soon as the firing was heard, a hundred men were ordered out to sustain him. They were all soon engaged in a brisk retreating skirmish with the superior numbers of the enemy, disputing their advance inch by inch, though too weak entirely to repulse them. Their gallant opposition, and the roughness of the ground, checked the progress of the enemy for a considerable time.

Meanwhile, the party under Lieutenant-Colonel Campbell was advancing, through the forest road, to the rear of Fort Montgomery. A party of one hundred and twenty men, accompanied by a single field-piece, which was all the artillery in the fort, was ordered out to meet them, in the hope of being able to hold them in check, until a reinforcement, which had been sent for, should arrive from Peekskill. From the advantageous position of this little party, they were enabled to do immense execution upon the enemy, who were several times driven back in his desperate attempts to gain the pass. At length, filing off through the woods, upon the right and left, they were about to surround the Spartan band, when, perceiving their danger, they made good their retreat to the fort.

It was now about two o'clock in the afternoon ; and the enemy, in full force, approached the works, and began a furious assault, which continued about three hours. At five o'clock, a flag was sent up, to demand a surrender, in order to prevent the further effusion of blood. A spirited refusal was returned, and the attack was renewed. The defence was ably sustained until the dusk of the evening, when the enemy, by the superiority of their numbers, forced the works on all sides, the garrison being too small to man the lines in their whole extent.

Through the treachery of the messenger, who had been despatched early in the day, to solicit a reinforcement from General Putnam, the message did not reach that officer ; and he was wholly unacquainted with the movements of the enemy on the western side of the river, and the perilous exposure of his friends there, until it was announced by the report of musketry and cannon in the first onset. He was then on his return from Verplanck's Point, whither he had gone in person, as before stated, to obtain certain intelligence of the numbers and position of the enemy. He hastened back with all speed, to order a suitable detachment to their support. In this he was partially anticipated by the promptness and decision of his Aid, Major Humphreys, who, being alone at Head Quarters when the firing commenced, hastened to Colonel Wyllys, then the senior officer in camp, and earnestly advised him, without waiting for orders from the General, to despatch all the men not on duty to Fort Montgomery. Five hundred men were instantly ordered on this service, under the command of the gallant Colonel Meigs, and were ready to march when General Putnam arrived. They were hurried forward with all possible despatch, having five or six miles to march to the place of debarkation. But it was too late. Major Humphreys, in company with Dr. Beardsley, a surgeon in his brigade, rode at full speed through a by-path to the river, to give notice to the garrison that a reinforcement was on its march. But, notwithstanding all their exertions, they did not reach the fort, till it was so completely invested, that it was impossible to enter ; and they had the misfortune to be idle, though not unconcerned spectators of the storm.

The works being carried, General Clinton, with a considerable number of his officers and men, who were well acquainted with the ground, were so fortunate as to effect their escape, under cover of the night, and to reach the other side of the river, where they found the reinforcement in the act of passing over for their relief. The loss sustained by both the garrisons, in killed, wounded and prisoners, was about two hundred and fifty, more than one third of their whole number. That of the enemy was about two hundred killed and wounded.

Governor Clinton arrived at Peekskill about an hour before midnight. A council was immediately called, in which it was decided to be impossible to maintain the post, against the superior numbers that would undoubtedly be brought down upon it the next day. It was consequently determined to retire with the troops to Fishkill, a strong post about twelve miles up the river, and to commence immediately the removal of the stores.

The Continental frigates, which had been stationed above for the defence of the chain, were ordered down for that purpose, by General Putnam, as soon as the manœuvres of the enemy's ships indicated a purpose to ascend. It being no longer possible to defend the chain, after the loss of the forts, the frigates were burned, lest they should

27

fall into the enemy's hands. The boom and chain were soon after removed by the British, and their ships, having nothing to obstruct their passage, moved up the river.

The forts on the east side having been evacuated immediately after the battle, as untenable against such a superior force, a large detachment of the British, which had been all the day previous resting at Verplanck's Point, under the command of General Tryon, marched up and reduced Continental Village to ashes, with several dwelling-houses and other public buildings at Peekskill—having first secured the valuable stores, which it had been necessary to leave behind. Another detachment, under General Vaughan, proceeded up the river, about thirty miles, to Esopus, a little below Kingston, on the western shore, which they also destroyed—laying waste in their progress many of the scattered dwellings, mills, and stores, of the defenceless inhabitants. The same was done at Livingston's Manor, and several other places. This wanton and useless destruction of private property, instead of striking terror—as they designed it should—into the hearts of the rebels, reacted powerfully against the royal cause, and gave a keenness to the resentment of the injured party, which outlasted many years the contest between the two nations.*

* It would be neither just nor judicious to charge upon the British nation an unusual want of humanity in the conduct of their wars. Yet there are many such scenes as this recorded against them in every part of the world. There was another circumstance, connected with the battle above described, which reflects but little honor on the victors at Fort Montgomery. While they gave to their own killed a decent soldier's burial, the Americans left upon the bloody field were thrown in heaps, like so much carrion, into a pool in the rear of the fort. Dr. Dwight who, in company with several officers, visited the spot in May, seven months after the battle, thus describes the painful scene which greeted them there : " The first object which met our eyes,

The purpose of General Vaughan's expedition was to form a junction with General Burgoyne, whom he hoped to meet at Albany. But having, instead of that, encountered, at some distance below Albany, the disagreeable and astounding intelligence of the surrender of that officer, with his whole army, the British general retired hastily down the river, abandoning all the advantages he had gained at so much cost to his enemy. Forts Montgomery and Constitution were entirely demolished, and fleet and army returned to New York, in twenty days after the battle.

When General Vaughan went up the river, General Putnam detached one division of his force, under Governor Clinton, to follow him on the west side, while he proceeded with the other, on the east side, to prevent their landing, and committing ravages in the country. He had advanced as far as Red Hook, about thirty miles, when, the enemy commencing his retreat, he returned to his

after we had left our barge and ascended the bank, was the remains of a fire, kindled by the cottagers of this solitude, for the purpose of consuming the bones of some of the Americans, who had fallen at this place, and had been left unburied. Some of these bones were lying, partially consumed, round the spot where the fire had been kindled; and some had evidently been converted to ashes. As we went onward, we were distressed by the fœtor of decayed human bodies. As we were attempting to discover the source from which it proceeded, we found, at a small distance from Fort Montgomery, a pond of a moderate size, in which we saw the bodies of several men, who had been killed in the assault upon the fort. They were thrown into this pond, the preceding autumn, by the British, when, probably, the water was sufficiently deep to cover them. Some of them were covered at this time; but at a depth so small, as to leave them distinctly visible. Others had an arm, a leg, or a part of the body, above the surface. The clothes which they wore when they were killed, were still on them, and proved that they were militia, being the ordinary dress of farmers."

post at Fishkill. The plan of this movement was communicated to General Gates, who, having nearly completed the terms of capitulation with Burgoyne, replied : " I shall now have nothing but General Clinton to think of. If you keep pace with him on one side, the Governor on the other, and I in front, I cannot see how he is to get home again."

It was in the midst of these stirring and absorbing scenes, when heavily burdened with public cares, and overwhelmed with the calamities which had befallen him in his official capacity, as Commander in the Highlands, that General Putnam was called again to experience the heaviest of domestic afflictions, in the loss of his wife. She died at his quarters, about a week after his removal to Fishkill ; and it is not improbable that her death was hastened, if not procured, by the exposure, inconvenience and fatigue, incident to this sudden change. General Washington, writing to him on the 19th of October, thus alludes to this severe bereavement : " I am extremely sorry for the death of Mrs. Putnam, and sympathize with you upon the occasion. Remembering that all must die, and that she had lived to an honorable age, I hope you will bear the misfortune with that fortitude and complacency of mind that become a man and a Christian

"I am, dear Sir, with great esteem, yours, &c.,
    " GEORGE WASHINGTON."

In the same despatch, which communicated these afflictive tidings to the Commander-in-chief, General Putnam announced the surrender of Burgoyne, and the retaking of Peekskill and the Highland passes on the east side of the river. His force had, in the meantime, been swelled by reinforcements of militia to six thousand. " Last Monday," he writes, " General Parsons, with about two thousand troops, marched down and took possession of Peeks-

kill, and the passes in the Highlands. . Yesterday, about
forty sail passed up the river crowded with troops, and are
at anchor above Poughkeepsie—the wind not favoring.
We were on our march after them, when I met the agreeable intelligence of the surrender of General Burgoyne—a
copy of which is enclosed.* I thereupon most sincerely
congratulate your Excellency. I have halted my troops,
and am now considering what ought to be my movement.
I have sent to Governor Clinton for his opinion, and ordered General Parsons to spare no pains to find out the situation and strength of the garrison at King's Bridge, in order
to direct my future operations most advantageously."

Rev. Dr. Dwight, then one of the most promising
young divines in the country, was at this time a chaplain
in the army, and attached to the brigade under General
Parsons. On Sunday, the 19th, the day after the receipt
of the cheering intelligence of the surrender of Burgoyne,
he preached a sermon at Head-Quarters from this text—
" I will remove far off from you the northern army."
Joel ii., 20. It was, of course, an excellent and eloquent
discourse, and, in the excitement of so interesting an occasion, gave infinite satisfaction to his hearers, the officers
and soldiers of the army. Putnam, in particular, who
was greatly attached to the preacher, was highly delighted
with it, and did not fail to show his pleasure, by expressive
looks and motions, during the progress of the service. On
leaving the church, he was very earnest in commending
the preacher's eloquence, and the remarkable appropriate-
ness of his discourse ; declaring, at the same time, that

* Washington received the first intelligence of this important
event from General Putnam. General Gates sent a copy of the
capitulation to him, and despatched a special messenger to communi-
cate the tidings to Congress, but gave no notice whatever of the
affair to the Commander-in-chief.

27*

there was no such text in the Bible, and the good minister
had been guilty of a pious fraud, in making up one for the
occasion.   It was not until the Bible was produced, and
the passage read by his own eyes, that he yielded the
point—adding, as he did so, " There is everything in that
book, and Dwight knows just where to lay his finger
on it."

General Clinton, in his despatch to General Washington,
informing him of the loss of Forts Montgomery and Clinton, concluded with the following remarks : " I have only
to add, that, where great losses are sustained, however
unavoidable, public censure is generally the consequence
to those who are immediately concerned.   If in the present instance this should be the case, I wish, so far as
relates to Fort Montgomery and its dependencies, it may
fall on me alone ; for I should be guilty of the greatest
injustice, were I not to declare, that the officers and men
under me, of the different corps, behaved with the greatest
spirit and bravery."

The censure did *not* fall on him alone.   General Put
nam received a large share of it, as well as the whole of
that which referred to the loss of the posts and valuables
on the east side.   The circumstances detailed above, which
have been collected with great care from the most reliable
sources, would seem to exonerate him from all blame.
In his own post, he waited with prudence and firmness an
expected attack, and would undoubtedly have resisted it
to the last, if it had been made.   To have attacked General Tryon at Verplanck's Point, whose numbers were fully
equal to his own, would have been to expose his defences
to the main body of the British, whom he supposed to be
still on board their ships in the river, aiming at those defences.   That he was deceived by their manœuvres, especially in the then state of the atmosphere, was his misfor-

tune, and not his fault.   Other able and judicious officers, who were with him, were equally deceived.

That he did not anticipate an attack in the rear of the western forts, and was surprised by it when it was made, indicated no want of that prudent consideration and watchfulness, which are essential requisites to the character of a great commander.   An attack from that quarter had been judged utterly impracticable by the able committee* of officers who had examined the ground, a few months before.   " We are very confident," say they, in their report, " that the enemy will not attempt to operate by land, the passes through the Highlands are so exceedingly difficult." This opinion is fully confirmed by the reports of the British officers, who were engaged in this daring and difficult enterprise.   A letter from one of them to his friend in London, published in Almon's Remembrancer, speaks feelingly of " the very many and extraordinary difficulties of this march over the mountains," and declares that they were obliged to contend with " every natural obstruction, and all that art could add to them."   The movements on that side of the river were not seen by General Putnam, nor reported to him.   As soon as the detachments had filed off from the landing, they were screened from his view by the mountains.

As soon as he was made aware of the real designs of the enemy, he hastened to do all in his power to defeat them ; and but for the distance, and the difficulty of crossing the river, would, in all probability, have been successful.   General Clinton says, " I can assure your Excellency, that I am well convinced, if night had not approached rather too fast to correspond with our wishes, the enemy would have been disappointed in his expectations, as a reinforcement of five hundred men from General Putnam's

* See page 291.

army, were at the east side of the river, ready to pass for our relief, when the works were forced."

Marshall says, "The whole force under General Putnam did not much exceed two thousand." This includes six hundred in the forts on the west side, and two hundred at the Clove, from which Colonel Malcom's regiment had been withdrawn by Washington's orders. "Yet this force," he continues, "*though far inferior to that which General Washington had ordered to be retained at the station*, was, if properly applied, more than competent to the defence of the forts against any numbers which could be spared from New York. To insure success, it was necessary to draw the attention of Putnam from the real object, and to storm the works before the garrisons could be aided by his army. This Sir Henry Clinton accomplished."

In reference to the above passage in Italics, it will be remembered, that the Commander-in-chief, on withdrawing the greater part of the forces from Peekskill, to aid his own operations on the Delaware, had directed General Putnam, " in case he was threatened with an attack, to get what aid he could from the militia." On the arrival of reinforcements to Sir Henry Clinton from Europe, this aid was immediately called for. But, to use the words of Governor Clinton, who was on the spot, " It being a critical time with the yeomanry, and as they had not yet sown their grain, and there being at that time no appearance of the enemy, they were extremely restless and uneasy. They solicited General Putnam for leave to return, and *many of them went home without his permission.* Urged by these considerations, he thought proper to dismiss a part of them." As they were New York militia, brought there by the order of Governor Clinton, who commanded in person at Fort Montgomery, it is not reasonable to suppose that they were discharged without his consent and approval. In speaking of it, he nowhere expresses or implies the slightest censure upon his superior. A subsequent order was issued by Governor Clinton for a portion of these militia to return ; but, before they could arrive, the post was lost.

With regard to the propriety of abandoning the posts on the east side of the river, and retiring to Fishkill, it was determined on in council, and has never been called in question by any respectable authority. Washington never expressed any dissatisfaction with the conduct of Putnam on this occasion. On hearing of the landing of the enemy at Verplanck's Point, he remarked, in a letter to Governor Livingston, of New Jersey, "This circumstance is somewhat alarming, as the situation of our affairs this way, has obliged us to draw off so large a part of our force from Peekskill, that *what now remains there may perhaps prove inadequate to the defence of it.*" It will be seen hereafter that a Court of Inquiry, ordered by Congress to investigate this case, reported, that the loss was occasioned by want of men, and not by any fault in the commanders. This want of men, Putnam had used every means in his power to supply. " He had repeatedly informed the Commander-in-chief," says Humphreys, " that the posts committed to his charge must, in all probability, be lost, in case an attempt should be made upon them ; and that, circumstanced as he was, he could not be responsible for the consequences." General Washington, in replying to Clinton's despatch, said, " I had the greatest hopes that General Putnam would draw in as many Connecticut militia, as would replace the Continental troops, and I make no doubt but he did all in his power to obtain them in time." Aid of this kind could not be drawn in at a moment's warning, to such an extent as to render essential service.

And, at this particular time, the orders had gone out for reinforcements of militia, and some detachments were on the march, but did not reach the post, till it had fallen into the hands of the enemy.

CHAPTER XXIV.

IMMEDIATELY after the defeat of Burgoyne, large detachments, no longer needed at the north, were sent forward to Peekskill, until General Putnam's force, exclusive of the militia from New York and Connecticut, amounted to nearly nine thousand men. Before General Washington had received full advices of the important movements in the north, he suggested to General Putnam, by letter, the propriety of an attempt to cut off the retreat of Sir Henry Clinton to New York, and to get possession of the city ; expressing entire confidence in his (Putnam's) judgment and ability to pursue the most proper and efficacious means to secure the end.

Although the British General had already secured his retreat to New York, General Putnam immediately called a council of his principal officers, in which it was unanimously determined, agreeably to the suggestions of the Commander-in-chief, that four thousand men should move down the west side of the Hudson, and take post near Haverstraw ; that one thousand should be retained in the Highlands, to guard the country and repair the works ; and that the remainder, under command of General Putnam, should march down on the east side of the river, towards King's Bridge. The object proposed by this disposition of the forces was to cause a diversion of the enemy in New York, and prevent a reinforcement being sent to General Howe ; and it was doubtless an ulterior purpose to attack the city, should a favorable opportunity present itself.

General Dickinson, at the same time, and with the same object in view, proposed a similar plan, in which he expected the co-operation of Putnam. This plan also Washington highly commended, and urged its immediate execution. General Putnam was deeply interested in this movement, and bent all his energies to secure it, but was prevented from even making the attempt—in the same manner as he had been a few months before—by the withdrawal of his force, to strengthen the main army on the Delaware. He was doubtless the more desirous to be the instrument of striking some important blow, at this time, as it would not only advance the good cause of his country, but in some degree make amends for the recent disasters in his department.

While these projects were in contemplation, Putnam sent out some small detachments, to annoy the enemy, and to protect the country from their ravages. In one of these, Colonel Meigs, with a division of General Parsons' brigade, made a forced march to Westchester, where he surprised a band of freebooters, making fifty prisoners, and recovering a large number of horses and cattle, which they had recently stolen.

General Howe was now in possession of Philadelphia, and the most vigorous measures were being made to open a communication with the fleet below. These measures it was Washington's principal aim to defeat ; and, supposing that the British had no further designs on the north, he felt that the army in that quarter ought to furnish him with large and effective reinforcements. To this end, agreeably to the decision of a council of war convened for that purpose, he commissioned Colonel Hamilton to proceed to Albany, to confer with General Gates on the subject, and procure all the aid he could. He was, at the same time, directed to call on General Putnam, and desire him to send forward two brigades—Nixon's and Glover's—with all possible despatch.

On arriving at Putnam's Head Quarters, Colonel Hamilton directed him, in the name of the Commander-in-chief, to forward the two Continental brigades named in his instructions, and another of Massachusetts militia, consisting of sixteen hundred men, under General Warner, whose term of service would expire in about four weeks. He also procured an order for the instant despatch of the regiments previously called for, which had been delayed partly by the hope, on the part of Putnam, of being able immediately to put in execution his project against New York. It was understood, also, that, in addition to these, Poor's New Hampshire brigade, then just arrived from Albany, should proceed at once to join the main army.

Hamilton then proceeded to Albany, to confer with Ge-

28

neral Gates.   On his return to New Windsor, just a week subsequent to his previous visit, he was greatly disappointed that the expected reinforcements had not gone forward The statement can be best understood from his own letter to Washington, dated New Windsor, November 10th : " I am pained beyond expression to inform your Excellency, that, on my arrival here, I find everything has been neglected and deranged by General Putnam, and that the two brigades, Poor's and Learned's, still remain here, and on the other side at Fishkill. Colonel Warner's militia, I am told, have been drawn to Peekskill, to aid in an expedition against New York, which it seems is at this time the hobby-horse with General Putnam. Not the least attention has been paid to my order in your name, for a detachment of one thousand men from the troops hitherto stationed at this post. Everything is sacrificed to the whim of taking New York.

" The two brigades of Poor and Learned, it appears, would not march for want of money and other necessaries ; several of the regiments having received no pay for six or eight months.   There has been a high mutiny among the former on this account, in which a captain killed a man, and was himself shot by his comrade.   These difficulties, for want of proper management, have stopped the troops from proceeding. * * * By Governor Clinton's advice, I have sent an order, in the most emphatical terms, to General Putnam, immediately to despatch all the Continental troops under him to your assistance, and to detain the militia instead of them.

" My opinion is, that the only present use of troops in this quarter, is to protect the country from the depredations of little plundering parties, and for carrying on the works necessary for the defence of the river.   Nothing more. ought to be thought of.   It is only wasting time, and mis-

applying men, to employ them in a suicidal parade against
New York.

"If your Excellency agrees with me in opinion, it will
be well to send instant directions to General Putnam, to
pursue the object I have mentioned ; for I doubt whether
he will attend to anything I say, notwithstanding it comes
in the shape of a positive order. I fear, unless you interfere, the works here will go on so feebly, for want of men,
that they will not be completed in time. I wish General
Putnam was recalled from the command of this post, and
Governor Clinton would accept it ; the blunders and ca-
prices of the former are endless."

In another letter, written two days later, he says, "I
believe the past delay is wholly chargeable to General
Putnam. Indeed, I owe it to the service to say, that
*every part of this gentleman's conduct is marked with blun-
ders and negligence, and gives general disgust.*"

Colonel Hamilton's order to General Putnam, above
alluded to, is in the following pointed and authoritative language : "I cannot forbear confessing, that I am astonished and alarmed beyond measure to find, that all his Excellency's views have been hitherto frustrated, and that no single step of those I mentioned to you has been taken, to
afford him the aid he absolutely stands in need of, and by
delaying which the cause of America is put to the utmost
conceivable hazard. I so fully explained to you the General's situation, that I could not entertain a doubt, you
would make it the first object of your attention, to reinforce him with that speed the exigency of affairs demanded ; but, I am sorry to say, he will have too much reason
to think, other objects, in connection with that insignificant, have been uppermost. I speak freely and emphati-
cally, because I tremble at the consequences of the delay
that has happened. Sir Henry Clinton's reinforcement is

probably by this time with General Howe.   This will give
him a decided superiority over our army.   What may be
the issue of such a state of things, I leave to the feelings
of every friend of his country, capable of foreseeing consequences.   My expressions may perhaps have more
warmth, than is altogether proper, but they proceed from
the overflowing of my heart, in a matter where I conceive
this continent essentially interested.

"I wrote to you from Albany, and desired you would
send a thousand Continental troops, of those first proposed
to be left with you.   This I understand has not been done.
How the non-compliance can be answered to General
Washington, you can best determine.   I now, sir, in the
most explicit terms, by his Excellency's authority, give it
as a positive order from him, that *all* the Continental
troops under your command may be immediately marched
to King's Ferry, there to cross the river, and hasten to reinforce the army under him.   The Massachusetts militia are
to be detained instead of them, until the troops coming
from the northward arrive.   When they do, they will
replace, as far as I am instructed, the troops you shall send
away in consequence of this requisition.   The General's
idea of keeping troops this way, does not extend further
than covering the country from any little irruptions of
small parties, and carrying on the works necessary for the
security of the river.   As to attacking New York, that
he thinks ought to be out of the question for the present.
If men could be spared from other really necessary objects,
he would have no objection to attempting a diversion by
way of New York."

The writer will yield to no man in respect for the talents,
and eminent public services, of Alexander Hamilton.   But
it is obvious to remark that, at the period when these letters were written, he was scarcely twenty years old, and

without any military knowledge or experience; while the person, of whom he speaks in terms of unsparing censure, and harsh disrespect, was an old soldier, a veteran officer, on whose head the frosts of three score winters had fallen, and whose martial virtues and martial deeds, in two wars, had won the admiration of friend and foe alike, and wreathed his brow with undying laurels. His opinions would certainly have lost no weight in this case, if they had been given in a tone and manner more becoming his relative position.

Among the published letters of Washington, there is no reply to these communications, from which his opinion of them may be gathered. In his letters to General Putnam, on the subject, while he makes it sufficiently appear that he was disappointed in not receiving earlier succor from that quarter, his language is uniformly respectful and kind.

General Putnam enclosed a copy of Hamilton's letter to General Washington, and added: "It contains some most unjust and ungenerous reflections, for I am conscious of having done everything in my power to succor you as soon as possible. I shall go to New Windsor this day, to see Colonel Hamilton, and, until I have orders from you, I cannot think of continuing at this post, and send *all* the troops away. If they should go away, I am confident General Howe will be further reinforced from this quarter." He then stated, in confirmation of this opinion, what he knew of the strength of the enemy in New York.

On the receipt of this letter, Washington replied as follows: "The urgency of Colonel Hamilton's letter was owing to his knowledge of our wants in this quarter, and to a certainty that there was no danger to be apprehended from New York, if you sent away all the Continental troops that were then with you, and waited to replace them by those expected down the river. I cannot but say

28*

there has been more delay in the march of the troops, than I think necessary ; and I could wish that, in future, my orders may be immediately complied with, without arguing upon the propriety of them. If any accident ensues from obeying them, the fault will be upon me, and not upon you."

It is not proposed to claim for General Putnam entire exemption from faults, either as a man, or an officer. He was probably somewhat remiss in his duty on this occasion. But he was, by no means, entitled to the severe remarks of Hamilton. It is evident that Washington, though he approved of the zeal and energy of his Aide-de-camp, must have viewed the whole matter, as it related to Putnam, in a totally different light. For it is hard to perceive how a measure proposed by General Putnam, in which General Dickinson was to bear a part, should be regarded worthy to be spoken of only as a " hobby," a " whim," and a " caprice ;" while the same measure, proposed by General Dickinson, at the same time, and embracing in its arrangements the co-operation of General Putnam, should meet with entire approbation and respect. " Your idea," says Washington to Dickinson, " I think an exceedingly good one, and I am very desirous that you should improve and mature it for immediate execution. I am in great hopes it will effect the valuable purpose which you expect ;"—which was, to prevent General Howe from receiving any further reinforcements from New York.* This letter was written on the 4th of November, two days after Hamilton's first interview with Putnam, and consequently while the former was at Albany. It was only one

* General Putnam had just learned from his spies, and communicated to Washington, the fact, that four regiments were immediately to be sent round to the Delaware from New York. Writings, vol. v., page 127.

week before that interview, that Putnam himself had received the first suggestion of the Commander-in-chief, that a movement toward New York, if well conducted, might be safe and advantageous. It is impossible, therefore, to suppose, that Washington could have viewed the designs of Putnam in this contemptuous light, or justified the use of such reproachful terms in relation to it ; unless, for the time, he was wholly divested of that consistency and sense of justice, for which he was eminently distinguished.

It cannot fail to strike the most careless reader as singular, that while, in one paragraph, it is represented, that " everything had been neglected and deranged by General Putnam," and that Poor's and Learned's brigades were detained at Fishkill by his fault alone, the very next paragraph begins with the acknowledgment, that " the two brigades of Poor and Learned *would not march for want of money and other necessaries*—several of the regiments having received no pay for six or eight months. There has been a high mutiny on this account," &c. That this was the only real difficulty in the way, there is no doubt ; and there is ample evidence that Putnam used every means in his power to overcome it. His letters to the Commander-in-chief on the subject were frequent and pressing ; and Washington called the special attention of Congress to the matter, on the 10th of November—the very date of Hamilton's second and severe letter—in the following words : " I would beg leave to mention, that we are in great distress for want of money. This will be more urgent every day ; and it is probable there will be a good deal of pay due to the troops coming to reinforce us. *General Putnam writes pressingly for a supply, and says he is in the most disagreeable situation for want of it.*"

If the troops " *would not march* " without their arrears

of pay, resisting even to mutiny and blood; and if, with the aid of the eloquent Governor Clinton, Hamilton could not himself induce them to march, till he had borrowed six thousand dollars to meet this very difficulty, it would seem that he might have spared the old veteran some portion of those severe reflections. The mutiny took place before Hamilton's arrival. Against whom did they mutiny, if not against him who ordered them to march? And who had issued that order but the commander of the post?

The truth is, there was a prejudice against Putnam, among the people of New York, and the political leaders had determined to have him removed from the command in the Highlands.* The precise grounds of this prejudice do not distinctly appear. If it was an alleged incompetency to such a command, it is manifest that they differed widely in their judgment from Washington, who had had far better opportunities to know and judge of his qualifications. Colonel Humphreys says : "The indulgence which he showed, whenever it did not militate against his duty, towards the deserted and suffering families of the tories in the State of New York, was the cause of his becoming unpopular with no inconsiderable class of people in that State. On the other side, he had conceived an unconquerable aversion to many of the persons who were entrusted with the disposal of tory property, because he believed them to have been guilty of peculations, and other infamous practices."

Dr. Sparks observes : " It must be remembered, that at this station there were innumerable applications for passports to go into New York, under the pretence of urgent business, and various matters of a private concern ; and it was thought General Putnam's good nature was too pliant on these occasions, and that too many opportunities were

* Appendix, No. 3.

afforded for an improper intercourse between the disaffected and the enemy.   At any rate, the symptoms of uneasiness appeared from such high sources, and were so decidedly manifested, that General Washington deemed it
necessary to take notice of them, and change the command."

In recalling General Putnam from this command, Washington, by the clearest implication, disavows any and every
ground of censure or disapprobation, on his own part.
" My reason for making this change," he says, " is owing
to the prejudices of the people, which, whether well or
ill grounded, must be indulged ; and I should think myself
wanting in justice to the public, and candor towards you,
were I to continue you in a command, after I have been
in almost direct terms informed, that the people of the
State of New York will not render the necessary support
and assistance, while you remain at the head of that department."   Here is no intimation of incompetency or
unfaithfulness, or of any reason, so far as the Commander-
in-chief was concerned, why General Putnam should not
retain the station he had held.   It is clearly implied that,
but for " the prejudices of the people," he would not have
been removed, and consequently, that neither Washington's wishes, nor Washington's *private* views of the good
of the service, required his removal.   And this was written in March, five months after Hamilton's mission.

On the 28th of November, a Court of Inquiry was ordered by Congress, to investigate the causes of the loss of
Forts Montgomery and Clinton.   This order was not executed by Washington until the 16th of March following,
though he had long before decided, that the wishes of New
York should be regarded, in relation to the command of the
Highlands, as appears by his letter to General Gates, of
the 2d of December   Four days after the passage of this

order, Washington addressed a letter to Governor Clinton, requesting his acceptance of that post. In urging this point, he makes use of the following argument, which demands, in this connection, a word of explanation. " You may rest assured," says he, " that there are no impediments on the score of delicacy, or superior command, that shall not be removed."

Governor Clinton was a man of eminent ability, and unbounded influence in New York, and no better selection could have been made, on both these accounts. But his rank in the Continental army was only that of a brigadier-general, of recent appointment. Not only every major-general in the army, therefore, but all the brigadiers, among whom were some of the ablest and most popular men on the list, were implicated in this remark. It could not be tortured into a disrespectful reference to General Putnam, inasmuch as his removal had already been decided upon, on entirely different grounds, and an inquiry had been ordered, which rendered necessary a temporary suspension from all command.

To return to the narrative, though Putnam's force was now greatly reduced, he was not inactive. The continual changes which were taking place in his command—the removal of his men from place to place—the miserable, broken, half-hearted service rendered by the militia—and the extreme destitution, at times, of money, and of many of the comforts and necessaries of life, made it altogether an unenviable post, and occasioned considerable delay in the prosecution of the repairs on the defences, which had been demolished by the British.

Not long after the continental troops had been withdrawn, General Putnam moved down, with a part of the forces that remained, and approached the enemy's posts on the east side of the Hudson. On the 27th of November, General Dickinson made a descent upon Staten Island, with about fourteen hundred men. He landed, before daylight, at Halstead's Point, in three divisions, which marched into the island seven miles, by three different routes, and met at the appointed place of rendezvous. The principal object of this expedition was to surprise General Skinner, the celebrated tory refugee, and General Campbell, who were stationed there. The most profound secresy was observed as to the design of the expedition— few even of the officers knowing anything of their destination, till the very moment of starting. And yet General Skinner received intelligence of their approach, in season to effect his escape, with the main body of his force. Some skirmishes ensued, and five or six of the enemy were killed, and twenty-four taken prisoners. General Dickinson returned without effecting his object, but he received the commendation of Washington on his enterprise, and the judgment he had shown in arranging his plan.

To aid this enterprise, and at the request of General Dickinson, Putnam sent out Parsons and Warner, with their brigades, towards King's Bridge, to make a diversion in that quarter. Putnam reconnoitred in person within three miles of King's Bridge. But, finding no opportunity to operate with effect on that point, he diverged to New Rochelle, where he made a disposition to cross over to Long Island, and attack the forts at Huntington and Satauket. But the enemy received warning, in season to evacuate the forts before his preparations for embarkation were completed.

Having received intelligence that small parties of the enemy were out, under the orders of Governor Tryon, to lay waste the property of the unprotected, Putnam immediately detached three parties of one hundred men each, to prevent their depredations. Two of them were successful in their manœuvres, and returned, one with thirty five, and the other with forty prisoners. The third party of the enemy succeeded in effecting their purpose, so far as to burn the house of a Mr. Van Tassel, a noted whig, and a member of the committee of safety, compelling him to accompany them naked and barefooted, over frozen ground and ice, to their quarters. Determined to show the enemy that firing houses was a game which two could play at, and that the loss was not necessarily all on one side, General Putnam directed Captain Buchanan to cross over to York Island in a whale-boat, and fire the house of General Oliver Delancy, one of the leading loyalists of that place. This act of justifiable retaliation had, for a time, the desired effect, of arresting this species of unmeaning and wanton destruction.

About the same time, one of Putnam's scouting parties, learning that Colonel James Delancy was at West Farms, a little below Westchester, determined to make him a prisoner. They, accordingly, surrounded the house where he lodged, and proceeded to search it. When the alarm was given, he jumped out of bed, and endeavored to conceal himself under it. But he was soon discovered, dragged forth, and carried to Head-Quarters. He was a tory of too much value to be spared long, and Sir Henry Clinton soon found means to effect an exchange for him. He was afterward leader of a gang of irregulars, or bandits, known by the name of cowboys, and made himself infamously immortal, by every species of cruelty and excess.

Though the season was far advanced into winter, and the weather was very severe, another and more serious enterprise was undertaken by General Putnam, the execution of which was entrusted to General Parsons and Colonel Webb. The object was a descent upon Long

Island, having four objects in view : to destroy a quantity of lumber, which the enemy was preparing, at the east end of the island, for the erection of new barracks in New York—to set fire to a number of coasting vessels, at the same place, loading with wood for the British forces at Newport — to attack a regiment, then quartered about eight miles east of Jamaica—and to remove, or destroy, whatever public stores they should find on the island.

By the plan of operations, General Parsons was to execute the first part, at the east end of the island ; Colonel Meigs was to land at Hempstead Harbor, and attack the regiment near Jamaica ; and Colonel Webb was to land near Huntington, to support Meigs, and to render such aid to the eastern division, under Parsons, as might be required.   Meigs was prevented from crossing the Sound, by the unfavorable state of the weather.   The other two divisions started with fair prospects ; but, unfortunately for Colonel Webb, he encountered in his passage the British sloop-of-war Falcon.   Being only in a common transport, without guns, he could not offer battle, or attempt a defence.   In endeavoring to escape, he was driven on shore so far from the beach, that he and all his party were taken prisoners.   They attempted to reach the land in boats ; but the surf ran so high that the boats were swamped the moment they touched the water, and they had no remedy but to give themselves up to the foe.

General Parsons effected his landing in safety, and succeeded in destroying a large quantity of timber, boards, and wood, and one of the enemy's vessels.   Captain Hart, of this party, with a detachment of forty men, attacked a number of boats near the shore, killing eight, and wounding eleven—among whom was the captain of one of the British sloops-of-war.   General Parsons returned, with

29

his whole party unhurt, and twenty of the enemy prisoners. The loss of the other party, by the Falcon, was
sixty-five : viz. Colonel Webb, with four officers, twenty
privates of his continental regiment, and forty militia, all
picked men.

CHAPTER XXV.

ABOUT the middle of December, General Putnam, by
direction of the Commander-in-chief, returned to his post
in the Highlands, with instructions to employ his whole
force, and all the means in his power, for erecting and
completing, as far as possible, such works and obstructions
as might be necessary to defend and secure the river
against any future attempts of the enemy. With a view
to the more diligent prosecution of these works, he was
advised to confine his attention exclusively to them, without attempting any active measures to annoy the enemy,
or to protect the country against his incursions.

All the forts, and other works of defence in the Highlands, had been entirely demolished by the British, during
their twenty days' occupancy ; and it now became a question of importance whether these should be restored in
their former positions, or new and more eligible places
selected for the purpose.   There were differences of opinion on this subject, among those whose interest and co-
operation were essential to its progress.   And it was this,
together with the pressing want of money, and the poverty
and hard fare of the soldiers, which occasioned the delay
in the prosecution of the works, so often complained of by
Washington in his letters ; and not any want of activity or
zeal on the part of General Putnam.

With a view to settle this question definitely and for
ever, and proceed vigorously with the work, a thorough
survey of the whole region was made in the early part of
January, by General Putnam, accompanied by Governor
Clinton, General James Clinton, and several other distinguished gentlemen—among whom was Colonel Radière,
a French engineer of some celebrity.   All, except Radière, united in the opinion that West Point was the most
eligible place to be fortified.   Radière opposed this decision with considerable vehemence, and drew up a memo-
rial, designed to show that the site of Fort Clinton possessed advantages much superior to West Point.   The
British commander, Sir Henry Clinton, and his associates,
seem to have entertained the same high opinion of the
advantageous position of Fort Clinton ; for, while they
demolished all the other forts, they commenced repairing
and strengthening that, for future operations.   It is possible that this circumstance may have had some influence in
affecting the decision of Radière.

As the French engineer was a man of science, and possessed the confidence of Congress and the Commander-in-

chief, it was deemed expedient by General Putnam to consult the Council and Assembly of New York, before he came to a final determination. At his suggestion, a committee was appointed by those bodies, who were employed three days in carefully reconnoitring the borders of the river in the Highlands, and attending to all the suggestions of the more experienced military men who accompanied them, in reference to the several points deemed most capable of defence. After a patient and careful examination of every position, and every argument, they decided unanimously in favor of West Point—thus agreeing with every person authorized to act in the affair, except the engineer. It was accordingly decided, on the 13th of January, that the fortifications should be erected at West Point. Colonel Radière was sorely piqued at this result, and manifested his ill-will on the occasion by a petulant, unaccommodating behavior, and by the overbearing manner in which he presented his estimates and requisitions,—which were altogether disproportioned to the finances of the government, and only served, as Humphreys remarks, " to remind them of their poverty, and satirize their resources." He was not long after replaced by the celebrated Kosciusko ; after which the works went forward with more spirit.

Colonel Humphreys, who was on the spot at the time, claims for General Putnam the whole merit of the selection of this post ; and adds—" It is no vulgar praise to say, that to him belongs the glory of having chosen this rock of our military salvation. The position for water-batteries, which might sweep the channel where the river formed a right angle, made it the most proper of any for commanding the navigation ; while the rocky ridges that rose in awful sublimity behind each other, rendered it impregnable, and even incapable of being invested by less

29*

than twenty thousand men. The British, who considered this post as a sort of American Gibraltar, never attempted it but by the treachery of an American officer."

It is impossible to say to whom the credit of originality, in this case, belongs; nor is it a matter of much importance with reference to men who had so many other and more substantial titles to fame. The first recorded suggestion in reference to this point, of which we have any knowledge, is contained in the letter of Governor Clinton to General Washington, dated December 20th, about two weeks before the survey above spoken of. After declining, for reasons of state, the proffered command in the Highlands, he freely offers his advice and assistance, wherever and by whomsoever they may be needed — gives several important hints respecting the construction of new works on the river—and especially recommends that a " strong fortress should be erected at West Point, opposite to Fort Constitution."

Before the close of January, when the snow was two feet deep, General Parsons, with his brigade, went over to West Point and broke ground. It is difficult, at this day, to conceive of the many impediments which then existed, in the way of completing such necessary works ; or the toil and suffering involved in their prosecution. The better to understand and appreciate it, the reader should remember that it was the same memorable season, when Washington, with his wasted, half-clothed, half-fed army, was freezing in his comfortless winter quarters, at Valley Forge. The marvel is, how such an army was held together at all, under such circumstances ; and how works of any description could go forward by the agency of men so poorly paid, so miserably provided for. And yet, such was the energy and zeal displayed by all concerned, that the works went forward with unexpected rapidity and success.   It was in forwarding and encouraging these works, observes Colonel Humphreys, " that the patriotism of Governor Clinton shone in full lustre.   His exertions to forward supplies can never be too much commended.   His influence, arising from his popularity, was unlimited; yet he hesitated not to put all his popularity at risk, whenever the federal interests demanded it.   Notwithstanding the impediments that opposed our progress, with his aid, before the opening of the campaign, the works were in great forwardness."

Fortifications alone were not regarded as sufficient for the purpose of guarding the river, without other contrivances to obstruct the passage of ships.   Resort was, therefore, to be had to chains, booms, and *chevaux-de-frise*, as before at Fort Montgomery.   All these works were in the course of preparation together.

On the thirteenth of February, one month after the site had been determined upon, General Putnam wrote to the Commander-in-chief, as follows : " At my request, the Legislature of this State have appointed a committee, to fix the places and manner of securing the river, and to afford some assistance in expediting the work.   The state of affairs now at this post, you will please to observe, is as follows :   The chain and necessary anchors are contracted for, to be completed by the first of April ; and, from the intelligence I have received, there is reason to believe they will be finished by that time.   Parts of the boom intended to have been used at Fort Montgomery, sufficient for this purpose, are remaining.   Some of the iron is exceedingly bad ; this I hope to have replaced with good iron soon.   The *chevaux-de-frise* will be completed by the time the river will admit of sinking them.   The batteries near the water, and the fort to cover them, are laid out.   The latter is within the walls six hundred yards around, twenty-one feet base, fourteen feet high, the *talus* (or slope) two inches to the foot. This, I fear, is too large to be completed by the time expected. Governor Clinton and the committee have agreed to this plan, and nothing on my part shall be wanting, to complete it in the best and most expeditious manner. Barracks and huts for about three hundred men are completed, and barracks for about the same number are nearly covered. A road to the river has been made with great difficulty."

He then proceeds to enumerate some of the difficulties with which he had to contend, in the prosecution of his work. "Meigs's regiment, except those under inoculation with the small-pox, is at White Plains ; and, until the barracks can be fitted for their reception, I have thought best to continue them there, to cover the country from the incursions of the enemy. *Dubois's regiment is unfit to be ordered on duty, there being not one blanket in the regiment. Very few have either a shoe or a shirt, and most of them have neither stockings, breeches, nor overalls. Several companies of enlisted artificers are in the same situation, and unable to work in the field.* Several hundred men are rendered useless, merely for want of necessary apparel, as no clothing is permitted to be stopped at this post. General Parsons has returned to camp some time since, and takes upon himself the command to-morrow, when I shall set out for Connecticut."

That these statements are in no way exaggerated, there is evidence enough in all the chronicles of the day. For the painful counterpart, in all its hideous nakedness, see Washington's letters to Congress, of the 23d of December*—to Governor Livingston of the 31st of the same month—to Governor Clinton of the 16th, and to Congress

* Writings, vol. v., pages 197 and 206.

of the 27th of February.* The latter, in direct allusion to the above, says : "The enclosed extract of a letter from General Putnam will show how great the distresses are in that quarter for want of money. He has described their necessities so fully, that it is unnecessary for me to add upon the subject. I shall only observe, that his account *is more than justified* by many other letters, and that I am persuaded the earliest possible supply will be forwarded, and that the very important and interesting works carrying on there may not be the least retardéd."

As soon as General Putnam could conveniently return from Connecticut, where his private affairs demanded attention at this time, the Court of Inquiry, which had been ordered in November, was organized. It consisted of Major-General McDougall, Brigadier-General Huntington, and Colonel Wigglesworth.† The following is an extract from Washington's letter to General McDougall, apprizing him of this appointment : " You will observe by the words of the resolve (of Congress), that the inquiry is to be made into the loss of Forts Montgomery and Clinton, in the State of New York, and into the conduct of the principal officers commanding those forts. Hence the officer commanding-in-chief in that department will be consequentially involved in the inquiry ; because, if he has been deficient in affording the proper support to those posts, when called upon to do it, the commandant and

* Writings, vol. v., pages 238 and 244.
† It may be well to remark that such inquiries are almost invariably instituted in relation to military enterprises which are attended with disastrous results. They do not by any means necessarily imply a diminution of confidence in the officers whose conduct is implicated in the inquiry. They are part of a great system, as necessary to the reputation of the officers, as to the due adjustment of discipline and reward in the army.

principal officers will of course make it appear, by the
evidence produced in their own justification."

General McDougall was at the same time invested with
the command in the Highlands, respecting which it was
remarked: "I am sensible this command will not be in
itself the most agreeable piece of service, and that you
would prefer a post on the principal theatre of action; but
the vast importance of it has determined me to confide it
to you, and I am persuaded your object is to be useful to
the public." General Putnam had fully realized the
truth of these remarks, respecting the character of the post
in the Highlands. But it was always a principle with
him, never to shrink from any service, or complain of any
duty, because it was disagreeable.

It was on this occasion, when it became necessary to
suspend his command for a season, in order to subject him
to this trial, that Washington explained to Putnam the
necessity he was under, growing out of the prejudices of
the people of New York, of recalling him altogether from
that post.

The Court of Inquiry, after a patient and careful examination of all the facts in the case, were unanimously of
opinion, and made report accordingly, that the disaster
of the fifth of October, 1777, in which Forts Montgomery
and Clinton were lost, was occasioned only by the want
of men sufficient for their proper defence, and not by any
fault of the commanders.

This investigation being satisfactorily terminated, General Putnam was requested—partly, no doubt, with reference to his own convenience—to return to Connecticut,
and hasten with all possible expedition, the march from
that quarter of the new levies of militia for the coming
campaign, which Washington apprehended would open
early, and prove an active and decisive one. This seemed

the more certain, when, about the 1st of May, intelligence was received of the conclusion of a treaty of alliance between France and the United States. It was the first formal recognition, by any of the nations, of American Independence, and was responded to, in all parts of the country, by universal acclamations of joy. It inspired all hearts with confidence. Washington, writing to Putnam on the occasion, ever as watchful and prudent as he was firm and hopeful in the goodness and ultimate success of his cause, said : " I hope that the fair, and, I may say, *certain* prospect of success will not induce us to relax."

Except a few ordinary skirmishes, and the able retreat of Lafayette from Barren Hill, nothing of any moment occurred till the last of June, when the successful attack upon the retreating foe at Monmouth, gave fresh éclat to the American cause. Immediately after this felicitous event, General Putnam returned to the camp, and took the command of the right wing of the army, recently commanded by General Lee, who was then under arrest for his conduct in the battle of Monmouth. Without any action of importance, the army was concentrated about the North River, as the enemy retired to New York. The season passed away with little else than marches and countermarches, with the view of being always ready for any decided movement on the part of Sir Henry Clinton.

About the first of September, when the preparations known to be making in New York indicated a combined attack, by sea and land, on the French fleet at Boston, dispositions were made to move in that direction. With this view General Gates, with three brigades, was ordered to proceed to Danbury, in Connecticut. Washington moved as far as Fredericksburg, about thirty miles from the river, on the way to Boston. General Putnam, with two brigades, was left in the neighborhood of West Point,

for the defence of the North River, which, in the language
of Washington, was one of the three capital objects at
which the enemy would necessarily direct his force, and
which it was *his* first duty to defend. General McDougall, with two other brigades, was ordered to join General
Gates at Danbury.

As no serious demonstrations were made by the enemy
in either of these directions, the whole army, after remaining in this position more than two months, retired into
winter quarters. General McDougall returned to his
command in the Highlands, and General Putnam, with
three brigades, composed of the New Hampshire and Connecticut troops, together with Hazen's corps of infantry
and Sheldon's of cavalry, was posted in the vicinity of
Danbury, for the threefold purpose of protecting the country lying along the Sound—covering the magazines on the
Connecticut River—and being ready to reinforce the
Highlands, on any serious movement of the enemy in that
direction.

In the course of the winter, a spirit of insubordination,
arising from the many hardships they had suffered, and
the long arrearages of pay now due, manifested itself
among a portion of the troops at Danbury; and, but for
the vigor, promptness and address of their veteran commander, whom they loved and respected, it might have
been attended with the most serious results. The General
Assembly of Connecticut was then in session at Hartford;
and a plan was matured by the two brigades belonging to
that State, of marching to that place in a body, and demanding redress, at the point of the bayonet, for the grievances under which they labored. The second brigade
was already under arms for this purpose, when intelligence
of their proceedings was brought to General Putnam. He
instantly mounted his horse, galloped down to their can-

tonment, and, in his plain, blunt manner, thus addressed them : " My brave lads, whither are you going ? Do you intend to desert your officers, and to invite the enemy to follow you into the country ? In whose cause have you been fighting and suffering so long ? Is it not your own ? Have you no 'property ? no parents ? no wives ? no children ? You have thus far behaved like men—the world is full of your praises—and posterity will stand astonished at your deeds ; but not if you spoil it all at last. Don't you consider how much the country is distressed by the war ; and that your officers have not been any better paid than yourselves ? But we all expect better times, and then the country will do us ample justice. Let us all stand by one another, then, and fight it out like brave soldiers. Think what a shame it would be for Connecticut men to run away from their officers !"

The General then rode along the line, and was received by the several regiments in the usual manner, with presented arms and beat of drum. The acting Major of Brigade was then ordered to give the word for them to shoulder arms, march to their regimental parades, and there lodge arms ; all of which was done promptly and with apparent good humor. One soldier only, who had been a ringleader in the mutiny, was confined in the quarter-guard. He attempted to make his escape in the night ; but the sentinel, though he had himself taken part in the mutiny, was so entirely convinced of his error, and won back to his duty, that he shot him dead upon the spot.

During this season, the British, as usual, sent out an occasional foraging party, to sweep away from the unprotected portion of the country whatever they could find of stock or provisions. Unfortunately for their reputation for humanity, these parties did not confine themselves to this species of justifiable plunder, but burned and laid

30

waste the property of the defenceless.   A corps of fifteen
hundred men, under command of Governor Tryon, was,
on one of these occasions, approaching the town of West
Greenwich, more familiarly known as *Horseneck*, from a
peninsula on the Sound, anciently used as a pasture for
horses, but now the richest and most populous part of the
township.

This was one of Putnam's outposts, and he chanced to
be there, in person, when Tryon advanced. He had no
force to oppose him but a picket of one hundred and fifty
men, with two pieces of artillery. With these, he took
his station on the brow of a steep declivity, near the Pres-
byterian church, resolved to do the enemy what mischief
he could and then retire. As they advanced, they received several well-directed volleys, that told with good effect
on their line ; upon which the dragoons, supported by a
corps of infantry, prepared to charge. Putnam immediately ordered his men to provide for their own safety, by
retiring to a swamp inaccessible to cavalry, while he secured his, by forcing his well-trained horse, at full speed,
down the declivity. The road at that time turned to the
north, a little before it came to the brow of the hill, and,
after proceeding a considerable distance, bent again with a
sharp angle towards the south—having been dug along the
steep in such a manner, as to make the passage practicable and tolerably safe. General Putnam, under the influence of the same spirit with which he entered the wolf's
den, being hard pressed by his pursuers, forced his horse
directly down the precipice,—winding his course, however, in such a zig-zag direction, as enabled him to keep
his feet. His pursuers, when they came to the top of the
precipice, struck with astonishment at his daring attempt,
stopped short, and fired upon him as he effected the perilous descent ; when, despairing of overtaking him by the

Perilous Descent at Horseneck.   PAGE 350.

circuitous course of the road, they gave over the chase. He escaped the sharp firing of his pursuers, only one ball taking effect; and that, fortunately, passed through his beaver, without hurting a hair of his head.   The road is so much altered at the present time as to prevent the eye from fully realizing the extent of the hazard.   It is now blown through the rocks above at a great expense; and continued by a causeway from the foot of the chasm to the valley below, in the very direction where the General descended.

The story of the seventy stone steps, by which this hill is ascended, and of the magnificent church on the top, to which that wonderful stairway was designed to lead, is a sheer fabrication, originating in what Dr. Dwight calls, " that mass of folly and falsehood, *Peters's History of Connecticut*." The truth is, there is a small Episcopal church on the brow of the hill, and the members of the congregation, who lived below the hill, being unwilling to take the tedious circuit of the road, when walking to the church, and being unable to ascend the hill in its original state, gathered a collection of stones from the road, and the neighboring enclosures, and placed them at convenient distances, to aid them in climbing this steep.   The number is commonly reported to be seventy, though sometimes magnified to a hundred; but, instead of being a magnificent flight of steps, the regularity of their arrangement would not distinguish them from the common stones of the street.

Putnam continued his route, unmolested, to Stamford— about ten miles.   Calling out a party of militia at this place, he returned with all despatch, formed a junction with the little band he had left behind, and hung upon the rear of Tryon, in his retreat, with such effect, as to take about fifty of his party prisoners.   Some of these being wounded, were treated with such special humanity and kindness, that Governor Tryon addressed a handsome note to Putnam in acknowledgment, accompanied with a present of a complete suit of clothes.*

* There is an apparent anachronism in the common narratives of this adventure. Colonel Humphreys places it in the winter of 1778-9. A note attached to the Boston edition of his memoirs, printed in 1818, says, that the whole party of prisoners, taken from Tryon, on this occasion, was sent, *the next day*, to the British lines for exchange. This could hardly have happened at the time named by Humphreys; for Putnam had, a year before, received specific instructions from Washington on this very point. In a letter of the 25th of January, 1778, after congratulating Putnam on the success of his two little parties against the enemy, which he hoped would have the effect to prevent their making so extensive excursions in future, he remarks: " One circumstance I cannot avoid taking notice of, that our officers who have been but a very short time in the enemy's hands, reap the advantages of any captures which happen to be made by us. This must not be practised in future, as it is the height of injustice, and will, if continued, draw upon us the censures of the officers who have been for a long time suffering all the rigors of a severe captivity. The proper mode of procedure is, to deliver them into the hands of the commissary of prisoners, who must be best acquainted with the propriety of complying with the claims of our officers in their hands." It is manifest, therefore, either that the whole enterprise is post-dated a whole year by Humphreys, or that the Boston editor is in error, in connecting the summary exchange of prisoners with this occasion. The former is most probable; since the incident of the suit of clothes received from Governor Tryon, which is also mentioned by Humphreys, connects the two events together, while Washington's letter, alluding both to the success of Putnam's two parties, and to the premature exchange of prisoners, establishing the date of the one, necessarily decides that of the other. It will be remembered that, at that period, Putnam sent out three parties from New Rochelle, against the parties of Tryon, and that two of them were successful. The number of prisoners taken by both, as represented by Humphreys, was seventy-five. One of those parties might have been the party at Horseneck, increased by the picket to one hundred and fifty men. And, as that party took *forty* prisoners,

In the latter part of March, 1779, before General Putnam received orders to move from his winter quarters at Danbury, he was apprized by the Commander-in-chief of the probable designs of the enemy to commit extensive depredations on the towns along the coast, and warned to be on his guard, to prevent their ravages as far as possible. But, having the advantage of vastly superior numbers, and armed ships, by which they were easily and safely transported from place to place, it was not easy to follow or check them in their cruel designs. It was expected, by the short-sighted administration of that day, that this species of predatory warfare—keeping the country in a state of constant alarm and suffering — would wear out the rebellious provinces, and induce them to return to their allegiance. The effect was just the reverse, exasperating even the timid, and rousing the whole community to an indignant and hearty co-operation in sustaining the war.

As the season for active operations approached, Sir Henry Clinton formed a plan for opening the campaign with a brilliant *coup de main* up the North River. Washington was immediately informed of the preparations making for this object, and penetrating, at once, their design, took measures to counteract them. Generals Putnam and McDougall were ordered to hold themselves in readiness to march ; and, on the 26th of May, the army under Washington moved by divisions from Middlebrook towards the Highlands. On the 30th, the British army, commanded by Sir Henry Clinton in person, proceeded up the river ; and General Vaughan, at the head of the largest

it would leave but a slight difference to be adjusted in the two statements. This is rendered more probable from the circumstance, that, in describing the Horseneck expedition, Colonel Humphreys makes no mention of prisoners, which, as an honest man, he would not do, if he had previously accounted for all the prisoners taken.

30*

division, landed, the next morning, near Verplanck's
Point.   The other division, under General Patterson,
accompanied by Sir Henry, landed on the west side, near
Stony Point.   The works at this place, which were in an
unfinished state, were abandoned at once to the enemy.
The garrison at Fort Lafayette, on the opposite side, consisting of seventy men, being invested by General Vaughan
on the land side, and by the galleys on the water side,
was compelled to surrender as prisoners of war.

The design of this expedition was evidently to get possession of West Point, and the river.   But, while these
movements were in progress, that post was so strongly
reinforced, that it was deemed too hazardous to prosecute
the design any farther.   The whole army, under the immediate command of Washington, was now concentrated
in the Highlands.   General Putnam, with his division,
had crossed the river, and joined the main body in the
Clove.   On the 23d of June, General Washington removed his head-quarters to New Windsor, leaving the main
body at the former place, under the immediate command
of Putnam.

The two posts on the river, recently taken by the enemy, were important to both parties.   The possession of
them by the British was a great inconvenience to the
American army, as it cut off one of their best communications, by King's Ferry, between their principal posts on
the two sides of the river, besides affording to the enemy
convenient vantage ground, from which to advance higher
up.   They were immediately put into a condition of
defence, and ably garrisoned ; while, at the same time,
measures were adopted by Washington to recover them.

On the 15th of July, Stony Point was gallantly stormed
and recovered by General Wayne, and the whole garrison
made prisoners—consisting of nearly six hundred men.

The attempt upon Verplanck's Point was to have been made at the same time. But it failed; and in consequence of this failure, it became necessary to abandon Stony Point again to the enemy. It was then more strongly fortified and garrisoned than before; but was again, in a short time, with the opposite post at Verplanck's, finally evacuated, and left to the quiet possession of the Americans.

On the 21st of July, Washington established his head-quarters at West Point, and remained there until December, when the army went into winter quarters. It was during this period that the strong works at West Point and its vicinity were chiefly constructed. During a considerable part of the time, twenty-five hundred men were daily on fatigue duty. The right wing of the army, consisting of the Pennsylvania, Maryland and Virginia troops, was commanded by General Putnam. His post was at Buttermilk Falls, about two miles below West Point. As the fatigue parties were furnished alternately by each division of the army, and as General Putnam was experienced in this department, he took an active and efficient part in completing the fortifications which had been laid out under his own eye, and the site for which had been selected chiefly through his agency. He had the honor of giving his own name to the principal fort. It is still to be seen, though in ruins, reminding the multitudes who annually visit the spot, of the labors, sufferings and sacrifices, as well as of the virtues and honors of that noble band of heroes, who achieved our Independence.

With the exception of Wayne's enterprise at Stony Point, and another of equal merit, under the gallant Major Henry Lee, at Paulus Hook (Jersey City), the campaign of 1779 was productive of no important events, so far as the main body of the army under Washington was concerned. That commander, under date of the 30th of September, thus characterizes the campaign in a letter to Lafayette : " The operations of the enemy have been confined to the establishment of works of defence, taking a post at King's Ferry, and burning the defenceless towns of New Haven, Fairfield and Norwalk, on the Sound, within reach of their shipping, where little else was, or could be opposed to them, than the cries of distressed women and helpless children ; but these were offered in vain.   Since these notable exploits, they have never stepped out of their works, or beyond their lines.   How a conduct of this kind is to effect the conquest of America, the wisdom of a North, a Germain, or a Sandwich, can best decide.   It is too deep and refined for the comprehension of common understandings, and the general run of politicians."

CHAPTER XXVI.

RETIREMENT AND LAST DAYS OF THE HERO.

Putnam visits his family in Connecticut—Sets out on his return to the army—Is struck with paralysis, and retires—His interest in public affairs—Correspondence with Washington—His efforts to promote temperance—His abhorrence of duelling—His mode of accepting challenges—His peaceful enjoyment of the evening of life—Public and private estimation of his character—Testimony of Drs. Dwight and Whitney—A Christian's death—Funeral honors—Epitaph.

WHEN the army went into winter quarters at Morristown, early in December, General Putnam took leave of absence, for a few weeks, and went, with his Aids, to visit his family in Connecticut. Before the end of that month, he set out on his return to the camp. He had proceeded but a few miles, on the way to Hartford, when his progress was arrested by an attack of paralysis, by which the use of his limbs on one side was temporarily lost. He was enabled to reach the house of his friend Colonel Wadsworth ; where, unwilling to admit the real character of his disease, he endeavored, by active exertion, to shake it off. It refused to yield to so simple a remedy, and the old soldier, with a mind wholly unimpaired by his years and labors, and a heart warmly devoted to the cause of his country, was compelled to submit, for the remainder of his days, to a life of comparative inaction.

General Putnam survived this attack somewhat more

than eleven years. He was never so disabled, as to be
deprived of the power of enjoying moderate exercise in
walking and riding ; and even in the last year of his life,
and but a few weeks before he was called away, he travelled, by slow stages, on horseback, to Danvers, the
place of his birth, a distance of one hundred miles. With
his accustomed independence, on arriving at the house
of his relative, he refused assistance in dismounting, and
jumped to the ground with something of the agility of
youth. His mental faculties, his relish for social enjoyment, his love of pleasantry, and, more than all, his love
of country, he retained, undiminished, to the last. Few
men had more or firmer friends, or shared more largely in
the confidence and respect of those who knew him.

With the liveliest interest he watched the motions of
the army, and the progress of public affairs, and maintained a free correspondence with the Commander-in-chief,
and his old comrades in the camp. It would appear that,
at one time, about six months after his first attack, he
entertained strong hopes of being able to rejoin the army.
In reply to a letter, expressing such a hope as this, General Washington wrote, on the 5th of July, 1780, as follows :

    " Dear Sir :

    " I am very happy to learn from your letter of the
29th, that the present state of your health is so flattering,
and that it promises you the prospect of being in a condition to make a visit to your old associates some time this
campaign. I wish it were in my power to congratulate
you upon a complete recovery. I should feel a sincere
satisfaction in such an event, and I hope for it heartily,
with the rest of your friends in this quarter.

        " I am, dear Sir, &c.

            " GEO. WASHINGTON."

Three years after, on the conclusion of the treaty of peace, and the final establishment of American Independence, and in response to the hearty congratulations of Putnam on that interesting occasion, the Father of his country addressed him in the following affectionate and respectful terms. The whole letter is in the highest degree complimentary to his military standing and services, and indicates, in terms which cannot be mistaken, the estimation in which he was held by the writer and his associates.

"*Head Quarters, 2d June,* 1783.

" DEAR SIR :

" Your favor of the 20th of May I received with much pleasure. For I can assure you, that, among the many worthy and meritorious officers with whom I have had the happiness to be connected in service through the course of this war, and from whose cheerful assistance and advice I have received much support and confidence, in the various and trying vicissitudes of a complicated contest, the name of Putnam is not forgotten ; nor will be but with that stroke of time, which shall obliterate from my mind the remembrance of all those toils and fatigues, through which we have struggled, for the preservation and establishment of the *Rights, Liberties,* and *Independence* of our *Country.*

" Your congratulations on the happy prospects of our peace and independent security, with their attendant blessings to the UNITED STATES, I receive with great satisfaction ; and beg that you will accept a return of my gratulations to you on this auspicious event—an event, in which, great as it is in itself, and glorious as it will probably be in its consequences, you have a right to participate largely, from the distinguished part you have contributed towards its attainment

" But while I contemplate the greatness of the object for which we have contended, and felicitate you on the happy issue of our toils and labors, which have terminated with such general satisfaction, I lament that you should feel the ungrateful returns of a country in whose service you have exhausted your bodily health, and expended the vigor of a youthful constitution. I wish, however, that your expectations of returning sentiments of liberality may be verified. I have a hope that they may—but should they not, your career will not be a singular one. Ingratitude has been experienced in all ages ; and Republics, in particular, have ever been famed for the exercise of that unnatural and sordid vice.

" The SECRETARY AT WAR, who is now here, informs me that you have been considered as entitled to full pay since your absence from the field, and that you will still be considered in that light till the close of the war ; at which period you will be equally entitled to the same emoluments of half-pay, or commutation, as other officers of your rank. The same opinion is also given by the Paymaster-General, who is now with the army, empowered by Mr. Morris for the settlement of all their accounts, and who will attend to yours, whenever you shall think proper to send on for that purpose, which it will probably be best for you to do in a short time.

" I anticipate, with pleasure, the day—and that I trust not far off—when I shall quit the busy scenes of a military employment, and retire to the more tranquil walks of domestic life. In that, or whatever other situation Providence may dispose of my future days, *the remembrance of the many friendships and connections I have had the happiness to contract with the gentlemen of the Army, will be one of my most grateful reflections. Under this contemplation, and impressed with the sentiments of benevolence*

*and regard, I commend you, my dear Sir, my other friends,
and with them the interest and happiness of our dear country, to the* KEEPING AND PROTECTION OF ALMIGHTY GOD
   " I have the honor to be, &c.,
             " GEORGE WASHINGTON
   " *To the Honorable Major-General* PUTNAM."

That the old veteran was a good citizen, as well as a
brave soldier and an able officer, and, in retiring from the
army, did not lose sight of the interests of society around
him, will appear from the following letter ; which will
commend itself especially to the Washingtonians, Recha-
bites, and other temperance reformers of the day.   Though
it does not come up to the standard of this tetotal age, it
was certainly in advance of the age in which he lived
The original letter is among the papers of the Connecticut
Historical Society, at Hartford.

                           " *Brooklyn,** *Feb.* 18, 1782.
   " GENTLEMEN :
      " Being an enemy to Idleness, Dissipation and Intem-
perance, I would object against any measures which may
be conducive thereto ; and, the multiplying of public
houses, where the public good does not require it, has a
direct tendency to ruin the morals of youth, and promote
idleness and intemperance among all ranks of people, especially as the grand object of the candidates for licenses is
money ; and, when that is not the case, men are not over
apt to be tender of people's morals or purses.   The au
thorities of this town, I think, have run into a great error,
in approbating an additional number of public houses,
especially in this parish.   They have approbated two
houses in the centre, where there never was custom (I
mean travelling custom) enough for one.   The other cus-

                  * Brooklyn was set off from Pomfret.
         31

tom (the domestic) I have been informed, has, of late years, increased ; and the licensing another house, I fear, would increase it more. As I kept a public house here myself, a number of years before the war, I had an opportunity of knowing, and certainly do know, that the travelling custom is too trifling for a man to lay himself out so as to keep such a house as travellers have a right to expect. Therefore, I hope your Honors will consult the good of this parish, so as to license only one of the two houses. I shall not undertake to say which ought to be licensed. Your Honors will act according to your best information.

> " I am, with esteem,
> " Your Honor's humble servant,
> " ISRAEL PUTNAM.

" To the Honorable County Court, to be holden at Windham, on the 19th instant."

Though he had passed so great a portion of his life in the camp, amidst the demoralizing influences and false maxims which prevail in that arbitrary and unnatural state of society, General Putnam, with one exception only, maintained a high standard of moral virtue. During most of his military life, he was addicted to the soldier's habit of profaneness ; and most of the anecdotes related of him, are freely interlarded with oaths. This sin he acknowledged, lamented, and wholly abjured in his later years. To duelling, that worst and most heartless species of legalized murder, he was always and utterly opposed—holding in hearty abhorrence every principle of the so-called code of honor. It was a practice which few men could better afford to hold in supreme contempt ; for his courage was above suspicion.

It once happened that, without intending an insult, he

The Duel. PAGE 363.

grossly offended a brother officer. The dispute arose at a wine table, and the officer demanded instant reparation. Putnam, being a little excited, expressed his willingness to accommodate the gentleman with a fight; and it was stipulated that the duel should take place on the following morning, and that they should fight without seconds. At the appointed time, the officer went to the ground, armed with sword and pistols. On entering the field, Putnam, who had taken a stand at the opposite extremity, and at a distance of thirty rods, levelled his musket, and fired at him. The gentleman now ran toward his antagonist, who deliberately proceeded to reload his gun.

" What are you about to do ?" exclaimed he. " Is this the conduct of an American officer, and a man of honor ?"

" What am I about to do ?" exclaimed the General, attending only to the first question. " A pretty question to put to a man whom you intended to murder ! I'm about to kill you ; and if you don't beat a retreat in less time than 'twould take old Heath to hang a tory, you are a gone dog ;" at the same time returning his ramrod to its place, and throwing the breach of his gun into the hollow of his shoulder.

This intimation was too unequivocal to be misunderstood ; and the valorous duellist turned and fled for dear life.

An English officer, who was a prisoner on his parole, being offended at some remarks of General Putnam, in which he had reflected with some severity upon the character of the British, demanded satisfaction, as for a personal insult. Putnam accepted the challenge, and having his choice of the weapons, agreed to meet his antagonist the next morning, at a certain place which he named, prepared with arms for both parties. On the arrival of the Englishman at the appointed place, he found Putnam seat-ed by the side of what appeared to be a barrel of powder, smoking his pipe—a common match being inserted into a small opening in the top of the barrel. Requesting the Englishman to sit down on the other side of the cask, he set fire to the match with his pipe, and coolly remarking that there was an equal chance for both of them, went on with his smoking. The Englishman watched the match, for a moment, as the fire crept slowly down towards the powder, and then starting hastily up, made a precipitate retreat.

" You are just as brave a man as I took you to be," said Putnam. " This is nothing but a barrel of onions, with a few grains of powder on the head, to try you by. But you don't like the smell."

In following out the *tableaux vivants* of history, we are so often compelled to leave our chosen hero weltering in his blood on an untimely field, or wearing away the prime of his days in captivity, that we take unusual satisfaction in contemplating the long evening of calm and dignified repose, that closed the active and adventurous career of Putnam. Though incapacitated for further service in the stirring scenes of the camp and the field, he retained, in full vigor, his power to enjoy and promote the tranquil pleasures of social life. Fortunately, the thrift and industry of his early years, and the prudent management of his temporal affairs, had secured an ample competency for his declining years, and placed him above that painful and humiliating embarrassment, which embittered the last days of so many of his worthy compeers in that glorious struggle. In a pleasant home, which his own industry had procured and adorned ; in the midst of a kind and affectionate family, happy in themselves and in him ; and of a free and prosperous people, who looked up to and vene-

rated him, as one of the authors of their freedom and
prosperity; with a wide circle of admiring and confiding
friends among the best and worthiest in the land; and in
the cheerful, conscientious performance of all the duties
of a kind father, a faithful friend, a good neighbor, a wor
thy citizen, a high-minded patriot, and a devout Christian,
he diligently improved his long furlough from the scenes
of earthly strife and toil, in maintaining a spiritual warfare
against inward foes, and preparing for a spiritual rest.

The narrative of his adventurous life sufficiently illustrates his martial virtues, his intrepid bravery, and consummate skill, and his humane and generous regard for
the unfortunate victims of war. "But," as Mr. Peabody
beautifully and justly remarks, "his military reputation,
high as it was, concealed no dark traits of personal character beneath its shadow. In all the domestic relations,
the surest test of habitual virtue, he was most exemplary;
and his excellence in this respect deserves the more notice,
as the stern discipline and wild adventure, in which so
much of his life was spent, were more favorable to the
growth of severer qualities. His disposition was frank,
generous and kind; in his intercourse with others, he was
open, just, sincere and unsuspecting; liberal in his hospitality, and of ready benevolence, wherever there was occasion for his charity. Those who knew him best were the
most forward to express their admiration of his excellence."

Dr. Dwight, who was personally and intimately acquainted with him, in private as well as public life, bears
this testimony to his character.

"With only the advantages of a domestic education, in
a plain farmer's family, and the usual instruction of a
common parish school, he raised himself from the management of a farm, to the command of a regiment, in the
31*

last Canadian War ; and in the Revolutionary War, to the second command in the armies of the United States. To these stations he rose solely by his own efforts, directed steadily to the benefit of his country, and with the cheerful, as well as united, suffrages of his countrymen.

"Every employment in which he engaged, he filled with reputation. In the private circles of life, as a husband, father, friend and companion, he was alike respected and beloved. In his manners, though somewhat more direct and blunt than those of most persons who have received an early, polished education, he was gentlemanly, and very agreeable. In his disposition he was sincere, tender-hearted, generous, and noble. It is not known that the passion of fear ever found a place in his breast. His word was regarded as ample security for anything, for which it was pledged ; and his uprightness commanded absolute confidence. His intellect was vigorous ; and his wit pungent, yet pleasant and sportive. The principal part of his improvements, however, were derived from his own observation, and his correspondence with the affairs of men. During the gayest and most thoughtless period of his life, he still regarded Religion with profound reverence, and read the Scriptures with the deepest veneration. On the public worship of God he was a regular and very respectful attendant. In the decline of life, he publicly professed the religion of the Gospel ; and in the opinion of the respectable clergyman of Brooklyn, the Rev. Dr. Whitney, from whose mouth I received the information, died hopefully a Christian."

Dr. Whitney, in a sermon preached immediately after General Putnam's death, says : "He was eminently a person of public spirit, an unshaken friend of liberty, and was proof against attempts to induce him to betray and desert his country. The baits to do so were rejected with the utmost abhorrence. He was of a kind, benevolent disposition ; pitiful to the distressed, charitable to the needy, and ready to assist all who wanted his help. In his family he was the tender, affectionate husband, the provident father, an example of industry and close application to business. He was a constant attendant upon the public worship of God, from his youth up. He brought his family with him, when he came to worship the Lord. He was not ashamed of family religion. His house was a house of prayer. For many years he was a professor of religion. In the last years of his life, he often expressed a great regard for God, and the things of God. There is one, at least, to whom he freely disclosed the workings of his mind—his conviction of sin—his grief for it—his dependence on God, through the Redeemer, for pardon—and his hope of a future happy existence, whenever his strength and heart should fail him. This one makes mention of these things, for the satisfaction and comfort of his children and friends ; and can add, that, being with the General a little before he died, he asked him whether his hope of future happiness, as formerly expressed, now attended him. His answer was in the affirmative ; with a declaration of his resignation to the will of God, and his willingness even then to die."

In this hope, and in the full possession of his faculties to the last, he died, on the 19th of May, 1790, in the seventy-third year of his age. He was borne to his grave with the martial honors usually accorded to a brave and patriotic soldier. His death was noticed, with every mark of respect, in the public prints ; while the people, as they met, said one to another, " Know ye not that there is a Prince and a great man fallen this day in Israel ?"

His tomb bears the following inscription, from the pen and heart of his friend Dr. Dwight :

SACRED BE THIS MONUMENT
TO THE MEMORY
OF

ISRAEL PUTNAM, Esquire,

SENIOR MAJOR-GENERAL IN THE ARMIES
OF
THE UNITED STATES OF AMERICA,
who
was born at Salem,
in the Province of Massachusetts,
on the 7th day of January,
A. D. 1718,
and died
on the 19th day of May,
A. D. 1790.

Passenger,
if thou art a Soldier,
drop a tear over the dust of a Hero,
who,
ever attentive
to the lives and happiness of his men,
dared to lead
where any dared to follow;
if a Patriot,
remember the distinguished and gallant services
rendered thy country,
by the Patriot who sleeps beneath this marble;
if thou art honest, generous, and worthy,
render a cheerful tribute of respect
to a man,
whose generosity was singular,
whose honesty was proverbial;
who
raised himself to universal esteem,
and offices of eminent distinction,
by personal worth,
and a
useful life.

APPENDIX.

NUMBER I.

MAJOR ROGERS.

THE story of Major Rogers, as far as it relates to the War of the Revolution, is furnished in the following extracts from the letters of General Washington, and the notes attached to them in Sparks' edition of his Writings.

" To MAJOR-GENERAL SCHUYLER.
" *Cambridge*, 18*th December*, 1775.

" In a letter from Rev. Dr. Wheelock, of Dartmouth College, of the 2d instant, I had the following intelligence : ' That the day before, two soldiers returning from Montreal informed him, that our officers were assured by a Frenchman (a captain of the artillery whom they had taken captive), that Major Rogers was second in command under General Carleton, and that he had been, in an Indian habit, through our encampment at St. John's. You will be pleased to have this report examined into, and acquaint me as to the authenticity or probability of the truth of it. If any circumstances can be discovered to induce a belief that he was there, he should be apprehended. He is now in this government." * * *

Note by Dr. Sparks.—" Major Rogers had been celebrated for his adventures and feats of valor in the French War, as the companion of Putnam and Stark. He wrote a journal of those events, which is not without ability and interest. He was once Governor of Michilimackinac. After the peace, he lived in New Hampshire, and continued an officer on half-pay. Dr. Wheelock's letter, from which the above is an extract, contains. some other curious particulars about him ; whether true or fabulous, the reader must judge.

" On the 13th ultimo," says Dr. Wheelock, " the famous Major
Rogers came to my house, from a tavern in the neighborhood where
he called for refreshment. I had never seen him before. He was in
but an ordinary habit, for one of his character. He treated me with
great respect; said he came from London in July, and had spent
twenty days with the Congress in Philadelphia, and I forget how
many at New York; had been offered and urged to take a commission in favor of the colonies, but, as he was now on half-pay
from the crown, he thought proper not to accept it; that he had fought
two battles in Algiers under the Dey; that he was now on a design to
take care of some large grants of land made to him; that he was
going to visit his sister at Moor's Town, and then to return by Mer-
rimac River to visit his wife, whom he had not yet seen since his
return from England; that he had got a pass, or license to travel,
from the Continental Congress; that he called to offer his services to
procure a large interest for this college; that its reputation was great
in England; that Lord Dartmouth, and many other noblemen, had
spoken of it in his hearing, with expressions of the highest esteem
and respect; that Captain Holland, surveyor-general, now at New
York, was a great friend to me, and the college, and would assist me
in the affair; and that now was the most favorable time to apply for
large grants of land for it.

" I thanked him for these expressions of his kindness; but, after I
had shown some coldness in accepting it, he proposed to write to me
on his journey, and let me know where I might reply to him; and he
should be ready to perform any friendly office in the affair. He said
he was in haste to pursue his journey that evening."

" About a month after visiting Dr. Wheelock, the Major appeared
at Medford, near the camp, and wrote to General Washington,
requesting him to sign a certificate, permitting him to travel unmolested in the country. Such a certificate, or permit, had first been
granted by the Committee of Safety in Philadelphia; who, from suspicious circumstances, and because he was actually a British officer,
had made him a prisoner, when he arrived in that place from England. The certificate was furnished to him, in consequence of a
parole, wherein he ' solemnly promised and engaged, on the honor
of a gentleman and a soldier, that he would not bear arms against the
American United Colonies in any manner whatsoever, during the
American contest with Great Britain :' and, in his letter to Washington, he says, ' I love America; it is my native country and that of
my family, and I intend to spend the evening of my days in it.'

"These professions being apparently sincere, Washington sent General Sullivan to examine him on certain points, and report the result. He owned the accuracy of Dr. Wheelock's letter, except the part relating to Canada, which he denied, though he had been to the west of Albany. As no good reason appeared, why he came to camp, or why he wished to travel through the country, the General did not think it expedient to receive a visit from him, nor to sign his permit; but, as this had already been signed by the President of the New York Congress, and the Chairman of the New Hampshire Committee of Safety, he suffered the Major to depart at his option, and to enjoy such security as his papers, thus authenticated, might procure him.

"There was a suspicion, strengthened by his subsequent conduct, that he was at this time a spy, or at least practising a very unworthy artifice for acquiring a confidence, to which his political sentiments did not entitle him. Be this as it may, he soon after joined the enemy's ranks, and was raised to be a colonel in the British army, notwithstanding his parole of honor, and his love of America. It may be said, perhaps, in extenuation, that he considered his parole extorted from him at a time when there were no just grounds for questioning his motives, and by an authority which he did not feel bound to respect."— *Vol. iii., p.* 208.

The "subsequent conduct" referred to above, as calculated to awaken suspicions, may be illustrated by the following extract from a letter of General Washington to the President of Congress, dated New York, June 27, 1776:

"Upon information that Major Rogers was travelling through the country under suspicious circumstances, I thought it necessary to have him secured. I, therefore, sent after him. He was taken at South Amboy, and brought up to New York. Upon examination, he informed me that he came from New Hampshire, the country of his usual abode, where he had left his family; and pretended he was destined to Philadelphia on business with Congress.

"As, by his own confession, he had crossed Hudson's River at New Windsor, and was taken so far out of his proper and direct route to Philadelphia, this consideration, added to the length of time he had taken to perform his journey, his being found in so suspicious a place as Amboy,* his unnecessary stay there, on pretence of getting some baggage from New York, and an expectation of receiving

* The most convenient point of communication with the British on Staten Island.

money from a person here of bad character, and in no circumstances to furnish him out of his own stock, the Major's reputation, and his being a half-pay officer, have increased my jealousies about him. The business which he informs me he has with Congress, is a secret offer of his services, to the end that, in case it should be rejected, he might have his way left open to an employment in the East Indies, to which he is assigned; and in that case, he flatters himself he will obtain leave of Congress to go to Great Britain.

"As he had been put upon his parole by Congress, I thought it would be improper to stay his progress to Philadelphia, should he be in fact destined thither. I, therefore, send him forward, but, to prevent imposition, under the care of an officer, with letters found upon him, which, from their tenor, seem calculated to recommend him to Congress. I submit it to their consideration, whether it would not be dangerous to accept the offer of his services."

Note by Dr. Sparks.—"Congress directed, that Major Rogers should be sent to New Hampshire, to be disposed of as the government of that Province should judge best. He soon afterwards went over to the British."—*Vol. iii., p.* 439.

In September following, Major Rogers was found actively employed in the British service, and against the American interests, notwithstanding his parole, and his love of America. He had abandoned his position in the East Indies, if he ever had any, and was engaged in drumming up British recruits, from among the American tories on Long Island. The following, from a letter of Washington to Governor Trumbull, of Connecticut, establishes this fact.

" Haerlem, 30th September, 1776.

"Having received authentic advices from Long Island, that the enemy are recruiting a great number of men * * * I have directed * * an expedition to the island, to check and suppress, if possible, a practice so injurious to our cause. * * * The influence of their money and their artifices, has already passed the Sound, and several persons have been detected of late, who have enlisted to serve under their banner, and the particular command of Major Rogers."

Governor Trumbull, in writing to Colonel Livingston on the subject, says: "I have received intelligence, which I believe may be depended on, that Major Rogers, now employed by General Howe, and who you know was a famous partizan, or ranger, in the last war, is collecting a battalion of tories on Long Island and from the main, many of whom have joined him at Huntington, and that he proposes soon to make a sudden attack in the night on Norwalk, to take the continental stores, and lay waste the town. I hope we shall be able to frustrate his designs. I have no need to apprise you of the art of this Rogers. He has been a famous scouter, or woods-hunter, skilled in waylaying, ambuscade, and sudden attack."—*Vol. iv., page* 128.

Major Rogers, on his return to the British camp, was immediately promoted to the rank of a Colonel, with the command of a regiment of loyalists, called the *Queen's Rangers.* General Howe wrote, on the 6th August, " Major Rogers, *having escaped to us from Philadelphia,* is empowered to raise a battalion of rangers, which, I hope, may be useful in the course of the campaign." The following is a copy of enlisting orders, sent out by him :

" *Valentine's Hill,* 30 *December,* 1776.

" Whereas his Majesty's service makes it absolutely necessary that recruits should be raised, this is to certify that Mr. Daniel Strang, or any other gentleman, who may bring in recruits, shall have commissions, according to the number he or they shall bring in for the Queen's American Rangers. No more than forty shillings bounty is to be given to any man, which is to be applied towards purchasing necessaries ; *to serve during the present* REBELLION, and no longer. *They will have their proportion of all* REBEL *lands,* and all privileges equal to any of. his Majesty's troops. The officers are to be the best judges in what manner they will get their men in, either by parties, detachments, or otherwise, as may seem most advantageous; which men are to be attested before the first magistrate within the British lines.

" ROBERT ROGERS,
" *Lieutenant-Colonel Commandant of the Queen's Rangers.*

" Strang, who had the above paper in his possession, was taken up near the American camp, at Peekskill. He was tried by a court-martial, and making no defence, was condemned to suffer death, on the charge of holding correspondence with the enemy, and lurking round the camp as a spy. General Washington approved the sentence. But, notwithstanding this rigor, and the danger of the service beyond the enemy's lines, yet persons were found to in engage it, who met with some success, though much less than had been anticipated by General Howe. Recruits for the British provincial regiments were raised, even as high up the North River as Dutchess county, and Livingston's Manor. The Island of New York, Long Island, Sta-

ten Island, and a large part of Westchester county, were wholly subject to the power of the enemy; and, as these were populous districts,
they doubtless afforded the chief portion of the provincial troops, enlisted into the king's service, whiie General Howe's head-quarters
were in New York."—*Vol. iv., page* 521.

Near the end of October, Colonel Haslet was despatched, with
seven hundred and fifty men, by order of Lord Stirling, "to attack
the enemy's outposts at Mamaroneck; which was done, and their
guards forced. We brought in thirty-six prisoners, a pair of colors,
sixty stand of arms, and a variety of other plunder besides. The
party we fell in with was *Colonel Rogers*, the late worthless Major.
On the first fire, he skulked off in the dark. His lieutenant, and a
number of others, were left dead on the spot. Had not our guards
deserted on the first outset, he and his whole party must have been
taken."—*Page* 526.

In November, General Lee formed a plan for attacking and carrying off Rogers, at a moment when he was ordered by General Washington to move in another direction. It was while aiming to accomplish this object, that he was surprised by Colonel Harcourt, and
carried to Brunswick, a prisoner of war.

NUMBER II.

THE BATTLE OF BUNKER HILL.

COLONEL SWETT's admirable, and ably fortified sketch of this great battle, which, to use the language of the Christian Examiner, " is now classical authority on the subject"—which Bradford refers to, as " the most correct and perfect account which has been given"—and which the Boston Courier cites, as " one of the most valuable and authentic records connected with the History of the Revolution"—would seem to have put for ever at rest, the question of the presence and active services of General Putnam, on that memorable occasion. The ample notes appended to the third edition of that sketch, furnish an amount and variety of testimony that is absolutely overwhelming. Referring to them, I take leave to add, in this place, a few more of the same character, which have been kindly furnished by several friendly correspondents—not because they are necessary to establish the point in dispute, but just to preserve them from oblivion.

" I, Sylvanus Conant, of Mansfield, in the County of Tolland and State of Connecticut, testify and say, that I am now in my ninety-second year; that I was a soldier in the Revolutionary War; that I was in the battle of Bunker's Hill, on the seventeenth day of June, 1775; that I was acquainted with General Israel Putnam, of Connecticut, and know that he was in the battle. Saw him at the commencement of the battle, riding about the hill, and giving orders to the troops, and heard him sharply reproving a soldier for cowardice, or neglect of duty; and was told by others, though this I did not see myself, that near the close of the battle, General Putnam, seeing a field-piece deserted by the company, dismounted from his horse and fired the piece once or twice with his own hands, and then remounted his horse, and rode off the hill with the retreating troops.

" Subscribed and sworn to this 5th day of January, 1843.

" SYLVANUS CONANT.

" *Mansfield, Jan.* 5, 1843."

" State of Connecticut, ⎱ ss.
" Tolland County." ⎰

[*From the Mercantile Journal, Boston.*]

"MR. SLEEPER, *Dear Sir:* I understand from the public papers, that Mr. Bancroft stated in a late lecture before the Charlestown Lyceum, that he found no evidence to prove that General Putnam had the chief command in the battle of Bunker Hill, or even took any part in the engagement. For his information and that of the public, please give currency, through your journal, to the following facts, which I lately obtained from Major John Burnham, of this town. Major Burnham, I would remark, is a Revolutionary soldier and officer; is in his ninety-fourth year, and yet retains his mental faculties in a wonderful manner. He is a very worthy man, and a humble disciple of Christ. I assure you the most implicit confidence can be placed in his statements.

"I paid him a visit the other day, and he informed me that he took an active part in that ever memorable engagement of the 17th of June; that he was lieutenant of a company from Gloucester, commanded by Captain Warner; that he arrived on the battle-ground a few minutes before the firing commenced; that his Captain was met by General Putnam and directed where to go; that he frequently saw the General, riding among the troops and giving orders; that he never knew or heard, at the time of the battle, of any other individual taking the chief command but General Putnam; and that he has no more doubt of the fact than he has of his own existence. Such is the testimony of one who had the best possible means of knowing the truth of his statements.

"A. F. H.

"*Derry, January 27th,* 1843."

Letter of H. Burbeck, now upwards of ninety years old, to C. S. Davies, Esq., of Portland, Me.:

"Figure to yourself a man of sixty—six feet high and somewhat round-shouldered; sun-burnt from exposure; with coarse leather shoes, and blue stockings; coarse homespun small-clothes, a red waistcoat, and calico 'Banian' (answering to the sack worn at the present day), a three-cornered hat, with a red cockade, and a bandelier, or belt, with a sword hung high up under the left arm. You will say that it is a complete caricature—but such was the fact, and such the dress of the Heroes, who fought at the Battle of Bunker Hill.

"On that day, General Putnam rode between Charlestown and Cambridge without a coat, in his shirt sleeves, and an old white felt

hat on, to report to General Ward, and to consult upon further operations. I never understood that he was in the engagement, but was
very active in forwarding troops, ammunition, &c. In short, he was
the great gun of the day. Colonels Prescott and Stark were warmly
engaged in the battle; but General Putnam forwarded the materials
to them, to support the action. For that reason he is justly entitled to
equal praise and honor on that eventful day, for without his assistance nothing would have been done.

"H. BURBECK."

It is not surprising that there should be differences of opinion, in
relation to the nature of Putnam's command, among the multitude of
irregular troops collected on that day. The greater part of them
were ready to obey the orders of any one in whom they had confidence, and did not stoop to ask if he was regularly invested with the
command by the proper authorities. The officers were equally ready
to take command, where they could render good service by doing so.
The only matter of surprise is, that any should have been found, who
were willing to deny that Putnam was on the field at all, because
they did not happen to see him, at particular times and places. It is
probable that most of the soldiers, if they were true to their own
duty, had other and more absorbing employment, than taking notes
of the proceedings of their commanders, with a view to calling them
to account for their conduct. The field was an irregular one. The
action was in all parts of it, and it was impossible for any one to
say who was, or was not, present at any particular time, except in
the immediate vicinity of his own post. And even then, amid the
smoke, and din, and confusion of battle, an officer might have passed and repassed many times, and ordered some of the most important
movements of the day, without being noticed, or even seen, by one
in ten of the soldiers.

In all such cases as this, it is manifest, that testimony of a merely
negative character can have no weight at all against that which is
positive. The evidence of one competent witness, testifying that he
saw General Putnam in the heat of the engagement, discharging the
duty of a brave and able commander, would be allowed, in any court
of justice, to overbalance that of any number, who could only say
they did not see him. The amount and character of positive testimony to this point, furnished by Colonel Swett's notes, is such as
should satisfy the most determined skeptic.

With reference to the same point, Dr. Dwight says: "It is not so
32*

extensively known, as it ought to be, that General Putnam commanded the American forces at the Battle of Breed's Hill; and that, to
his courage and conduct, the United States are particularly indebted
for the advantages of that day; one of the most brilliant in the annals
of this country."

The following is a note to Rev. Dr. Whitney's sermon on the
death of General Putnam.

"The friends of the late General Putnam feel themselves not a
little obliged to his worthy and respectable biographer, for giving to
the public the distinguishing features in the General's character, and
the memorable actions of his life; yet wish that a more perfect and
just account had been given of the Battle of Bunker's Hill, so far as
General Putnam was concerned in it. In page 107 of his life, are
the following words: 'The provincial Generals having received
advice that the British Commander-in-chief designed to take possession of the heights on the peninsula of Charlestown, detached a thousand men, in the night of the 16th of June, under the orders of General Warren, to intrench themselves upon one of those eminences:'
and on page 110: 'In this battle, the presence and example of General Putnam, who arrived with the reinforcements, were not less conspicuous than useful.'

"From the first of these passages, the reader is led to conclude,
that the detachment was first put under the orders of General Warren; from the second, that General Putnam came to General Warren's aid, with a reinforcement. The true state of the case was this.
—The detachment at first was put under the command of General
Putnam. With it he took possession of the hill, and ordered the
battle from the beginning to the end. General Warren (one of the
most illustrious patriots) arrived alone on the hill, and as a volunteer joined the Americans just as the action commenced; and within
half an hour, received a mortal wound, while he was waxing valiant
in battle, and soon expired. These facts General Putnam himself
gave me, soon after the battle, and also repeated them to me after his
life was printed. Colonel Humphreys, page 109, justly observes:
'Few instances can be produced, in the annals of mankind, where
soldiers who have never before faced an enemy, or heard the whistling of a ball, behaved with such deliberate and persevering valor.'
The General who encouraged and animated them by his words and

example to prodigies of bravery, is highly to be honored, and the praise not given to another, however meritorious in other respects. Other evidence to confirm what I have said here, I am able to produce, if any should call for it."

Extract from a letter, written by an officer in the British army, at Boston, to his friend in England, dated 25 June, 1775:

" After the skirmish of the 17th, we even commended the troops of Putnam, who fought so gallantly *pro aris et focis.* When we marched to attack their redoubt, they called out, " General Abercrombie, are the Yankees cowards ?" nor did they discharge a gun until we were within fifteen yards. The fire on our left wing was so hot, that our troops broke. * * * So very secretly was the action conducted, that Generals Clinton and Burgoyne knew nothing of it till the morning. The town did in general, and Putnam in particular. This man served under Prussia, and does honor to his master. He is 63, and brave to the back-bone."—*Am. Archives, 4th Series, vol. ii., page* 1092.

Putnam was at this time in his fifty-eighth year, and had never seen Prussia. It is possible that one of the distinguished men, under whom he served in the French war, may have been familiarly designated by this title. None of the American officers, of that period, had seen foreign service. General Lee was not then with the army, nor was he known by the English to have accepted a continental commission. These inaccuracies, however they may be explained, do not invalidate the evidence here furnished, that Putnam was active and prominent in that engagement, and that his military character was held in the highest estimation by his old commanders and comrades of the British army.

Sandford, who published his history within a year after the first appearance of the article, in which Putnam's position and conduct in this battle were called in question, has the following remarks, at page 291 et seq.:

" It has been recently discovered, that 'Old Put' was a coward. So stupid a calumny could only have found place in the pages of a stupid journal; and a short review of that soldier's life, during the period in which this new trait is said to have displayed itself, will show, at least, that, if he was a coward, he was a coward to some purpose. The news from Lexington found him working at stone-fence, in his leathern frock and apron. He immediately mounted his horse, to spread the intelligence through the adjoining towns; and, when he returned to make a little preparation for the march, a body of several hundred of persons, already under arms, appointed him their commander. He ordered them to march with a quick step; and, setting off himself, in his check-shirt, arrived at Concord by sun-rise next morning.

"Men, who were stationed at one particular spot, in the battle of Bunker's Hill, pretend to trace the movements of General Putnam; and have charged him with a fear of powder and ball, for being seen once in a particular situation, when, in fact, he was at different times in every part of the field. It may be true, that the army was not under any general, who had been regularly commissioned; but it is equally true, that Putnam discharged the duties, though he might not have held the diploma, of a commander-in-chief. 'General Warren joins the Massachusetts forces in one place,' says Hubley; ' and General Pomeroy in another, whilst General Putnam was busily engaged in aiding and encouraging here and there as required.' Since he was the most experienced, and had not yet shown himself a coward, it was natural that the other two generals should give him the precedence; and we know not that the historian could have chosen language more pointedly expressive of the conduct which a brave commander is always found to adopt. That Putnam was, at one time, seen with entrenching tools before him, we would rather admit than deny. It might have been necessary to carry them from one part of the works to another: the length of the redoubt was eighty rods: a man, who had come from making stone-fence, was not likely to shrink from a spade or a pick-axe; and, since the sooner they were carried the better, we think nothing more probable than that Putnam, being on horseback, took a part of them himself.

"It was not Colonel Gerrish alone, who was tried for cowardice at the battle of Bunker's Hill. The colonists had not yet been separated from England long enough to distinguish, with certainty, the friends from the foes: the conduct of every individual was watched with the strictest scrutiny; and court martials continued to be held upon officers and men, from the 7th of July to the 5th of October. The same rigor was extended to the camp. Offences, which would now be overlooked, were then punished with severity. One captain was fined eight shillings for two oaths; and a private received twenty lashes for abusing Colonel Gridley, and forging Putnam's order for a quart of rum. If Putnam himself was a coward, he was certainly a most conspicuous coward. Had he dodged, or turned pale, there was not an officer or a man in the army, who would not have been a witness to the fact.

"On the 22d of July, 1775, the army was marshalled into three divisions; and it is a remarkable instance of successful cowardice, that the left wing was given to Major-General Putnam. Indeed, so little was his character known, at this time, that, when General Washington, early in 1776, had formed a bold and hazardous plan of taking Boston by storm, he designated Putnam for his leader, though he was youngest, in rank, of four major-generals. 'In expectation,' says Marshal, 'that the flower of the British troops would be employed against the heights of Dorchester, General Washington had concerted a plan for availing himself of that occasion, to attack the town of Boston itself. Four thousand chosen men were held in readiness to embark at the mouth of Cambridge river, on a signal to be given, if the garrison should appear to be so weakened by the detachment from it, as to justify an assault. These troops were to embark in two divisions; the first to be led by Brigadier-General Sullivan; the second, by Brigadier-General Green; and the whole to be under the command of Major-General Putnam.' In fine, a lack of courage was the last accusation which could be expected to succeed against General Putnam; and, until a man has voluntarily descended to fight a wolf in her own den, let him never think himself entitled to call the hero of Pomfret a coward.

NUMBER III.

On this subject Dr. Sparks has the following note, appended to the letter in which Washington announces to General Putnam his removal from the command in the Highlands, and the causes of that removal.

" General Putnam's advanced age, his good nature, and easy temperament, were among the chief causes of the ill success of his command on the North River. His proceedings were not marked with the promptness, decision, and energy, nor even with the military address which had characterized his early years. If all these had been combined, it is probable there would still have been dissatisfaction, after the enemy had forced their way up the river, and laid waste its borders. Not only were complaints uttered by the popular voice, but the political leaders of the State expressed discontent. Robert R. Livingston, then Chancellor of New York, wrote to General Washington on the subject in a pointed manner.

"'Your Excellency,' said he, 'is not ignorant of the extent of General Putnam's capacity and diligence; and how well soever these may qualify him for this most important command, the prejudices to which his imprudent lenity to the disaffected, and too great intercourse with the enemy, have given rise, have greatly injured his influence. How far the loss of Fort Montgomery and the subsequent ravages of the enemy are to be attributed to him, I will not venture to say; as this will necessarily be determined by a court of inquiry, whose determinations I would not anticipate. Unfortunately for him, the current of popular opinion in this and the neighboring States, and, as far as I can learn, in the troops under his command, runs strongly against him. For my own part, I respect his bravery and former services, and sincerely lament that his patriotism will not suffer him to take that repose, to which his advanced age and past services justly entitle him.'—*MS. Letter, Jan. 14th.*

" It must be remembered, that at this station there were innumerable applications for passports to go into New York, under the pretence of urgent business, and various matters of a private concern; and it was thought General Putnam's good nature was too pliant on these occasions, and that too many opportunities were afforded for an improper intercourse between the disaffected and the enemy. At any rate, the symptoms of uneasiness appeared from such high sources, and were so decidedly manifested, that General Washington deemed it necessary to take notice of them, and change the command."

The case of General Schuyler, and many others, afford easy proof how readily such prejudices arise among the masses of the people, without any good foundation; and how the best and ablest officers, and most devoted patriots, may be temporarily involved in the shadows of public censure, and even removed from the sphere of their useful efforts, without in the least diminishing their claims to the gratitude and respect of posterity. The history of General Washington is not wanting in lessons of this kind; and, if some distinguished and talented officers in his own army, and others who stood high in the confidence of the American people, could have prevailed in their designs, even *he* would have been superseded in that lofty command, of which it is difficult to say, whether the station conferred dignity upon the man, or the man upon the station.